The

Hermetic

Tradition

. . . .

Other books by Julius Evola

The Doctrine of the Awakening
Eros and the Mysteries of Love
Revolt against the Modern World
The Yoga of Power

. . . .

THE HERMETIC TRADITION

Symbols and
Teachings of the Royal Art

Julius Evola

Translated from the Italian by E. E. Rehmus

Inner Traditions International
Rochester, Vermont

Inner Traditions International
One Park Street
Rochester, Vermont 05767

LIBRARY OF CONGRESS CATALOGING-IN-PUBLICATION DATA

Evola, Julius.
    [Tradizione ermetica. English]
    The hermetic tradition : in its symbols, doctrine, and "royal art" / Julius Evola ; translated from the Italian by E. E. Rehmus.
       p.   cm.
    Includes bibliographical references and index.
    ISBN 978-089281451-0
    1. Hermetism.   2. Symbolism.   I. Title
  BF 1611.E9613   1994
  135'.4--dc20   94-4085
                                                CIP

Printed and bound in the United States

10 9

Text design and layout by Virginia L. Scott
This book was typeset in Italian Electric, with Thor as a display face

CONTENTS

. . . .

PART TWO: The HERMETIC ROYAL ART

FOREWORD

. . . .

For Julius Evola (1898-1974) alchemy was *not*—as is generally believed—a single specialized subject concerning itself exclusively with metals and their correspondences in man, but rather a comprehensive physical and metaphysical system embracing cosmology as much as anthropology (in the sense of a complete knowledge of man in body, soul, and spirit).[1] Everything—nature and supernature—can be found in it. To Evola, hermetism and alchemy are one and the same.

The goal of this system is the understanding and *experiencing* of an ensouled "holy" organism, replete with living powers, in whom everything is wonderfully interwoven, connected to and communized with everything else. Man stands in the middle where he is microcosm in analogy to the whole macrocosm: As above, so below—in the words of the Emerald Tablet. The alchemical symbol language as the expression of this universal system must therefore also have correspondences in all the other mysteriosophic spheres and can consequently serve as a universal key in these spheres, just as, vice versa, any other mystery teaching has the power to fill in the lacunae of esotericism in alchemy.

Alongside Arturo Reghini (1878-1946)—and surely also at his suggestion—Evola was one of the few in those years who were aware of this parallel, especially to ancient theurgical practice. In 1926 Evola published an article in *Ultra* (the newspaper of the unusually liberal Theosophical lodge in Rome) on the cult of Mithras in which he placed major emphasis on the similarities of these mysteries

---

[1] This foreword first appeared in Ansata-Verlag's *Die Hermetische Tradition* (Interlaken, Switzerland, 1989). It is translated from the German by E. E. Rehmus and H. T. Hansen.

with hermetism. In the UR group (1927-29), of which Evola was a member, specific alchemical symbols were employed in the teaching of "Magic."[2] It is this practical aspect that is emphasized here, for alchemy cannot be grasped by abstract thought alone, much less is it just a psychic process in the unconscious (C. G. Jung's theory),[3] but much more than that: it is an *exercise* of soul and spirit in the best Platonic tradition.

Where did Evola's early preoccupation with alchemical symbolism come from? After his Dadaist and philosophical period, Evola came in contact with Theosophical and Freemason circles.[4] Here we can especially point to Reghini, of whom Evola writes in his autobiography,[5] that he either lent him the essential alchemical texts or at least informed him of them. Through the very significant esoteric magazines, *Athanor* and *Ignis* (1924-1925), edited by Reghini, Evola became acquainted with a whole series of contributions to alchemy that were enough to give him his first hints of knowledge.[6] Reghini's influence must have been decisive because so many of his quotations are also favorite quotations of Evola's.[7] In his autobiography Evola quotes from early translations of René Guénon's *Le voile d'Isis* (later the *Études traditionelles*), which also gave him suggestions for his vision of alchemy.

Jacopo da Coreglia[8] writes that it was a priest, Father Francesco Oliva, who had made the most far-reaching progress in hermetic science and who—highly prizing the keen spirit and intellectual honesty of the young seeker—gave Evola access to records strictly reserved for adepts of the narrow circle. These were concerned primarily with the teachings of the Fraternity of Myriam (Fratellanza Terapeutica Magica di Myriam), founded by Doctor Giuliano Kremmerz (pseudonym of Ciro

---

[2] In 1985 Ansata-Verlag published the first volume of the UR group data reports and documents under the title Magie als Wissenschaft vom Ich (Magic as science of the ego). The second and third volumes of these monographs are to be published by Ansata in forthcoming years. Many passages difficult to understand in the present book are explained in these monographs as these monographs are complemented in *The Hermetic Tradition*.

[3] Alchemy is *not* a psychotherapeutic path in the classical sense. It is actually intended for the absolutely spiritually healthy person, in whom "individuation" has already been accomplished. Only then is its practice permitted in order to make of "life" a "super-life." Where nature alone can do nothing more, there must the alchemical "art" take over. The alchemical work is psychotherapeutic only to the extent that the great healing (reintegration of man in transcendence) stands in analogy to the small healing (making the psyche well).

[4] See our introduction to Evola's *Revolt against the Modern World* (Rochester, Vt . 1994)

[5] *Il cammino del cinabro* (Milan, 1972), 109.

[6] Most prominent of these are Reghini's "Brevi note sul Cosmopolita ed i suoi scritti" (Brief notes on the Cosmopolite and his writings) in *Ignis* nos. 3, 4, 5, and "Ode alchemica di Fra Marcantonio Crassellame Chinese" (The alchemical ode of Fra Marcantonio Crassellame Chinese) in *Ignis* nos. 8 and 9.

[7] Especially those of Braccesco, Sendivogius, and Michel Potier's, *Philosophia pura*.

[8] Arthos, no. 16 (Genoa), 48ff.

Formisano, 1861-1930). Evola mentions in the notes to chapter 11 that the Myriam's "Pamphlet D"[9] laid the groundwork for his understanding of the four elements. Where this group in turn got its knowledge remains a secret. In its own view, and Jacopo da Coreglia also shares this opinion, the Myriam (which seems to have split into many groups) is the last torch-bearer of a tradition that has been handed down—under constantly changing names—from the classical times of Pythagorean paganism and it is independent of the Freemasons or similar contemporary movements. In his *Pour la Rose Rouge et la Croix d'Or* Count J. P. Giudicelli de Cressac Bachellerie reveals its inner structure and current grading process.

In addition, there is the decisive influence of Ercole Quadrelli, who under the pseudonyms of Abraxas and Tikaipos, made some especially important contributions to the UR group. And it should be mentioned in this regard that Quadrelli was trained by Giuliano Kremmerz and the Myriam.[10]

The freely accessible works of Kremmerz—*I dialoghi sull'ermetismo* (Dialogues on hermetics) and his magazine *Commentarium* (1910-12)—also did much for Evola's spiritual development in the realm of alchemy. His acquaintance with the *Chymica vannus* and with the alchemist Philalethes probably go back to these works.

The strongest and perhaps decisive influence on the Evolian conception of alchemy as a universal system is probably Cesare Della Riviera's *Il mondo magico degli heroi* (The magical world of the heroes), (Mantua, 1603; Milan, 1605). This is one of the few texts of that time that helps itself to a hermetico-alchemical language, but is of an unequivocally holo-cosmological character. Alchemy is always placed in perspective with the other hermetic disciplines—such as magic and astrology—and is not regarded as an autonomous and specific teaching. For an alchemical book the unusually many references to the Abbot Johannes Trithemius (1462-1516) in this work point also in this direction.

The first tangible result of these studies was shown in the periodical *Krur* (sequel to *UR*).[11] There Evola presented a first shot at discussing the hermetic tradition and anticipated the essential content of the later book. The alchemical tradition was still portrayed only as pagan and not as a *royal* tradition, an attribute that in the final edition received so central a position that it brought Evola into conflict with other representatives of the traditional weltanschauung.

A broader and altogether different influence on Evola at this time came as a result of his meeting the Indian alchemist C. S. Narayana Swami Aiyar of Chingleput,

---

[9] Appeared only as private publication for the inner circle. In his *Eros and the Mysteries of Love: The Metaphysics of Sex* (Rochester, Vt., 1991) Evola describes some of the sex magic practices of this group.

[10] See Dr. Renato del Pontés' introduction to *Magie als Wissenschaft vom Ich*.

[11] *KRUR, 1929* (reprint, Teramo, 1981), 154ff., 201ff., 251ff., 307ff.; see also p. 374ff.

who expounded on the great importance of the breathing techniques in alchemy and how it helped to ingest certain substances.

In 1930 Evola wrote "The Doctrine of Transmutation in Medieval Hermetics" for Bilychnis (no. 275). In abridged form, the articled contained the fundamental precepts of *La tradizione ermetica*, which was published by Laterza in 1931. (The 1931 edition was insignificantly altered and expanded in 1948. This was followed in 1971 by Evola's last revision, which is the basis for this translation.)

It is interesting in this regard that Benedetto Croce was instrumental in helping Evola to make contact with this eminent publishing house. In the archives of Laterza are several of Evola's unpublished letters that refer to *The Hermetic Tradition*, and in which Croce's mediation appears again and again. One letter in particular is important, for in it Evola seems to answer the publisher's reproaches that the work was overloaded with annotations and had too little public appeal. Evola argued that it was not written for public appeal but only and simply to show for the first time that alchemy was not just the beginning of chemistry, but a profound and forgotten mystery-science; and without the abundance of quotations Evola would be marked as a visionary and the publisher criticized for not being serious.

Evola's conviction that alchemy was a universal system clarifies his endeavor to see this work as the completion and synthesis of all his earlier works in philosophy, magic, and Tantrism. Hence his emphasis on the pre- or, more correctly, super-Christian character of the hermetic tradition.

Naturally, Evola's belief in the all-inclusive character of hermetism did not go unchallenged. Certainly his most important critic was the second great herald of Tradition, René Guénon, to whom Evola, nevertheless, was indebted for outstanding insights (and the idea of the Tradition in the first place).

In his review of *The Hermetic Tradition* in the *Voile d'Isis* in April of 1931,[12] though basically positive, Guénon rejects quite strongly the idea that alchemy is a complete metaphysical doctrine and reduces it to the status of a mere cosmological system. According to him, a true tradition could never have come from an Egypto-Hellenic origin, then passed on to Islamic esotericism, and from there to Christian esotericism. In addition, alchemy had always been integrated into these various currents, whereas a pure and complete tradition has no need for some other tradition serving as an auxiliary vehicle. Moreover, it is an indication of the special character of alchemy that this path of knowledge in traditional societies should be a domain of the second caste, of the Kshatriyas (warrior caste), whereas only the Brahmins were truly dedicated to metaphysics. The last argument was correct, as far as Evola was concerned, for he had always seen himself as Kshatriya

---

[12] Contained in *Formes traditionelles et cycles cosmiques* (Paris 1970), 119ff.

and for him alchemy and the possibility of continuing to experiment on the spiritual plane—the "art" aspect—were extremely important. Nevertheless, the present work and its representation of alchemy is no willful or special interpretation on Evola's part, although on the ground of his "personal equation" some aspects may have been given a stronger emphasis—especially the active and the inner alchemy (nei-tan).

Guénon's opposition was consistent; it is known that the "Redness" represents the highest stage in alchemy and is above the "Whiteness." The Red (or Purple) embodies an active state, which naturally stood in a contrast to the White, which the contemplative Brahmin exhibits. (Evola points this up quite clearly in chapter 23). Against Guénon's view that the "white" Brahmin caste unequivocally held the highest place in the traditional world, Evola set the "purple" king as "pontifex" (bridge-builder) uppermost between Heaven and Earth. With the priority of the symbolic color red over white in hermetism, Evola seems to have a point. But Guénon could only call alchemy a specialization and he could never assign it the universal character that Evola did.

In spite of Evola's decided rejection of Jung's psychological interpretation of alchemy, Jung described *The Hermetic Tradition* as a "detailed account of Hermetic philosophy," and he cites approvingly an entire section in translation.[13] Evola never saw himself as a shaper or creative interpreter of alchemy, but only as one who did no more than deliver this knowledge, clarifying it, to be sure, but broadcasting it unchanged.

Guénon repeated the reproach against universality in his review of Evola's 1932 edition of Della Riviera's *Il mondo magico degli heroi* (published with Evola's commentary). Guénon also blamed Evola for the assimilation of alchemy by magic.[14]

To be sure, Guénon's authority to judge alchemy has now and then been questioned, considering that he himself had never written a work on the subject. Eugène Canseliet, for example, the alleged disciple and publisher of the works of Fulcanelli,[15] doubted Guénon's competence on this matter.[16] On the other hand, neither does Guénon hold his criticism back from Fulcanelli, especially his *Frères d'Héliopolis*.[17]

---

[13] C. G. Jung, *Psychology and Alchemy*, vol. 12 of the *Collected Works* (Princeton, N.J., 1968), 228, 242n.

[14] *Comptes rendus* (Paris, 1973), 7ff.

[15] See especially Pauwels/Bergier, Aufbruch ins dritte Jahrtausend (Bern, 1962) and Kenneth Rayner Johnson, *The Fulcanelli Phenomenon* (St. Helier, 1980).

[16] Robert Amadou, *Le feu du soleil* (Paris, 1978).

[17] R. Guénon, *Formes traditionelles*, op cit., 166.

Evola's work after the publication of *Mondo magico degli heroi* was more and more politically defined, and aside from the insignificant changes in the revised editions of *The Hermetic Tradition* and single reviews and articles, Evola was silent about alchemy. Mention is found of course in his *Eros and the Mysteries of Love: The Metaphysics of Sex*, where the sexual background of alchemical symbolism is illuminated.

An essential complement of Evola's alchemical work was his interest in Chinese alchemy, revealed in his editions of two Chinese alchemical treatises.[18] This interest is also evident in the title of his spiritual autobiography, *Il cammino del cinabro* (The path of cinnabar). In Chinese alchemy the path of liberation is the journey from the "lower" to the "higher" cinnabar; chemically as well as alchemically cinnabar derives from the union of Sulfur (the masculine principle) and Mercury (the feminine principle).

· · · · · ·

Despite the widest coverage in the present work by the author himself, one point must also be emphasized here again: if we are now really to understand the following—not just intellectually, but also spiritually and in body and soul, in a word, completely—our consciousness must risk a leap. In its profundity the metaphorical world of alchemy is simply not accessible to the contemporary abstract understanding. We must, for once, turn off the continual din of reason and listen with the "ear of the heart" if we want to have the symbols strike responsive chords in ourselves. Two worlds are met with here: on the one hand a timeless world, lying beyond reason, prehistorical, and beyond history, and on the other, a time-bound, historical world that is chained to dialectical reason. Between them there is now no gradual passage, but an abyss, which we must leap over. What does Friedrich Wilhelm Schelling say? "Accordingly *historical* and *prehistoric* times are *not merely relative differences between one and the same time,* they are *two essentially different kinds of time completely removed from one another,* and mutually exclusive. We call it completely different time . . . full of events, but of *quite another sort,* and conforming to *quite a different law.*"[19]

Since modern man is so slow to lay aside his belief in progress, which stamps his thought patterns and distorts his yardsticks—it seems to him almost monstrous

---

[18] Lu-Tsu, *Il mistero del fiore d'oro* (The secret of the golden flower [Rome, 1971]), and with Lu Kwan Yu (Charles Luk), *Lo yoga del tao* (Rome, 1976). Both works appear with commentary (the second, necessarily only in part, because of his death) by Evola. Not without importance in this context are the Evolian editions of the famous *Tao te Ching*: First as *Libro della via e della virtu* (Lanciano, 1923), and then in a completely revised version under the title of: *Il libro del principe e della sua azione* (Milan, 1959).

[19] *Einleitung in die Philosophie der Mythologie* in *Sammelte Werke* (1856; reprint, Darmstadt, 1976), 1:233–36.

that there also exist completely different ways of thinking—and that is why the astronomer does not understand the astrologer (in the ancient sense), the modern priest does not understand the Egyptian hierophant, the philosopher does not understand the initiate, and the chemist does not understand the alchemist. Alchemical symbolism has now admittedly been found to have widely influenced literature, painting, and sculpture in the past. Literati and art historians concern themselves about the interpretation of this work. They can immediately discover worthwhile suggestions in this book, if they wish to penetrate this other world.

H. T. Hansen

TRANSLATOR'S NOTE

· · · · · · · · · · · ·

T itles of works that appear in English in the text will appear in their original languages in the notes, following the sources and editions from which Evola cites. No attempt has been made to include publication data on English translations for the many works to which Evola refers. (Some of these works are available in English, but many of them are no longer in print.)

Brackets in the quoted material in the text proper contain Evola's own glosses and interpolations; other brackets in the text and footnotes are clarifications and notes from the translator.

PREFACE

· · · · · · · · · · · ·

n the present work we shall use the expression "hermetic tradition" in a special sense that the Middle Ages and the Renaissance gave it. It will not refer to the ancient Greco-Egyptian cult of Hermes, nor will it refer solely to the teachings comprising the Alexandrian texts of the *Corpus Hermeticum*. In the particular sense that we shall use it, *hermetism* is directly concerned with the *alchemical tradition*, and it is the hermetico-alchemical tradition that will be the object of our study. We shall attempt to determine therein the real sense and spirit of a secret doctrine, a practical and workable wisdom that has been faithfully transmitted from the Greeks, through the Arabs, down to certain texts and authors at the very threshold of modern times.

At the outset, we must draw attention to the error of those historians of science who want to reduce alchemy to mere chemistry in an infantile and mythological stage. Against this notion are raised the explicit exhortations of the most quoted hermetic authors not to deceive ourselves by taking them literally, because their words are drawn from a secret language expressed via symbols and allegories.[1] These same authors have repeated, to the point of weariness, that the "object of

---

[1] Artephius speaks for all those authors in the following: "Isn't it only too well known that ours is a cabalistic Art? That is, to be revealed only orally and overflowing with mysteries? Poor fool! How can you be so naive as to believe that we would teach you openly and clearly the greatest and most important of our secrets? I assure you that whoever tries to explain in the ordinary and literal sense of the words what the [hermetic] philosphers have written will find himself caught in the meanderings of a labyrinth from which he can never escape, because he lacks Ariadne's thread as guide." From *Livre d'Artephius* in Salmon, ed., *Bibliothèque des philosophes chimiques* (Paris, 1741), 2:144.

our precious art is concealed"; that the operations to which we allude are not done manually; that its "elements" are invisible and not those the vulgar recognize. The same authors refer contemptuously to the "puffers" and "charcoal burners" who "ruined the science" and whose manipulations could expect "nothing more than smoke," and to all those ingenuous alchemists who, in their incomprehension, surrendered to experiments of the sort that moderns now attribute to the hermetic science. The proper alchemists have always laid down ethical and spiritual conditions for their operations. In view of their living sense of nature, their ideal world is presented as inseparable from that other—which we can call Gnosticism, Neoplatonism, Qabalah, and theurgy—anything but chemistry. Likewise, with a multitude of half-expressed formulas, they have given to understand "to those who can read between the lines," for instance, that alchemical sulfur represents the will (Basil Valentine and Pernety), that smoke is "the soul separated from the body" (Geber), that "virility" is the mystery of "arsenic" (Zosimos)—and in this wise we could cite an infinite number of texts and authors. So it is that with a bewildering variety of symbols the "Sons of Hermes" all manage to say the same thing and to repeat proudly the *quod ubique, quod ab omnibus et quod semper.*[2]

Jacob Boehme reveals to us the axiom on which this unique knowledge rests, this tradition that claims for itself universality and primordiality: "Between Eternal Birth, Restoration from the Fall and the discovery of the Philosopher's Stone there is no difference."[3]

Are we standing perhaps before a mystical mainstream? If so, why the disguise and hermetic concealment? Holding ourselves to the conventional idea of "mysticism" (a sense which in the West it has acquired since the period of the classical Mysteries and especially with Christianity), we must point out that it is *not*

---

[2] Cf., for example, Geber (*Livre du mercure oriental* in Berthelot, ed., *La chimie au moyen-age* [Paris, 1893], 3:248): "In reality, there is accord between the authors, though to the uninitiated it appears that they have differences"; also A. J. Pernety (*Fables égyptiennes et grecques dévoilées* [Paris, 1786], 1:11): "The hermetic philosophers are all in agreement; none contradicts the principles of the others. And one who wrote thirty years ago, speaks as one who wrote two thousand years ago. They never tire of repeating the Church axiom: '*Quod ubique, guod ab omnibus et quod semper.*'" And even clearer is the *Turba philosophorum*, one of the oldest and most quoted of western hermetico-alchemical texts (in C. Puini, ed., *Introduzione alla magia* [Rome, 1971], 2:245): "Be it noted that whatever the manner in which [the hermetic philosophers] have spoken, nature is one, and they find themselves in accord and all say the same thing. But the ignorant take our words exactly as we say them without understanding the why or wherefore. Instead, they should consider whether or not our words are reasonable and natural and then take them [as they are]; *and if our words are not reasonable, they should try to raise themselves to our intention instead of holding to the letter.* In any case, you must know that we are in agreement, whatever we say. So bring one another together accordingly and study us; because in one it may be clear what in another remains hidden and who truly searches will find everything."

[3] J. Boehme, *De signatura rerum*, 7, §78: ["*Wie die ewige Geburt in sich selber ist, also ist auch der Prozeß mit der Wiederbringung nach dem Falle, und also ist auch der Prozeß der Weisen mit ihrem Lapide Philosophorum, es ist kein Unterschied dazwischen.*"—Trans.]

mysticism. We will demonstrate rather that it is a *real science,* in which reintegration (with the primordial state) does not have an intended moral, but is concrete and ontological, even to the point of conferring certain supernormal powers, one of whose incidental applications may even be the famous transmutation involving metallic substances.

This characteristic of the hermetic process constitutes the first reason for its concealment. Not for superficial monopolistic purposes, but for inner technical reasons, any science of this type always protects itself by initiatory secrets and expression through symbols. But there is a second reason, which to be understood requires the fundamental knowledge of a general metaphysic of history. Hermetico-alchemical knowledge has been described as a "sacred" science, but the prevailing designation that better characterizes it is that of Ars Regia or "Royal Art." Anyone who studies the varieties of spirituality that have evolved in what we call historical times can verify that there is a fundamental opposition, one that we can reduce analogically to the conflict between "royalty" and "sacerdotality"

The "royal" initiatory tradition, in its pure forms, can be considered the most direct and legitimate link to the unique, primordial Tradition.[4] In more recent times, it appears to us in its heroic variants, that is, as a realization and reconquest conditioned by analogous virile qualities suitable, on the plane of the spirit, to the warrior. But, on the other hand, there is the sacerdotal position in the narrow sense, with different qualities from the first, and at times opposite to it. This is especially so when, brought to the profane in its theistic-devotional forms, it confronts what we referred to above as the "heroic" variations of the royal tradition. From the point of what we symbolize as the original "divine royalty," this second tradition now appears as something crumbling to pieces, the blame for which must be attributed to the sentimental, emotional, theistic-devotional and mystical elements—especially in the West—who are constantly gaining ground in their attempt to keep its esoteric elements in almost total darkness.

It is no accident that the hermetico-alchemical tradition should call itself the Royal Art, and that it chose Gold as a central royal and solar symbol, which at the same time takes us back to the primordial Tradition. Such a tradition presents itself to us essentially as the guardian of a light and a dignity that cannot be reduced to the religious-sacerdotal vision of the world. And if there is no talk in this tradition (as in a cycle of other myths) of *discovering* gold, but only of *making* it, that only goes to show how important, in the already indicated sense of reconquest and reconstructon, the heroic moment had become.

---

[4] To understand better those ideas that are contrary to the traditional and the primordial state, of the heroic, etc., reference to our work *Revolt against the Modern World* (Rochester, Vt., 1994), and to the books and texts of R. Guénon is almost indispensible. Cf. as well our *Maschera e volto dello spiritualismo contemporaneo* (Rome, 1971), particularly the chapter on the notion of returning to Catholicism.

Thus we can easily understand the second reason for disguising the doctrine. With the fall of the Roman Empire, the predominating principles of the West went on to become the basis for the other tradition—the sacerdotal—which in its decadence was almost completely stripped of its entire esoteric and metaphysical range in order to convert itself into a doctrine of "salvation" in the name of a "Redeemer." Things being so, the hermetists, in contrast to other initiatory organizations that were tributaries of the same secret royal vein, instead of coming out into the light and presenting themselves for battle, chose to go into hiding. And the Royal Art was presented as the alchemical art of transmuting base metals into gold and silver. By so doing it no longer fell under the suspicion of heresy, and even passed as one of the many forms of "natural philosophy" that did not interfere with the faith; even among the ranks of Catholics we can discern the enigmatic figures of hermetic masters, from Raymond Lully and Albertus Magnus to Abbot Pernety.

In a narrower sense, and leaving aside the fact that the various Western alchemical authors declare that they have each employed a different ciphered language to refer to the same things and the same operations, there is no question that alchemy is not simply a Western phenomenon. There are, for example, a Hindu alchemy and a Chinese alchemy. And anyone who is at all in touch with the theme can see that the symbols, the "matters," and the principle operations correspond to one another; but especially does the structure of a physical (and ultimately metaphysical) science correspond inwardly and outwardly at the same time. Such correspondences are explained by the fact that once present, the same conceptions with respect to the general and "traditional" view of the world, life, and man, lead quite naturally to the same consequences, even in consideration of special technical problems like that of transmutation. So, as long as this "traditional" conception persists—even when only residually in lifeless philosophical and logical distortions with respect to which the differences between Orient and Occident were minimal in comparison with those that would exist later between alchemy and the modern mentality—while it has continued to remain alive, we will find alchemy recognized and cultivated by illustrious spirits, thinkers, theologians, "natural philosophers," kings, emperors, and even popes. Dedication to a discipline of this kind has not been considered incompatible with the highest spiritual or intellectual level. One proof, among many others, is that more than one alchemical treatise has been attributed to the "angelical master," Thomas Aquinas.[5]

An alchemical tradition has enigmatically extended itself not only across at least fifteen centuries of Western history, but even across the continents, as deeply into the Orient as into the West.

---

[5] See M.-L. von Franz, *Aurora consurgens*, vol. 3 of *Mysterium Coniunctionis* (Zurich, 1957).

. . . . . .

Our work will not be directed toward convincing those who do not wish to be convinced. But it will supply firm points of support for anyone who reads it without prejudice. On the other hand, anyone who is in accord, be it only with a single one of our conclusions, will not fail to recognize its entire importance. It is like the discovery of a new land whose existence was previously unsuspected—a strange land, alarming, sewn with spirits, metals, and gods, whose labyrinthine passages and phantasmagoria are concentrated little by little in a single point of light: the "myth" of a race of "kingless" and "free" creatures, "Lords of the Serpent and the Mother" to use the proud expressions of the same hermetic texts.

Apart from the introduction, the purpose of which is to clarify what we have called the "heroic" expression of the royal tradition, the present work consists of two parts: the first dedicated to the symbols and the doctrine, the second to practice.

The limits of the present edition have obliged us to forego a quantity of quotations from Greek, Latin, and Arabic texts, so that we have saved only what is essential. We have also tried to be as clear as possible. But the reader should have no illusions. Rather than being simply read, this book demands *study*. For this reason, after having acquired a coherent vision, one must go back over basic teachings and particular symbols, which can never be understood isolated from the rest, in order to exhaust all their possible and different meanings. For our part we can assure the reader that in the present book he will find a solid basis for dealing with any hermetico-alchemical text no matter how obscure and sybilline. For the rest, we will insist only that in the practice section there is good deal more than appears at first glance, should the reader really want to know by experience the reality and possibilities the "Sons of Hermes" are talking about. In any case, elsewhere[6] we have given everything necessary for integrating all that can be learned from this book, with a view to the evocation and effective contacts of the spirit with the metaphysical, superhistorical elements of the hermetic tradition.

---

[6] Cf. the three volumes of the collective work *Introduzione alla magia*.

Part One

the symbols and teachings

che cRee,
che seRpenc,
AnÒ
che cicAns

One of the symbols that we encounter in diverse traditions remote in both time and space is that of the *tree*. Metaphysically, the tree expresses the universal force that spreads out in manifestation the same way that the plant energy spreads out from its invisible roots to the trunk, branches, leaves, and fruit. Consistently associated with the tree are on the one hand, ideas of immortality and supernatural consciousness, and on the other, symbols of mortal, destructive forces and frightening natures such as dragons, serpents, or demons. There also exists a whole cycle of mythological references to dramatic events in which the tree plays a central part and in whose allegory profound meanings are hidden. The biblical myth of the fall of Adam, among others, is well known. Let us highlight some of its variants, but not without first pointing out the *universality* of the symbolical elements of which it is composed.

In the Vedas and Upanishads we find the "world tree," inverted sometimes to suggest the origin of its power in "the heights," in the "heavens."[1] Here we discover a ready convergence of many elements and ideas: from this tree drips the nectar

---

[1] Cf. *Kathā-Upanishad*, 6 1; *Bhagavad-Gita*, 15 1-3, 10 26

of immortality (*soma* or *amrita*) and whoever sips it is inspired with a vision beyond the reaches of time, a vision that awakens the memory of all the infinite forms of existence. In the foliage of the tree hides Yama, the god of beyond the grave, whom we also know as the king of the primordial state.[2]

In Iran we also find the tradition of a double tree, one of which comprises, according to the *Bundahesh*, all seeds, while the other is capable of furnishing the drink of immortality (*haoma*) and spiritual knowledge;[3] which leads us immediately to think again of the two biblical trees of Paradise, the one of Life, and the other of Knowledge. The first, then, is equivalent (Matt. 13:31–32) to the representation of the kingdom of heaven that sprouts from the seed irrigated by the man in the symbolical "field"; we encounter it again in the Apocalypse of John (22:2), and especially in the Qabalah as that "great and powerful Tree of Life" by which "Life is raised on high" and with which is connected a "sprinkling" by virtue of which is produced the resurrection of the "dead": a patent equivalence to the power of immortality in the Vedic *amrita* and Iranian *haoma*.[4]

Assyro-Babylonian mythology also recognizes a "cosmic tree" rooted in Eridu, the "House of Profundity" or "House of Wisdom." But what is important to recognize in these traditions—because this element will be useful in what follows— is another association of symbols: the tree also represents for us the personification of the Divine Mother, of that same general type as those great Asiatic goddesses of Nature: Ishtar, Anat, Tammuz [*sic*], Cybele, and so forth. We find, then, the idea of the *feminine* nature of the universal force represented by the tree. This idea is not only confirmed by the goddess consecrated to the Dodona oak—which, besides being a place of oracles, is also a fountain of spritual knowledge—but also by the Hesperides who are charged with guarding the tree, whose fruit has the same symbolic value as the Golden Fleece and the same immortalizing power as that tree of the Irish legend of Mag Mell, also guarded by a feminine entity. In the *Edda* it is the goddess Idhunn who is charged with guarding the apples of immortality, while in the cosmic tree, Yggdrasil, we again encounter the central symbol, rising before the fountain of Mimir (guarding it and reintroducing the symbol of the dragon at the root of the tree), which contains the principle of all *wisdom*.[5] Finally, according to a Slavic saga, on the island of Bajun there is an oak guarded by a dragon (which we must associate with the biblical serpent, with the monsters of Jason's adventures, and with the garden of the Hesperides), that simultaneously is the residence of a feminine principle called "The Virgin of the Dawn."

Also rather interesting is the variation according to which the tree appears to us as the tree of *dominion* and of *universal empire*, such as we find in legends like

---

[2] Goblet D'Alviella, *La migration des symboles* (Paris, 1891), 151–206.

[3] Jaçna, 9 and 10.

[4] *Zohar*, 1.226b; 1.256a; 3.61a; 3.128b; 2.61b; 1.225b; 1.131a

[5] Cf. D'Alviella, *Migration*.

The Tree, the Serpent, and the Titans · · · · · · · · · · · · · · · · · · · 3

those of Holger and Prester John, whom we have mentioned elsewhere.[6] In these legends the Tree is often doubled—the Tree of the Sun and the Tree of the Moon.

Hermetism repeats the same primordial symbolic tradition and the same association of ideas, and the symbol of the tree is quite prevalent in alchemical texts. The tree shelters the "fountain" of Bernard of Treviso, in whose center is the symbol of the dragon Ouroboros, who represents the "All."[7] It personifies "Mercury," either as the first principle of the hermetic Opus, equivalent to the divine Water or "Water of Life" that gives resurrection to the dead and illuminates the Sons of Hermes, or else it represents the "Lady of the Philosophers." But it also represents the Dragon, that is, a dissolving force, a power that *kills*. The Tree of the Sun and the Tree of the Moon are also hermetic symbols, sometimes producing *crowns* in the place of fruits.

This quick glance at the stuff of religion, which we could expand indefinitely, is enough to establish the permanence and universality of a tradition of vegetable symbolism expressing the universal force, predominantly in feminine form. This vegetable symbolism is the repository of a supernatural science, of a force capable of giving immortality and dominion, but at the same time warns of a multiple danger that complicates the myth in turn to various purposes, different truths and visions.

In general, the danger is the same anyone runs in seeking the conquest of immortality or enlightenment by contacting the universal force; the one who makes contact must be capable of withstanding overwhelming grandeur. But we also know myths in which there are heroes who confront the tree, and divine natures (in the Bible, God himself is hypostasized) that defend it and impede access to it. And the result, then, is a battle variously interpreted, according to the traditions.

There is a double possibility: in one case the tree is conceived as a *temptation*, which leads to ruin and damnation for anyone who succumbs to it; in the other, it is conceived as an object of possible conquest which, after dealing with the dragons or divine beings defending it, transforms the darer into a god and sometimes transfers the attributes of divinity or immortality from one race to another.

Thus, the knowledge that tempted Adam[8] to "become as God" and that he attained only by immediately being knocked down and deprived of the Tree of Life by the very Being with whom he had hoped to equalize himself. Yet this is the same knowledge, supernatural after all, that the Buddha acquires under the tree, despite

---

[6] Evola, *Il mistero del Graal e la tradizione ghibellina dall'Impero* (Milan, 1964).

[7] Cf. the ex-libris hermetic reproduction by L. Charbonneau-Lassay, in *Regnabit*, no. 3-4, (1925). In the central space of the tree is found the Phoenix, symbol of immortality, who brings us back to *amrita* and *haoma*.

[8] Although we shall return to the topic, let us pause for a moment to allow the reader to intuit the profound meaning of the symbol, according to which "temptation" is represented by "woman"—the "Living Eve"—who orginally formed part of Adam.

all the efforts of Mara, who, in another tradition, stole the lightning from Indra.[9]

As chief of the Devas, Indra himself, in turn, had appropriated *amrita* from a lineage of anterior beings having characters sometimes divine and sometimes titanic: the Asuras, who with *amrita* had possessed the privilege of immortality. Equally successful were Odin (by means of hanging himself in self-sacrifice from the tree), Hercules, and Mithras, who after fashioning a symbolic cloak from the leaves of the Tree and eating its fruits, was able to dominate the Sun.[10] In an ancient Italic myth, the King of the Woods, Nemi, husband of a goddess (tree = woman), had to be always on guard because his power and dignity would pass to whomever could seize and kill him.[11] The spiritual achievement in the Hindu tradition is associated with cutting and felling the "Tree of Brahma" with the powerful ax of Wisdom.[12]

But Agni, who in the form of a hawk had snatched a branch of the tree, is struck down: his feathers, scattered over the earth, produce a plant whose sap is the "terrestrial soma"; an obscure allusion, perhaps, to the passing of the legacy of the deed to another race (now terrestrial). The same advantage Prometheus gained by similar daring, but for which he fell, was chained, and suffered the torment of the hawk or eagle lacerating his innards. And if Hercules is the prototype of the "Olympian" hero who liberates Prometheus and Theseus, we have a quite different personification in the heroic type of Jason, who is of the "Uranian" race. After Jason returns with the Golden Fleece, found hanging on the tree, he ends by dying under the ruins of the Argo, the ship which, built of Dodona's oak, conveyed the very power that had made the theft possible. The story is repeated in the *Edda* of Loki who stole the apples of immortality from the goddess Idhunn who was guarding them. And the Chaldean Gilgamesh, after cultivating the "great crystalline fruit" in a forest of "trees like those of the gods," finds the entrance blocked by guardians.[13] The Assyrian god Zu, who aspiring to the supreme dignity took unto himself the "tablets of destiny" and with them the power of prophetic knowledge, is nevertheless seized by Baal, changed into a bird of prey and exiled, like Prometheus, on a mountaintop.

The myth speaks to us of an event involving fundamental risk and fraught with

---

[9] Cf. Weber, *Indische Studien*, 3:466.

[10] Cf. F. Cumont, *Les mystères de Mithra* (Brussels, 1913), 133.

[11] This myth is the center around which is crystallized the exhaustive material of the famous work of J. G. Frazer, *The Golden Bough*.

[12] *Bhagavad-Gita*, 15.3

[13] Connection to the Hebrides is obvious. This text, incomplete as it is, does not exclude an ulterior phase of the adventure (cf. D'Alviella, *Migration*, 190). The better known text, *The Epic of Gilgamesh*, gives a negative unravelling of the adventure. Gilgamesh loses, while asleep, the plant of immortality that he had finally won after crossing the "waters of death" and arriving at the "primordial state" kingdom.

elemental uncertainty. In Hesiod's theomachies, typically in the legend of the King of the Forest, gods or transcendental men are shown as possessors of a power that can be transmitted, together with the attribute of divinity, to whomever is capable of attaining it. In that case the primordial force has a *feminine* nature (tree = divine woman). It conveys the violence which, according to the Gospels is said to be necessary against the "Kingdom of Heaven." But among those who try it, those who are able to break through, triumph, while those who fail pay for their audacity by suffering the lethal effects of the same power they had hoped to win.

The interpretation of such an event brings to light the possibility of two opposing concepts: *magical* hero and *religious* saint. According to the first, the one who succumbs in the myth is but a being whose fortune and ability have not been equal to his courage. But according to the second concept, the religious one, the sense is quite different: in this case bad luck is transformed into blame, the heroic undertaking is a sacrilege and damned, not for having failed, but for itself. Adam is not a being who has failed where others triumph, he has *sinned*, and what happens to him is the only thing that can happen. All he can do is undo his sin by expiation, and above all by denying the impulse that led him on the enterprise in the first place. The idea that the conquered can think of revenge, or try to maintain the dignity that his act has confirmed, would seem from the "religious" point of view as the most incorrigible "Luciferism."

But the religious view is not the only one. As we have already shown above, this point of view is associated with a humanized and secularized variation on the "sacerdotal" (as opposed to "royal") tradition and is in no way superior to the other—the heroic—which has been affirmed in both Eastern and Western traditions and whose spirit is reflected in great measure by hermetism. One exegesis gives us, in fact, the "rod of Hermes"[14] as a symbol of the union of a son (Zeus) with his mother (Rhea, symbol of the universal force), whom he has won after killing the father and usurping his kingdom: this is the symbol of "philosophic incest" that we shall encounter in all of the hermetic literature. Hermes himself is, of course, the messenger of the gods, but he is also the one who wrests the scepter from Zeus, the girdle from Venus, and from Vulcan, god of "Fire and Earth," the tools of his allegorical art. In the Egyptian tradition, as the ancient authors tell us, Hermes, invested with treble greatness—Hermes Trismegistus—is confused with the image of one of the kings and teachers of the primordial age that gave to men the principles of a higher civilization. The precise meaning of all this can escape no one.

But there is still more. Tertullian refers to one tradition that reappears in Arab-

---

[14] In Athenagoras (20.292) we find also an interference in the heroic cycle of Hercules; the one in which Rhea is bound by the "rope of Hercules."

Syrian alchemical hermetism and brings us back to the same point. Tertullian[15] says that the "damned and worthless" works of nature, the secrets of metals, the virtues of plants, the forces of magical conjurations, and "all those alien teachings that make up the science of the stars"—that is to say, the whole corpus of the ancient magico-hermetic sciences—was revealed to men by the fallen angels. This idea appears in the *Book of Enoch*, wherein it is completed within the context of this most ancient tradition, betraying its own unilaterality to the religious interpretation. Merejkowski[16] has shown that there is an apparent correspondence between the B'nai Elohim, the fallen angels who descended to Mount Hermon that are mentioned in the *Book of Enoch*,[17] and the lineage of the Witnesses and Watchers—ἐγρήγοροι—(about whom we are told in the *Book of Jubilees*,[18]) and who came down to instruct humanity. In the same way Prometheus "taught mortals all the arts."[19] Moreover, in *Enoch* (69:6-7), Azazel, "who seduced Eve," taught men the use of weapons that kill, which, metaphor aside, signifies that he had infused in men the *warrior spirit*. Here we can understand how the myth of the fall applies: the angels were seized with desire for "women." We have already explained what "woman" means in connection with the tree and our interpretation is confirmed when we examine the Sanskrit word *shakti*, which is used metaphysically to refer to "the wife" of a god, his "consort," and at the same time to his *power.*[20]

These angels were prey to the desire for power and, in "mating," fell—descended to earth—onto an elevated place (Mount Hermon). From this union were born the Nephelim, a powerful race (the Titans—τιτᾶνες—says the Giza Papyrus), allegorically described as "giants," but whose supernatural nature remains to be discovered in the *Book of Enoch* (15:11): "They need neither food, nor do they thirst and they evade [physical] perception."

The Nephelim, the "fallen" angels, are nothing less than the titans and "the watchers," the race that the *Book of Baruch* (3:26) calls, "glorious and warlike," the same race that awoke in men the spirit of the heroes and warriors, who

---

[15] *De cultu feminarum*, 1.2b.

[16] D Merejkowski. *Das Geheimnis des Westens* (Leipzig, 1929), chaps. 4 and 5

[17] *Book of Enoch*, 6:1-6; 7:1.

[18] *Book of Jubilees*, 4.5, in Kautzch, *Apokryphen und Pseudoepigraphen* (Tübingen, 1900), 2:47.

[19] Aeschylus, *Prometheus*, 506.

[20] Fabre d'Olivet (*The Hebraic Tongue Restored*) in his commentary on the biblical passage (Gen. 4:2), sees in "women" a symbol of the "creative powers." A special pertinence to what we will say about the compelling character of the hermetic art is shown in the Tibetan symbolism wherein Wisdom appears again as a "woman," while the "method" or "Art" plays the part of the male in coitus with her. Cf. *Shrichakrasambhara*, A. Avalon, ed. (London-Calcutta, 1919), xiv, 23; Dante (*Convivio*, 2.15.4) calls the Philosophers the "paramours" of the "woman," which in the symbology of the Fideli D'Amore represents Gnosis again, the esoteric Knowledge.

invented the arts, and who transmitted the mystery of magic.[21] What more decisive proof concerning the spirit of the hermetico-alchemical tradition can there be than the explicit and continuous reference in the texts precisely to that tradition? We read in the hermetic literature: "The ancient and sacred books," says Hermes, "teach that certain angels burned with desire for women. They descended to earth and taught all the works of Nature. They were the ones who created the [hermetic] works and from them proceeds the primordial tradition of this Art."[22] The very word *chemi*, from *chema*, from which derive the words *alchemy* and *chemistry*, appears for the first time in a papyrus of the Twelfth Dynasty, referring to a tradition of just this kind.

But what is the meaning of this art, this art of "the Sons of Hermes," this "Royal Art"?

The words of the theistically conceived God in the biblical myth of the tree are the following: "The man has become as one of us, to know good and evil; and now, lest he put forth his hand, and take also of the tree of life, and eat, and live forever." (Gen. 3:22-24). We can distinguish two points in this quotation: first of all, the recognition of the divine dignity of Adam, which he has won; and after that the implicit reference to the possibility of transferring this achievement to the rank of universal power, symbolized by the Tree of Life, and of confirming it in immortality. In the unfortunate result of Adam's adventure, God, being hypostatized, was unable to interfere but he could keep him from the second possibility: access to the Tree of Life would be barred by the flaming sword of the cherubim. In Orphism, the myth of the Titans has an analogous sense: lightning strikes & scorches "with a thirst that burns and consumes" those who have "devoured" the god, a thirst that is itself symbolized by the bird of prey that pecks at Prometheus. And in Phrygia Attis was mourned, χηρεὸν στάχυν ἀνηθέντα, "corn cut while still green," and his emasculation, that is to say, the deprivation of the virile power that Attis suffers, corresponds well enough to the prohibition "of the powerful tree at the center of Paradise" and to the chaining of Prometheus to the rock.

But the flame is not extinguished, rather it is transmitted and purified in the secret tradition of the Royal Art, which in certain hermetic texts is explicitly identified with magic, extending even to the construction of a second "Wood of

---

[21] In the more original conception, which we also find in Hesiod, "the watchers" are identified as beings of the primordial age, the Golden Age, who never died but simply made themselves invisible to men down through the ages thereafter.

[22] In M. Berthelot's anthology, *La chimie au moyen-âge* (Paris, 1893) 2:238 (hereafter cited as *CMA*). The same tradition is found in the Koran (2:96), which speaks of the angels Harut and Marut, both "enamored" of the "woman" and who descended to teach magic to men; and who fell into a hole with their feet sticking up. This could be interpreted as the Vedic tree, whose head is below and its roots are "above."

Life" as a substitute for the lost one.[23] It persists in seeking access "to the center of the tree in the midst of the terrestrial paradise" with all that that terrible struggle implies.[24] It is no more and no less than a repetition of the old temerity, in the spirit of the Olympian Hercules, conqueror of the Titans and liberator of Prometheus; of Mithras, subjugator of the Sun; in a word, of that very personality that in the Buddhist Orient received the name of "Lord of Men and Gods."

What distinguishes the Royal Art is its character of *necessity* or compulsion. Berthelot, by way of Tertullian's statements cited above, tells us: "Scientific law is fatalistic and indifferent. The knowledge of nature and the power derived from it can be turned equally to good or evil," and this is the fundamental point of contrast with the religious vision that subordinates everything to elements of devout dependency, fear of God and morality. And Berthelot continues, "Something of this antinomy in the hatred for the [hermetic] sciences runs through the *Book of Enoch* and Tertullian."[25] Nothing can be more exact than this: although hermetic science is not material science, which is all it could have been in Berthelot's view, the amoral and determining character that he sees in the latter pertains equally to the former. A maxim of Ripley in this regard is quite significant: "If the principles on which it operates are true and the steps are correct, the effect must be certain, and none other is the true secret of the [hermetic] Philosophers."[26] Agrippa, quoting Porphyry, speaks of the determining power of the rites, in which the divinities are *forced* by prayer, *overcome* and *obliged* to descend. He adds that the magical formulae *force* the occult energies of the astral entities to intervene, who *do not obey prayers* but act solely by virtue of a natural chain of necessity.[27] Plotinus's idea is no different: the fact in itself of the oration produces the effect according to a deterministic relationship, and not because such entity pays attention to the words or intention of the prayer itself.[28] In a commentary of Zosimos, we read: "Experience is the supreme taskmaster, because on the foundation of proven results, it teaches those who understand what best leads to the goal."[29] The hermetic Art consists, then, in an obligatory method that is exercised

---

[23] Cesare Della Riviera, *Il mondo magico degli heroi* (Milan, 1605), 4, 5, 49.

[24] Basil Valentine, *Azoth,* in Manget, *Biblioteca chemica curiosa* (Genoa, 1702), 2:214 (hereafter cited as *BCC*). In S. Trismosin's *Aurum vellus* (Rohrschach, 1598) is an illustration of great significance: we see a man in the act of climbing the Tree whose trunk is traversed by the symbolic stream. References to Hercules, to Jason, and their deeds are explicit and frequent in the literature, and in them—which is even more important—the soul is unexpectedly called *Prometheus.*

[25] M. Berthelot, *Les origines de l'alchimie (Paris, 1885),* 10, 17–19.

[26] Philalethes, *Epist. di Ripley,* §8.

[27] *De occulta philosophia,* 2:60; 3:32.

[28] *Enneads,* 4.42.26.

[29] Cit. in M. Berthelot, *Collection des anciens alchimistes grecques* (Paris, 1887), 2:284 (hereafter cited as *CAG*).

over the spiritual powers, by supernatural means if you will (the symbolic hermetic Fire is often called "unnatural" or "against nature"), but always excluding every kind of religious, moral, or finalistic tie or any relationship that is alien to a law of simple determinism between cause and effect. To return by way of the tradition to those who "are watching"—ἐγρήγοροι—those who have robbed the tree and possessed the "woman," this reflects a "heroic" symbolism and is applied in the spiritual world to constitute something that—as we shall see—is said to possess a worthiness higher than anything we have mentioned before;[30] and this is not defined by the religious term "holy," but by the warrior of the "King." It is always a king, a being crowned with a royal color, the purple, the final color of the hermetico-alchemical opus, and with the royal and solar metal, gold, that constitutes, as we have said, the center of all this symbolism.

And as for the worthiness of those who have been reintegrated by the Art, the expressions in the texts are precise. Zosimos calls the race of Philosophers: "autonomous, nonmaterialistic and without king," and "custodians of the Wisdom of the Centuries"—ἀβασίλευτος γὰρ αὐτῶν ἡ γενεὰ χαὶ αὐτόνομος.[31] "He is above Destiny"—τὶ φιλόσοφως γένος ἀνωτερον τῆς εἱμαρμένης ἔιπον[32]—"Superior to men, immortal," says Pebechius of his master.[33] And the tradition passed on as far as Cagliostro will be: "Free and master of Life," having "command over the angel natures."[34] Plotinus has already mentioned the temerity of those who have entered into the world, that is, who have acquired a body, which, as we can see, is one of the meanings of the fall,[35] and Agrippa[36] speaks of the terror that inspired man in

---

[30] It must be borne in mind that this superiority depends on the specific perspective of the heroic point of view; to which, in the final analysis, it is relative. The dark ages of the primordial tradition can be seen here, with their "generations." From the purely metaphysical point of view the essence of all authentic initiation is always the reintegration of man with the "primordial" state.

[31] *CAG*, 2:213

[32] Ibid., 229

[33] *CMA*, 2:310. That the alchemists were conscious of fashioning an immortality contrary to the intention of "God," is observed, for instance, in Geber, who in the *Livre de la miséricorde* (*CMA*, 3:173), says, "If he [God] has put in him [man] diverging elements it is because he wanted to assure the purpose of the created being. God did not want every being to survive forever, apart from him, so he inflicted on man this disparity of the four natures, which lead to man's death, and the separation of his soul and body." But elsewhere (*Livre des balances*, *CMA*, 3:147-8), the same author proposes to equilibrate the natures in man, once decomposed, to give him a new existence "such that he will no longer be able to die," because "once this equilibrium is attained, beings do not change, nor become corrupt nor ever modify themselves again."

[34] See this text in the magazine *Ignis* (1925), 227, 305.

[35] *Enneads*, 5.9.14; cf. 5.1.1; in the *Corpus Hermeticum* we see the analogous audacity in "leaving the spheres" in the same sense that Lucifer (Boehme, *De signaturarerum*, 16, §40) had exited from the "harmony" of the world.

[36] *De occulta philosophia*, 3:40.

his *natural* state, that is before his fall, when instead of instilling fear, he himself succumbed to fear: "This fear, which is the mark imprinted on man by God, makes all things submit to him and recognize him as superior" as carrier of that "quality called *Pachad* by the Qabalists, the left hand, the sword of the Lord."

But there is something else: the dominion of the "two natures" that contain the secret of the "Tree of Good and Evil." The teaching is found in the *Corpus Hermeticum*: "Man loses no worthiness for possessing a mortal part, but very much on the contrary, mortality augments his possibility and his power. His double functions are possible for him precisely because of his double nature: because he is so constituted that it is possible for him to embrace both the divine and the terrestrial at the same time."[37] "So let us not be afraid to tell the truth. The true man is above them [the celestial gods], or at least equal to them. For no god leaves his sphere to come to earth, whereas man ascends to heaven and measures it. Let us dare to say that a man is a mortal god and a celestial god is an immortal man."[38]

Such is the truth of the "new race" that the Royal Art of the "Sons of Hermes" is building on earth, elevating what has fallen, calming the "thirst," restoring power to the enfeebled, bestowing the fixed and impassive gaze of the "eagle" to the wounded eye blinded by the "lightning flash," conferring Olympian and royal dignity to what used to be a Titan. In a gnostic text pertaining to the same ideal world in which Greek alchemy received its first expressions it is said the "Life-Light" in the Gospel of John is "the mysterious race of perfect men, *unknown to previous generations.*" Following this text is a precise reference to Hermes; the text recalls that in the temple of Samothrace there stood two statues of naked men, their arms raised to heaven, their members erect,[39] "as in the statue of Hermes on Mount Cyllene," which represented the primordial man, Adamas, and reborn man, "who is completely of the same nature as the first." And it is said: "First is the blessed nature of Man from above; then the mortal nature here below; third the *race of those without a king* that is raised up, where Mary resides, the one whom we seek."[40] "This being, blessed and incorruptible," explains Simon Magus, "resides in

---

[37] *Corpus Hermeticum*, 9.4; cf. Boehme, *Aurora 11*, §72: "The soul of man sees much more deeply than the angels, because it sees as much of heaven as of hell"; and he adds that "because of that man lives in great danger in this world." In the *Sepher Yetzirah* (chap. 6) the seat of the heart is assimilated to that of the "King in war."

[38] *Corpus Hermeticum* 10.24–25.

[39] By way of constituting the figure **Y** schematically, which is the sign of "Cosmic-man-with-upraised-arms," one of the fundamental symbols of the Hyperborean, Nordic-Atlantic tradition has been preserved as a rune (Rune of Life) in the Norse-Teutonic tradition.

[40] Hippolytus, *Philosophumena*, 5.8. This Mariam is evidently the equivalent of the symbolic "woman" with whom the "Philosophers" joined, the "Virgin" who is mentioned in this passage of d'Espagnet (*Arcanum hermeticae philosophiae opus*, §58, in *BCC* 2): "Take a winged Virgin, impregnated with the semen of the First Male but still preserving the glory of her virginity intact"; whose meaning is, in turn,

every being, hidden; potential rather than active. It is precisely the one who keeps standing; who has kept standing above and who will continue to remain standing; who has continued standing here below, having been engendered by the image [reflection] in the flood of waters; and who will again stand on high, before infinite potentiality, whereupon he will be made perfectly equal to it."[41]

This same teaching is repeated in the many texts of the hermetic tradition,[42] and holds the key to all its meanings, as we shall attempt to illustrate in its principle aspects in the pages that follow.

---

the same as Rhea—the shakti aspect or "power" aspect of the One—which, the father having been killed (the First Male of whom d'Espagnet speaks), Zeus possesses, making of his mother his wife. Also in the Qabalah the "Matrona" is mentioned in whom all the powers of the king have been entrusted, (that is to say, Jehovah), who is the wife (shakti) also of the king and who was "espoused" by Moses as well (*Zohar*, 2.144b, 145a; 3.51a).

[41] Hippolytus, *Philosophumena*, 6.17.

[42] Cf., for example, the "Tables of the Theorems," §23 of J. Dee, *Monas hieroglyphica* (Antwerp, 1564), wherein are also mentioned three stages: the first refers to a "seed of power" prior to the elements and self-conceived"; the second to "punishment and sepulcher"; the third to a state "existing after the elements," which is resurrection by one's own power and "triumph of glory."

. . . .
One
. . . .

the plurality
and duality
of civilizations

Recently, in contrast to the notion of progress and the idea that history has been represented as the more or less continuous upward evolution of collective humanity, the idea of a plurality of the forms of civilization and of a relative incommunicability between them has been confirmed. According to this second and new vision of history, civilization breaks down into epochs and disconnected cycles. At a given moment and within a given race a specific conception of the world and of life is affirmed from which follows a specific system of truths, principles, understandings, and realizations. A civilization springs up, gradually reaches a culminating point, and then falls into darkness and, more often than not, disappears. A cycle has ended. Perhaps another will rise again some day, somewhere else. Perhaps it may even take up the concerns of preceding civilizations, but any connection between them will be strictly analogical. The transition from one cycle of civilization to another—one completely alien to the other—implies a jump, which in mathematics is called a discontinuity.[1]

Although this view is a healthy reaction to the superstition of history as

---

[1] The best known exponent of this concept is O. Spengler (*The Decline of the West*). Since de Gobineau, this theory has had further developments in connection with the doctrine of race.

progress—which came into fashion more or less at the same time as materialism and Western scientism[2]—nevertheless, we should be cautious, for in addition to a plurality of civilizations we have to recognize a duality—especially when we limit ourselves to those times and essential structures that we can embrace with some measure of certainty.

Modern civilization stands on one side and on the other the entirety of all the civilizations that have preceded it (for the West, we can put the dividing line at the end of the Middle Ages). At this point the rupture is complete. Apart from the multitudinous variety of its forms, premodern civilization, which we may as well call "traditional,"[3] means something quite different. For there are two worlds, one of which has separated itself by cutting off nearly every contact with the past. For the great majority of moderns, that means any possibility of understanding the traditional world has been completely lost.

This premise is indispensable for the examination of our subject. The hermetico-alchemical tradition forms part of the cycle of premodern "traditional" civilization and in order to understand its spirit we need to translate it inwardly from one world to the other. Who undertakes this study without having acquired the ability to rise above the modern mind-set or who has not awakened to a new sensitivity that can place itself in contact with the general spiritual stream that gave life to the tradition in the first place, will succeed only in filling his head with words, symbols, and fantastic allegories. Moreover, it is not just a question of intellectual understanding. We have to bear in mind that ancient man not only had a different way of thinking and feeling, but also a different way of *perceiving* and *knowing*. The heart of the matter that will concern us is to reevoke, by means of an actual transformation of the consciousness, this older basis of understanding and action.

Only then will the unexpected light of certain expressions dawn on us and certain symbols be empowered to awaken our interior perception. Only then will we be conducted through them to new heights of human realization and to the understanding that will make it possible for designated "rites" to confer "magical" and operant power, and for the creation of a new "science" that bears no resemblance to anything that goes by that name today.

---

[2] In fact, the extraordinary idea of a continuous evolution could only have been born of an exclusive contemplation of the material and technical aspects of civilizations, completely overlooking their qualitative and spiritual elements.

[3] The source for the precise concept of "traditional civilization" as opposed to "modern" is René Guénon's *The Crisis of the Modern World* (London, 1942).

Two

Livinɢ ᴅᴀᴄᴜʀᴇ

The fundamental issue in our study is the human experience of nature. The average modern man's relationship with nature is not the one that prevailed in the premodern "cycle," to which, along with many other traditions, the hermetico-alchemical tradition belongs. The study of nature today devotes itself exhaustively to a conglomeration of strictly reasoned laws concerning various "phenomena"—light, electricity, heat, etc.—which spread out kaleidoscopically before us utterly devoid of any spiritual meaning, derived solely from mathematical processes. In the traditional world, on the contrary, nature was not thought about but *lived*, as though it were a great, sacred, animated body, "the visible expression of the invisible." Knowledge about nature derived from inspiration, intuition, and visions, and was transmitted "by initiation" as so many living "mysteries," referring to things that today have lost their meaning and seem banal and commonplace—as, for example, the art of building, medicine, cultivation of the soil, and so forth. *Myth* was not an arbitrary or fantastic notion: it arose from a *necessary* process in which the same forces that shape things acted upon the plastic faculty of the imagination, unfettered by the bodily senses, to dramatize themselves in images and figures that were woven into the tapestry of sensory experience and resulted finally in a "significance" of moment.[1]

"Universe, hear my plea. Earth, open. Let the Waters open for me. Trees, do not tremble. Let the heavens open and the winds be silent! Let all my faculties

---

[1] Cf. F. W. Schelling, *Einleitung in die Philosophie der Mythologie* in *Sammelte Werke*, 2:192, 215–17, 222; also C. Puini, *Introduzione alla magia* (Lanciano, 1919), 3:66.

celebrate in me the All and One!"—these are the words of a hymn that the "Sons of Hermes" recited at the beginning of their sacred operations;[2] such was the height to which they were capable of elevating themselves. The following is an even more emphatic version:

> The gates of Heaven are open;
> The gates of Earth are open;
> The Way of the Current is open;
> My spirit has been heard by all the gods and genii;
> By the spirit of Heaven—and Earth—the Sea
> —and the Currents.[3]

And such is the teaching of the *Corpus Hermeticum*: "Rise up above every height; descend deeper than any depth; concentrate into thyself all the sensations of created things of Water, Fire, Dry and Wet. Think of finding yourself simultaneously everywhere, in the earth, sea or sky; think of having never been born, of still being an embryo: young and old, dead and beyond death. Embrace everything at the same time: all times, places, things, qualities and quantities."

These possiblities of perception and communication, this aptitude for connections, despite what we believe today, were not "fantasies," wild superstitions, or extravagant exaggerations. On the contrary, they were part of an experience as real as that of physical things. More precisely: the spiritual constitution of the man of "traditional civilizations" was such that any physical perception had simultaneously a psychic component, which "animated" it, adding to the naked image a "meaning" and at the same time a special and powerful emotional overtone."[4] This is how ancient "physics" could be both a theology and a transcendental psychology: it derived from quite universal metaphysical essences, primarily from the superconscious world, in sudden flashes of light wherein matter was provided by the sense organs. Natural science was a corollary spiritual science and the many meanings of its symbols reflected different aspects of a single knowledge.

---

[2] *Corpus Hermeticum*, 13.18.

[3] Leiden papyrus V in M. Berthelot, *Introduction à l'étude de la chimie des anciens* (Paris, 1889).

[4] Investigations undertaken by sociologists (Durkheim, Lévy-Bruhl, etc.) have uncovered something very similar today in the ways that so-called primitive people perceive; which people, in reality, are not primitive, but the degenerating remains of a cycle of premodern civilization.

Three

Che hermetic
Knowledge

It is on the above basis that we have to understand the whole idea of the hermetico-alchemical science. In a certain sense it can also be called a "natural science," but completely disregarding all the present connotations such a term may evoke in our minds. Today the medieval designation of "natural philosophy" expresses rather the synthesis of two elements, now standing on two separate planes, one intellectually unrealistic (philosophy) and the other consciously materialistic (science). But, given the character of organic unity—of a *cosmos*—that the universe offered to traditional man, there was also an implicit *anagogical* power in this "natural" understanding, namely, the possibility of rising to a transcendent metaphysical plane. On this basis are to be understood such expressions as "hieratic science," "divine" and "dogmatic art"—τέχνη θεία, τέχνη δογματικὴ—"Mithraic mystery," "Divine Work"—θεῖον ἔργον—appearing with the origins of alchemy[1] and which are preserved within the entire tradition of what Zacharias would call "divine and supernatural science."[2]

And as psychic sensitivity to the deep forces of nature began to dwindle in later eras, it became common to avoid the ambiguity in the expressions of the hermetic tradition by distinguishing between the "vulgar" or "dead" elements and the

---

[1] Cf., e.g., *CAG*, 2:209, 124, 145; 188, 114.

[2] Zacharias, *De la philosophie naturelle des métaux*, §1.

"living" ones, which are "our elements" (the "our" refers to those who had preserved the original spiritual state of the tradition): "our" Water, "our" Fire, "our" Mercury, etc.—not "those of the vulgar or common"—a jargon for referring to elements that were (physically) invisible, occult, "magical," known only to the "Wise," those "of us who have kept in our hands" those "elements of creation" that must be recognized by us as distinct from the earthy, impure "created elements" that are merely the modifications of physical matter.

"The four Elements in which all things participate," says Flamel,[3] "are not apparent to the senses, but are known by their effects." Air and Fire, of which Bernard of Treviso speaks, are "tenuous and spiritual" and "cannot be seen by physical eyes"; his Sulfur, Arsenic, and Mercury "are not those that the vulgar think them to be" or that "pharmacists sell," but they are "the Philosopher's *spirits*."[4] So "Philosophical Alchemy" is that "which teaches how to investigate, not by appearances, but according to concrete truth, the latent forms [in an Aristotelian sense, the occult formative principles] of things"[5]—an idea confirmed by Razi in the *Lumen luminum:* "This Art is the study of *Occult Philosophy.* In order to follow it, one must be acquainted with hidden and internal natures. In it one speaks of the rise [incorporeal state] and fall [visible state] of the elements and their compounds."[6] The true elements "are as the *soul* of the mixtures," the others are "nothing but the body," explains Pernety.[7]

And if the spontaneous presence or absence of the necessary metaphysical sensitivity itself determined the dividing line between those initiates to whom alone the texts speak and for whom the techniques of the Royal Art bear fruition—and those who are not initiates (for whom it is written not to cast pearls before swine)[8]—for these last there still remained the possibility of attaining the necessary state by means of an appropriate asceticism, even if the miracle of illumination was missing.

We shall discuss this asceticism later, but for the moment we shall confine

---

[3] N. Flamel, *Le désir désiré,* §6.

[4] Bernard of Treviso, *La parole délaissée* in Salmon, ed., *Bibliothèque des philosophes chimiques* (Paris, 1741), 2:401, 416 (hereafter cited as *BPC*). Cf. d'Espagnet, *Arcanum hermeticae,* §44: "Who says that the Moon or the Mercury of the Philosophers is the vulgar Mercury, either wants to deceive or is himself deceived"; and Philalethes, *Epist. di Ripley,* §61: "They are also deluded, who look for our secret in vulgar substances and still hope to find the Gold."

[5] G. Dorn, *Clavis philosophiae chemisticae, BCC,* 1:210.

[6] In *CMA,* 1:312.

[7] A. J. Pernety, *Fables égyptiennes et grecques dévoilées* (Paris, 1786), 1:75.

[8] Cf. C. Agrippa, *De occulta philosophia,* 3:65; G. Dorn, op. cit., 244. This theme derives from the Greek alchemists (*CAG,* 2:62, 63) who declared that they spoke for those who were initiated and had trained the spirit—"those who have understanding," the Arab authors would say—"Everything we say here is strictly for the Sage, not for the ignorant" (*Livre du feu de la pierre, CMA,* 3:220); and J.S.

ourselves to pointing out that within the framework of hermetism, asceticism does not have a moral or religious justification. It is simply a *technique*. Its purpose is to provide an experience that is not limited to the "dead" or "common" aspect of the Elements—as happens in that empiricism on which the modern, profane sciences are based. Instead, a subtle, incorporeal, spiritual quality infuses it. Paracelsus describes this quality in this way: "She [Nature] knows me and I her. I have contemplated the light that is in her. I have verified it in the microcosm and have found it again in the macrocosm."[9]

As is said in the *Hermetic Triumph*, "To know the inner and outward properties of all things" and "to penetrate to the bottom of Nature's operations" is the condition that is imposed on whomever aspires to possess this knowledge.[10] And so it can be said that "who does not understand by himself, no one will ever be able to make understand, do what he will."[11] This science is not acquired through books or reason—others affirm—"but by action, *by an impetuosity of the spirit.*" "For this reason I declare that neither the philosophers who have preceded me nor I myself have written anything except for ourselves"—*nisi solis nobis scripsimus*— "for the philosophers, our successors, and for no one else."[12]

Weidenfeld (*De Secretis Adeptorum*, London, 1634, p. 47); "Alchemists! Open Your Eyes and Seize the Light of Nature!"

[9] *Thesaurus thesaurorum alchimistorum* in A. Poisson, *Cinq traités d'alchimie* (Paris, 1890), 86.

[10] *Entretiens d'Eudoxe et de Pyrophile sur le Triomphe Hermétique*, BPC, 3:225.

[11] B. Treviso, *De la philosophie des métaux*, BPC, 2:398.

[12] Geber, *Summa perfectionis magisterii*, BCC, 1:383.

Four

"ONE THE ALL" AND THE DRAGON OUROBOROS

Only when we have succeeded in recapturing a living and "symbolic" sensitivity toward everything modern man has fossilized as dead "nature" and abstract concepts will we arrive at the first principle of the true hermetic teaching. This principle is *unity*, and the formula that expresses it can be found in the *Chrysopoeia of Cleopatra*:[1] "One the All"—ἕν τὸ πᾶν—to which we can connect the "Telesma, Father of all things" of the Emerald Tablet. Certainly it is not a question, in this case, of a philosophical theory—a hypothesis reducing everything to a single principle—but of an actual *state* brought about by a certain suppression of the law of opposition between I and not-I and between "inside" and "outside" [subjective/objective]. These dualities, with rare exceptions, dominate the common and most recent perception of reality. The experience of this state is the secret of what the literature calls the "Materia of the Work" or "First Matter of the Wise." Only from this state is it possible to "extract" and "shape," by "ritual" and "art"— τεχνικως—everything that the tradition promises, in spiritual as well as operative (i.e., "magical") terms.

---

[1] Marciano codex (Venice), ms. 2325, fol. 188b; and ms. 2327, fol. 196.

The alchemical ideogram of "One the All," is O, the circle: a line or movement that encloses within itself and contains in itself both its end and beginning. In hermetism this symbol expresses the universe and, at the same time, the Great Work.[2] In the *Chrysopoeia* it takes the form of a serpent—Ouroboros—biting its own tail, containing within the space of the circle that it creates, the ἕν τὸ πᾶν. In the same palimpsest is found another pantacle formed by two rings, the inner bearing this inscription: "One is the serpent, which contains the *poison*, according to the double sign [εἰς ἐστιν ὁ ὄφις ὁ ἔχων τὸν ἰὸν μετὰ δύο συνθεματα]" while in the outer circle it says: "One is the all, the source of all and the culmination of all: if the all did not contain the all, it would be nothing."[3]

This "all" has also been called *chaos* ("our" chaos), and *egg*—ὠὸν πρωτόγονον—because it contains the undifferentiated potentiality of every development or generation: it sleeps in the depths of each being as a *sensed myth*, to use Olympiodorus's expression, and it extends to the chaotic multiplicity of scattered things and forms in space and time here below. The closed line O, the circle of Ouroboros, also has another meaning: it alludes to the principle of *exclusion* or "hermetic" sealing that metaphysically expresses the idea of a unilaterally conceived transcendence being extraneous to this tradition. Here the transcendence is conceived as a mode of being contained in the "one thing," which has a "double sign": it is both itself and ultimately the overcoming of itself; it is identity and at the same time *poison*, that is to say, it has the capacity to alter and dissolve; it is both dominating (male) principle and dominated (female) principle—κρατοῦσα καὶ κρατουμένη—and hence *androgynous*. One of the most ancient hermetico-alchemical testaments is the saying that Ostanes confided to Pseudo-Democritus as the key to the books of the "Art": "Nature rejoices in nature, nature triumphs over nature, nature dominates nature" [ἡ φύσις τῇ φύσει τέρπεται, ἡ φύσις τῆς φύσιν νικᾷ, ἡ φύσις τὴν φύσιν κρατεῖ]."[4] But Zosimos says in the same vein, "Nature fascinates [τέρπει], conquers, and dominates nature" and, he adds: "By the Sulfurs[5] are the Sulfurs dominated and restrained"—a principle found recurring throughout the development of the tradition, from the *Turba philosophorum*[6] on.

There proceeds from this a whole series of symbolical expressions intended to indicate the absolute self-sufficiency of the unique principle in every "operation":

---

[2] *Agathodaimon*, cited by Olympiodorus, *CAG*, 2:80; 3:27.

[3] Marciano codex, ms. 2325, fol. 188b.

[4] *CAG*, 2:43.

[5] This is a play on θεῖον, which in Greek means both "sulfur" and "divinity." We are referring to the "fires," the internal forces of things. These expressions, like those following, have both a microcosmic and a macrocosmic sense.

[6] *BCC*, 1:499; cf. *Rosinus ad Sarratantam episcopum*, in *Artis auriferae quam chemiam vocant* (Basel, 1572), 1:288.

Father and Mother of itself[7]—αὐτοπάτορα καὶ αὐτομήτορα—of itself it is the son, by itself it is dissolved, by itself is killed, and to itself it gives new life. The "unique thing that contains in itself the four elements and rules over them,"[8] the "matter of the Wise," also called their "Stone," contains in itself whatever we may need. It kills itself and then brings itself back to life. It weds itself, impregnates itself and dissolves in its own blood."[9] It is its own root—radix ipsius.

We must always bear in mind, moreover, what we've already said: we are not dealing with a philosophical concept, but with the traces of a nature sub specie interioritatis, that goes beyond the antithesis between matter and spirit, between world and superworld. And so Zacharias can say, "If we declare our matter to be spiritual, that is true and if we declare it to be corporeal, we do not lie. If we call it celestial, that is its true designation. If we name it terrestrial, we have spoken correctly."[10] The "egg," which is the image of the world—κόσμου μίματα—receives, in the Hellenistic alchemical texts, the name λίθον τὸν οὐ λίθον,[11] and Braccesco explains: "This is stone [or being, form, corporeality, tangibility] and not stone, it is found everywhere, is base and precious, hidden and visible to everyone."[12] "It is chaos or spirit in the form of a body [the cosmos, perceived nature], but nevertheless is not body."[13] In one brilliant stroke, these enigmatic yet illuminating words of Zosimos synthesize the knowledge of the marvelous thing, via the double pathway and the double expression. It is, again in the evangelic sense, the hermetic Stone of the "Lords of the Temple"—οἰκοδεσπότες—the "Engineers of the Spirit"—φύλαξ πνευμάτων.

Here then is the great divine mystery, the looked-for object. This is the All. From it and by means of it everything comes. It is two natures, one essence: because one is attracted by the other and one is dominated by the other. This is the luminous water (literally, "silver") that is forever fleeing from and attracted by its own elements. It is the divine Water, which no one knew, whose nature is difficult to contemplate because it is not a metal, nor the water of perpetual motion, nor a corporeality. It is indomitable. All in all, it possesses a path and a spirit, and the power of destruction.[14]

---

[7] Corpus Hermeticum, 4.5.8. Cf. Hippolytus, Philosophumena, 6.17

[8] Morienus, Entretiens du Roi Kalid, BPC, 2:86.

[9] Triomphe Hermétique, BPC, 3:196. Cf. Rosinus ad Sarratantem in Artis auriferae, 1:325; Braccesco, La espositione di Geber philosopho (Venice, 1551), fol. 25a; Turba philosophorum, BPC, 2:17, etc.

[10] Philosophie naturelle des métaux, BPC, 2:523.

[11] CAG, 2:18.

[12] Espositione, fol. 66b; cf. R. Bacon, De secretis operibus artis et natura, BCC, 1:622.

[13] A. J. Pernety, Dictionnaire mytho-hermétique (Paris, 1758), 281.

[14] Text in CAG, 2:143-144.

Five

Che hermetic
Presence

Once the combination of corporeal and spiritual has been understood as it must be understood—that is, not as two principle parts (though one of them is called spiritual) of a theoretical cosmos exterior to consciousness, but as a *living* process provided by real experience—we come to another fundamental hermetic teaching: that of immanence, the presence of the "marvelous thing" in man, the "living chaos" in which all possibilities reside. The hermetic texts continually refer to this immanence in the same terms, passing from a cosmico-natural meaning to an inner human meaning. Stone, Water, Mine, Matrix, Egg, Chaos, Dragon, Lead, First Matter, Tree, Spirit, *Telesma*, Quintessence, Woman, Heaven, Seed, Earth, and so on, are symbols in the hermetic cipher language that refer, often in the same passage, to one continuous object and thereby create an enormous difficulty for the inexperienced reader.

The literature is also clear about the "origin of immanence." The Emerald Tablet's "Telesma, Father of all things" is complemented by the redoubtable revelation of the *Corpus Hermeticum:*[1] "Thou art all in all, composed of all powers." Morienus, in answer to King Kalid, explains: "Oh, King, I will confess the truth to you. God, for his pleasure, created in you this most wonderful thing,[2] and wherever you go, it will

---

[1] *Corpus Hermeticum*, 13.2.

[2] This theistico-creationist motif, and various others similar to it in the medieval texts, are nothing but a concession to the dominating exoteric religious beliefs of the time.

be in you, and you will not be rid of it. . . . You are its mine and storehouse, for it is in you, and to tell the truth, you yourself are the one who receives it and gathers it in. And whoever seeks any other stone in the Teaching will be deceived in his labor."[3] Ostanes, in the Arab text of *Kitab el-Foçul*, says the same: "There is nothing in the world as common as this mysterious thing: it is found in rich and poor, accompanies the traveller and stays with one at home."[4] And he adds: "By God! If it were called by its true name, the ignorant would shout: "Lie!" and the intelligent would be perplexed." Moreover: "The stone speaks but ye heed it not. It calls to you and ye answer not. O ye sleepers! What deafness stops your ears? What vise grips your heart?"[5] The Cosmopolite says: "What you're looking for is in front of your eyes; no one can live without it, all creatures serve it, but few even notice it; and everyone has it in his power."[6] And in the *Seven Chapters of Hermes*: "I have come to tell ye what ye do not know: the Work is with you and within you: once ye find it in yourselves, where it continuously resides, you will possess it forever right there where ye stand."[7]

The word *heaven*, of which it is said in the Gospels, "the kingdom of heaven is within," is also used for the First Principle in the hermetico-alchemical tradition. But for this there is, as we've said and will see, another even more frequent and typical symbol: *water*. The mystical hermetism of Boehme says about it: "This water endures throughout eternity. It reaches every corner of this world and is the Water of Life which penetrates beyond death . . . nowhere is it perceptible or apprehensible ['difficult to contemplate,' Zosimos said]. But it fills everything equally. *It is found also in the body of man and when he thirsts for this water and drinks of it, the Light of Life shines in him.*"[8] Thus is affirmed once and for all that "man is the center in which everything winds up: the quintessence of the whole universe is locked in him. He participates in the virtues and properties of all individuals."[9]

But the *body* being the most concrete expression of the human entity, in hermetism the same cosmic symbols also designate the "mystery" of corporeality—and now we begin better to understand that which is "nearer than any other thing," which "all have before their eyes and at their fingertips," considered vile by the ignorant and held by the sages as most precious of all. The Buddhist

---

[3] *Entretiens, BPC*, 2:86, 87, 88.

[4] Text in *CMA*, 3:124.

[5] Text in *CMA*, 3:117, 124. Cf. *Commentatio de pharmaco catholico* (Amsterdam, 1666), 4, §8.

[6] *De sulphure* (Venice, 1644), 208; *BPC*, 3:273, 279.

[7] Text in *BPC*, vol. 1.

[8] J. Boehme, *Aurora*, 24, §38, 39.

[9] Pernety, *Fables*, 1:72.

saying: "This body, a mere eight hands tall, comprises the world, is the creation of the world, the end of the world and the path that leads to the resolution of the world" strongly complements the *Tabula Smaragdina*: "That which is above is as that which is below, and that which is below is as that which is above, for the performance of the miracles of the one thing." This is expressed in the Greek texts as: "Everything in the macrocosmos, is also in man"[10] and is echoed by Boehme: "The earthly body you inhabit is all one with the totality of the enflamed body [that is, the body living in the special state of the "fire" of the spirit] of this world."[11] Still another hermetic sentence: "Look, it is a unique thing, having a unique root, of a uniqueness to which nothing exterior to it has been added, but which in the working of the Art, many superfluous things have been removed."[12]

This fundamental principle of hermetism, as we shall see, provides various orders of correspondence: real, analogical, "magical." Certain structures of reality, certain metallic states—conceived as silent astral fecundations in the *gremium matris terrae*—certain natural phenomena of the urano-planetary world, are conceived as ossifications of forces that reveal their secret in corresponding states of the spirit that lie sleeping in the heart of corporeality.

In the Orient they teach that by following the traces left behind in us by the *ātman* we can attain the knowledge of the universe.[13] Agrippa, paraphrasing Geber, expounds on the same teaching with equal clarity: "No one can excel in the alchemical art without knowing the principles *in himself;* and the greater the knowledge of the self, the greater will be the magnetic power attained thereby and the greater the wonders to be realized."[14] "*Ambula ab intra*" is one of the mottoes of the *Commentatio de pharmaco catholico.*

And this "interior way," this *via sacra* that begins with the "black hieratic stone"—ἱερατικὴ λίθοσ μελαινα—the "stone that is not a stone" but an "image of the cosmos"—κόσμου μίμητα—"our black lead" (all symbols of the human body, from this point of view), and along the course of which will rise up Gods and Heroes,[15] "heavens and planets," elemental men, metallic and

---

[10] Olympiodorus, text in *CAG*, 2:100.

[11] *Aurora*, 24, §67.

[12] In *Theatrum chemicum* (Ursel, 1602), 1:855 et seq.

[13] *Brihadaranyaka-Upanishad*, 1.6.7.

[14] Agrippa, *De occulta philosophia*, 3.36.

[15] It is useful to recall that the Romans ritually put a black stone—*lapis niger*—at the beginning of the Via Sacra. The hermetic work in the Greek texts sometimes refers to itself as "the mystery of Mithras" and Mithras was conceived as a god, or hero, issuing out of a *stone*, who would subjugate the Sun. Upon "this stone"—evangelistically—must be built a "church"; while "lords of the temple," as we have said, were referred to as hermetic masters. We can go quite far with such meaningful associations.

sidereal[16]—this path is enigmatically contained in the sigil represented by V.I.T.R.I.O.L., explained thus by Basil Valentine: "*Visita Interiora Terrae Rectificando Invenies Occultum Lapidem*" (pass through the bowels of the earth [earth = "the body"], and by rectifying thou wilt find the hidden stone). Eventually, along that path the knowledge of self and the knowledge of the cosmos intersect and season one another, until they become the one and the same marvelous thing, the true goal of the Great Work. As above, so below, as in spirit, so in nature. Within the human organism, as outside it, are present the Three, the Four, the Seven, the Twelve; Sulfur, Mercury, Salt; Earth, Water, Air, Fire; the Planets; the Zodiac. "*The furnace is unique*"—affirm the Sons of Hermes enigmatically— "unique the path and unique, as well, the Work."[17] "There is but one Nature and one Art. . . . The Work is all there is, and beyond it there exist no other truths."[18]

In the *Hermetic Triumph* it is said that "our Stone" exists, but that it hides itself until the artist can lend a hand to Nature.[19] The hermetic Art is to illuminate anew the meaning of the analogies by reestablishing the reality of what they represent: self-sufficient and not needing anything but self-sufficiency. To need nothing at all is the "unique thing"[20] itself, the "divine" and operative technique,"$\tau\acute{\varepsilon}\chi\nu\eta$ $\theta\varepsilon\acute{\iota}\alpha,$ $\tau\acute{\varepsilon}\chi\nu\eta$ $\delta o\gamma\mu\alpha\tau\iota\kappa\acute{\eta}$." The latter, "via the affinity of natures, controls the natures of like substances."[21] For that which can be said with the greatest certainty is that "the Work is a third world, like the other two, but with the forces of the macrocosmos and of the microsmos reunited in it."[22]

---

[16] Cf. Boehme *Aurora*, 25, §83: ["*So man will recht urkunden der Sternengeburt oder Anfang, so muß man eigentlich wissen die Geburt des Lebens, weil sich das Leben in einem Leib gebähret, denn es ist alles einerlei Geburt.*" (In order to know the origin of the stars or the Beginning, you must understand the origin of life, and how life originates in the body, because in everything there is only one origination.)— Trans.]

[17] Pseudodemocritean texts, *CAG*, 3:37.

[18] *Novum lumen chemicum* (Venice, 1644), 62.

[19] Text in *BPC*, 3:272.

[20] The many hermetic expressions refer to this idea—according to one of their principle meanings—that nothing can be added to the symbolic "matters"; that they suffice to perfect themselves and nothing exterior to them can confer that perfection; that they contain in themselves the principles of all the operations. Citing Morienus (*Entretiens*, *BPC*, 2:62) for all: "Those who have what they need in themselves [the hermetic masters], require nobody's help."

[21] *CAG*, 2:209.

[22] *Livre de la miséricorde, CMA*, 3:179.

Six

CREATION
AND MYTH

We wish to call attention to one final aspect of the analogy. According to the hermetic conception, as the elements of the cosmos correspond to those within man, so both the *process of creation—and the process by which man, through the Art, reintegrates himself within himself—follow an identical path and have the same meaning.* The analogy between the alchemical Art— χημεία—and the Act of the Demiurge—κοσμοπιία—goes back to the first Greek texts of Pelagius, Comarius, Zosimos. We can easily recognize the phases of Creation in the different phases of the hermetic work: the initiation experience furnishes the key to cosmogony, and vice versa: according to the hermetic exegesis, every traditional cosmogony and mythology has, among other meanings, an explanation shaped and veiled by the enigmas of the different operations and transformations of the Art.[1]

In order to make sense of this teaching it is clearly necessary to abandon the idea

---

[1] Cf., *CAG*, 2:213–14. This idea is explicit in Crassellame, *Ode alchemica* (text in O. Wirth, *Le symbolisme hermétique* [Paris, 1909], 161): "Our Great Work shows clearly that God has made the whole in the same way that the physical elixir is made." Morienus, (*Entretiens, BPC,* 2:88): "It contains in itself the four elements and resembles the world and the composition of the world." Cf. Della Riviera, *Mondo magico,* 46, 98–99; Philalethes, *Introitus apertus ad occlusum regis palatium,* chap. 5; Pernety, *Fables,* 1:25; Hortulanus (*Commentatio Tabulae Smaragdinae, BPC,* 1, §11: "Our stone is made in the same way that the world was created."

of the Creation as a historical fact over and done with in the spatial and temporal past. We must conceive of it as functioning in an ongoing state, metaphysical in its own right and therefore beyond space and time, beyond past as well as future, which is more or less that same state that some mystics, even Christian mystics, have called *eternal creation*. On such a basis, creation is an ever-present event that consciousness can always recover by actualizing itself in states, which—according to the "principle of immanence"—constitute the possibilities of its profound nature—its "chaos"—while in the cosmogonic myth, they are presented to us in the form of symbols, gods, images, and primordial acts.[2] And given that the goal of the "*ambula ab intra,*" of the hermetic "inner path" descending to the "interior of the earth" is precisely that "profound nature," this aspect of the hermetic teaching is easily explained. And as the alchemists not only take the different phases of the Hesiodic, or even biblical, creation for a paradigm, but sometimes extend the analogy to the same episodes in the life of Christ and particularly to the Herculean and Jasonic labors, all of these to them are neither "historical facts" nor "fables" but allusions to extratemporal spiritual states and acts.

We must add to the above that this "living of the myth" has, in hermetism, nothing even vaguely "mystical" about it. Aside from all that has been said, "living the myth" means to arrive by means of symbols at a perception of that metahistorical order in which nature and man himself, so to speak, are found in a state of creation and which, among other things, contains for us the secret of the energies that activate within and behind visible things and human corporeality. We shall see that none other is the premise in all strictly alchemical (i.e., not simply initiatic) operations.

For now we shall confine ourselves to pointing out the connection between such ideas and the deepest understanding of the ancient traditions according to which gods, demons, or heroes are the introducers to "physical reality" or to living consciousness, of the mysteries of nature. Hermetically "to know" a god is to realize a "creative state" that is at the same time a metaphysical significance, the "secret soul" and the occult power of a specific process of nature.

---

[2] Hermetism, moreover, reaffirms the traditional idea of the internal unity of all myths, as expressed by J. M. Ragon (*De la Maçonnerie occulte et de l'initiation hermétique* [Paris, 1926], 44): "On recognizing the truth of the alliance of the two systems, the symbolic and the philosophical—in the allegories of the monuments of all ages, in the symbolic writings of the priesthoods of all nations, in the rituals of the mystery societies—we obtain a constant series, an invariable system of principles that proceed out of a vast, impressive, and genuine superstucture, which is the only framework in which they can be truly coordinated." Concerning the symbolic content of the myth, we will limit ourselves to reproducing just this one testimony from Braccesco (*Espositione,* fols. 77b, 42a): "The Ancients hid this science in poetical fables and spoke through similitudes . . . those who have no knowledge of this science cannot know what the Ancients intended, what they wished to indicate by the names of so many gods and goddesses, or by their generations, love affairs and mutations. Nor should you imagine that moral lessons are hidden in these fables."

The different references in the texts to "genii," gods, etc., which in dreams or visions have revealed to the "Sons of Hermes" the secrets of the Art, must be understood in the same sense.

Now we shall go on to consider the developments of the hermetic doctrine in regard to the principles comprising the "one knowledge."

Seven

"WOMAN," "WATER," "MERCURY," AND "POISON"

We have spoken of the ἕν τὸ πᾶν. But we need to begin by establishing the "chaos" or "everything" aspect of the "one." In the strictest sense, this is the First Matter: the undifferentiated possibility, the origin of all generation. In hermetism, although the symbolism that designates it is rather diverse, it recapitulates the symbols utilized by many ancient civilizations. It is "Night," the "Abyss," the "Matrix"; the place of the "Tree," and as we have also seen, the Woman—the Mother, the "Lady of the Philosophers," the "Goddess of sublime beauty."[1] But the technical and specific symbols of the hermetico-alchemical texts are, above all, those of *Water* and *Mercury*.

"Without the divine Water"—θεῖον ὕδατος—"nothing exists"—οὐδεν ἐστιν—says Zosimos:[2] "it works every operation through its components [that is to say, in that by which it takes form]." Water of the Abyss—ἐναβύσσαιον ὕδωρ, Mysterious Water, Divine Water, Permanent Water, Living Water (or Water of

---

[1] This last, in the third key of Basil Valentine (*Aurelia occultum philosophorum, BCC,* 2) is offered as the "Woman of the Sea," and at the same time, refers to the "center of the Tree that is in the center of Paradise," what "the Philosophers have sought so carefully."

[2] *CAG,* 2:144.

Life), Eternal Water, Silver Water (ὑδραργυρον), Ocean, *Mare Nostrum, Mare Magnum Philosophorum*, Aqua-Spirit, *Fons Perennis*, Heavenly Water, etc., are expressions found everywhere in the texts. On the other hand, between the symbols of the Feminine Principle and those of the Waters—"Mother Earth," "Waters," "Mother of the Waters," "Stone," "Cavern," "House of the Mother," "Night," "House of Profundity" or of "Strength" or of "Wisdom"—there is a connection that goes back to the beginning of time.[3] And this is what hermetism reclaims.

Meanwhile the Waters, the "Radical Wetness," the "Lady of the Philosophers," Chaos, the ἕν τὸ πᾶν, the "mystery sought for eons and finally found," etc. all come down, alchemically, to *Mercury*. Everything is composed of Mercury (or Mercurial Water), say the texts; it is what constitutes, they say, the Matter, the beginning and the end of the Work.

We have mentioned another association: the Serpent or Dragon. This is— καθολικός ὄφις—the "universal" or "cosmic Serpent" which, according to the gnostic expression, "moves through all things."[4] Its relation to the chaos principle—"our Chaos or Spirit is a Dragon of fire that conquers all"[5]—and to the principle of dissolution[6]—λείωσις—(the Dragon Ourobouros is the dissolution), goes back to the most ancient myths.

Hermetism, however, also uses more particular symbols for this. Venom, Viper, Universal Solvent, and Philosophical Vinegar designate the power of the undifferentiated, at whose touch all differentiation can but be destroyed. But at the time we find the word *menstruum* to indicate the same principle and, as such—that is, as the blood of the symbolic "Lady" which nourishes generation—it also takes on the opposite meaning of the Spirit of Life, the "Fountain of Living Water," the "Life in the bodies, that which attracts, the Light of lights."[7]

The principle in question, then, has a double meaning. It is Death and Life. It has the double power of *solve* and of *coagula:* it is the "Philosophical Basilisk," like a bolt of lightning burning all "imperfect metal" (Crollius); "Terrible Fountain," which if allowed to run over would lead to ruin, but which confers victory over all things to the "King" who knows how to bathe in it (Bernard of Treviso). It is

---

[3] Cf. H. Wirth, *Der Aufgang der Menschheit* (Jena, 1928), and J. J. Bachofen, *Urreligion und antike Symbole* (Leipzig, 1926).

[4] In Hippolytus (*Philosophumena*, 5.9; cf. 5.16), where the Serpent as the hermetic Mercury in Basil Valentine is assimilated to the river by the spring that issues from the center of Eden, and secondly to the Logos of John, whereby all things are made (an assimilation that we also find in hermetism); for Boehme Mercury is the Sound, the Verb, the "Word of God, manifestation of the eternal Abyss" (*Aurora*, 4, §§13, 14; *De signatura*, 8, §56).

[5] Philalethes, *Introitus apertus*, chap. 2.

[6] Pseudodemocritean texts, *CAG*, 3:22

[7] Syrian texts, *CMA*, 2:158.

the *Ruach*, Spirit or Breath, the "undifferentiated principle in every individual";[8] it is the "black Lead," and also the "Magnesia," the "Quintessence," that which can do everything in all things—*pHn Nn pHsi*—and that to those who know—*nown*—and who understand its use, it supplies Gold and Silver.[9]

In reality, by the same absolutely undifferentiated nature of that which it signifies, the symbolism used by the texts for this purpose is unlimited. The hermetic authors say explicitly that everything can be designated by anything—including the most extravagant things—with the aim of misleading the ignorant.

What is of interest, however, is how we relate these symbols to a spiritual state under the guise of an *experience*: given that for hermetism one must consider true what Aristotle said of the Mysteries, that perhaps one went to them not to learn, but to acquire a deep impression from a lived experience—οὐ μαθεῖν, ἀλλὰ παθεῖν.[10] It is in this sense that one must understand the expressions relative to the same priniciple of which we have just spoken, that we find in certain kindred currents of hermetism: "Water that produces trembling"—φρικτὸν ὕδορ;[11] "The darkness is a terrible Water!"—τὸ δὲ σκότος ὕδωρ ἐστὶ φοβέρον;[12] "Complete power of violent agitation, like water in constant movement"; that which brings "What makes permanent, frees what goes, destroys what grows"; and in whose image were made Cepheus, Prometheus and Japheth."[13] Boehme says it better, "The essence is squeezed wholly out of death through the death process, which is effected in the great anguish of the *impressure* where there is an existential death torment, which is the mercurial life . . . and this fearfulness comes from the Mercury, or the anguish of death."[14] It's a matter of coming into contact with the *venom*, with its dissolving force, as death, that breaks up the finite essences.

So, hermetic Mercury, the "Philosophical Basilisk," that acts like a bolt of lightning (recall the bolt that struck the Titans), corresponds to *prana*, the life force, which in the Hindu tradition is also called the "supreme cause of terror" and "brandished fireball," which, however, "makes who knows it immortal."[15] In Assyrian mythology, the god Marduk has thunderbolts in both hands when in combat against the Chaos monster, Tiamat. This symbolic combat leads us to the next phase, that of *separation*.

---

[8] Pernety, *Dictionnaire*, 141

[9] Cf. *CAG* 2:91, 94–96, 98, 144

[10] In Synesius, *Dion.*, 48.

[11] *The Great Magical Papyrus of Paris*, text in *Introduzione alla magia*, 1:144ff.

[12] In Hippolytus, *Philosophumena*, 5.19.

[13] Ibid., 5:14

[14] Boehme, *De signatura*, 3, §§19, 20: ["*Das Wesen gehet alles aus dem Tode durchs Sterben, welches geschieht in der großen Angst des Impressens, da eine sterbende Qual ist, welches das mercurialische Leben ist . . . und dieser Schreck ist aus dem Mercurio oder aus der Angst des Todes.*"—Trans.]

[15] *Kathā-Upanishad*, 2.4.2.

the

separation: sun

and moon

"**N**ature takes pleasure in itself" and "Nature dominates itself." Here is the possibility of "nature" being desire, abandonment to itself, spontaneity, and identification with self-gratification. At the same time it is the possibility of saying no to itself, of manifesting itself as that which acts against itself, that which dominates and transcends itself, to the point of actually making the distinction between that which *dominates* ("masculine," active) and that which *is dominated* ("feminine," passive), in which alone is found the ancient chaotic nature. Such are, *sub specie interioritatis*, the two poles that in splitting apart, release one from the other.

We can also say that in the One the All, the "One" and the "All" now crystallize as two distinct principles. The "One" takes on the meaning of a *center* that manifests in the heart of chaos (the "All") and affirms itself there as a principle of incorruptible fixity, stability, and transcendence. From the signature of O—"the first matter"—we move on to ☉, which is the ancient hieroglyph of the Sun. And that which in the originating matter was undetermined possibility, a passive potentiality for any quality, change, or chaotic transformation, is turned into a quite different principle, which in hermetism corresponds to the feminine symbol of the Moon ☽.

Sun ☉ and Moon ☾ is the fundamental hermetic duality. It can be said that the Serpent, upon multiplying itself, has opposed itself to itself[1] and the principle symbols that expressed themselves as the "prima materia"—Woman, Dragon, Mercury, the Waters—now serve only to express the lunar force. Separated from the center, this force becomes a blind impulse and savage flood. Its downward direction is the direction of the "fall" precisely indicated by the alchemical hieroglyphic of the Water principle ▽, under that aspect identical to the Moon ☾.

The dragons (like the Bulls) become those which the *solar* heroes—Mithras, Hercules, Jason, Apollo, Horus, etc.—fight against. They are called by the alchemists, in the hermetic interpretation of the myth, "green" and "undigested," because they have not yet suffered the "maturation" or domination that will transmute them to higher orders of power. In place of the Primordial Woman, of the solitary Virgin of the World, κόσμου κόρη, are introduced pairs in which is expressed the duality of the Tellurian and Uranian principle: Earth-Heaven. "Above, the celestial. Below, the terrestrial. The work is completed, masculine and feminine helping together."[2] Mercury is "fixed" and "coagulated": such is the sense of Flamel's sixth figure, which is a crucified Serpent.[3]

If the Dragon figures again in the center of the "Citadel of the Philosophers" of Khunrath, it is nevertheless a dragon that must be conquered and killed: the one that incessantly devours itself. This is Mercury as *burning thirst*,[4] covetousness, hunger, blind drive for gratification,[5] and thus the "viscous nature," the principle of identification and self-absorption—nature "fascinated" and conquered by nature.[6] Such is, macroscopically, the secret of the sublunary world of changing and

---

[1] Cf. Eliphas Levi, (*Histoire de la magie* [Paris, 1922], 138): "Life is a serpent that incessantly creates and devours itself. One must ignore fear and plant one's foot firmly on its head. Hermes, by doubling it, opposes it to itself, and in eternal equilibrium makes of it the talisman of his power and the glory of his caduceus."

[2] *CAG*, 2:147.

[3] Grillo de Givry, *Musée des sorciers, mages et alchimistes* (Paris, 1929), 398, 414, plate 347.

[4] Pseudodemocritean texts, *CAG*, 2:20. For the symbol of the dragon that devours itself, see Ostanes in *CMA*, 3:119-20.

[5] In *De signatura*, 2, §7, Boehme speaks of a craving or will that cannot satisfy itself outside of itself, that is the property of a "hunger that feeds on itself." Cf. 3, §3: "This desire was present in the Nothing before itself, cannot look for anything beyond itself, and cannot find anything in nature but itself." In 3, §12: "The desire leaps up out of the Abyss [cf. the alchemical "water of the Abyss"] and in that very desire we find the beginning of nature." This touches on the symbol of the dragon that devours itself and Mercury as "burning thirst."

[6] Apart from the quotations and comments in the Pseudodemocritean texts (*CAG*, 2:63), it is said that Mercury binds with the elements and cannot be separated from them, which is why it is "dominated and dominating" at the same time (amalgamation). "Viscous" soul is an expression to signify the spiritual state of man on which this force acts. Pernety (*Dictionnaire*, 202) speaks of a "Viscous Humidity," that is "the Mercury of the Philosophers," which is the basis for "all the individuals of the three kingdoms of nature."

becoming, opposed to the uranian region of *being*, of the discarnate stability of celestial natures reflecting the mode of pure spiritual virility.

Transposed to hermetic, metallurgical symbols, the principle of the Sun ☉ corresponds to Gold, that substance which no acid can alter; and the principle of the Moon ☾ corresponds to fluid Silver or Silver-Water (the ancient name for Quicksilver or Mercury).

Under a certain aspect the solar principle can be related to the color red and the second principle to white, referring, then, to Fire and Light, respectively. Fire is the proper virtue of the solar principle, not the fire of desire, generative ardor, or lust, but the *flamma non urens*, the nonmaterial principle of all animation.[7] Light, per se, is more closely related to the feminine, lunar principle as Wisdom which, with respect to ☉ has the same nature as the light that the Moon reflects from the solar principle.

There is a special alchemical symbol that is in part equivalent to the Sun, arsenic, which is explained by the Greek word ἀρσενικòν meaning both "arsenic" and "masculine" or "virile."[8] Still another symbol is Niter or Saltpeter, whose ideogram ⊕ indicates the predominance of a phallico-virile principle (the vertical | which cuts through the "prima materia" ◯. The symbolism of Niter (*Salitter*) is much used by Boehme, with which he expresses the "heat that activates the light," the "active, boiling virtue" of the divine powers in opposition to Mercurius or Sound (the corresponding Light principle), which is, we shall learn, the principle of all individuation.

---

[7] By virtue of this fire, which is "a part of celestial homogeneity," an "invisible spirit," a "soul not subject to the dimension of bodies," a "miracle that only the Philsophers can recognize," immense, invisible, apt by its virtue for action to be present everywhere. See Agrippa, *De occulta philosophia*, 1:514; Philalethes, *Epist. di Ripley*, §§56, 57; *Regulae*, chap. 10

[8] *CAG*, 2:417: "Symbolically, in enigma, arsenic was understood to mean virility."

Nine

FROZEN AND FLOWING WATERS

Once the two principles have been separated, the connection that can be made between them is of two kinds: ☉ (the Sun, Gold) *can be dominated by* ☾ (the Moon, the Waters), or *it can dominate them*. In the first case we have the law of *becoming*, proper to that world which, from ancient times to the scholastic era has been appropriately referred to as *sublunary*, and in the Hindu tradition, notably in Buddhism, the world of *samsara*—which is the hermetic "dissolution," the secret of those myths in which figure men and primordial beings devoured by dragons or other natures personifying the wet principle of chaos (for example, the Egyptian myth of Typhon-Seth and Osiris).

The second case refers to everything that reflects the immovable ☉ having the character of an ("exhaustively") completed, perfected thing, and to everything in which exists more cosmos than chaos through the predominance of a law of order, organization, and equilibrium over mere change.

From this there follows, in particular, a relation of the Gold principle—Sun, Fire, Niter, etc—to everything that is individual and corporeal, in the sense of a *signature* having the stable imprinting of a power; and of the Moon principle to everything that is "volatile" and unable to grasp the "vital spirit," the subtle energy of transformations. In the literature we find a multitude of allusions confirming such relationships—Frozen Waters and Flowing Waters: forces individualized and *fixed* by the Solar principle, and forces in the elemental state. In Aristotelian terminology, we can say that in general the Sun is "form" and the power of individuation, while the Moon—which preserves the archaic Mother and Woman symbols—expresses the "material" and universal: to the undifferentiated vitality, to the cosmic spirit or ether-light, corresponds the feminine. Everything, on the contrary, that opposes it as specialization, qualification, or concrete individuation reflects, then, the masculine solar principle. Here functions that power of limitation, the contracting virtue (the *coagula* in opposition to the *solve*) to which this passage of Boehme refers: "The universal divinity, in its most intimate and essential generation, in its nucleus, possesses a sharp and terrible asperity, which astringent quality is an excessive, radical, firm attraction . . . , similar to winter, when the cold is bitter and unbearable, to the point of *water being transformed into ice.*"[1]

The strange alchemical terms "cold fire" and "igneous cold" have an analogous meaning: the peculiarity of the Fire of the "primordial Masculine" as it opposes the moist and savage quality of the "impure matter" and of the Lunar Dragon, is precisely to be *frozen* at the same time. It animates, and also dominates, binds, projects a "fixation"; and from it detaches forms in which the Waters are chained together by a law, till they culminate in the miracle of the Mysterium Magnum, of a life with a central consciousness that says to itself: "I." In pages to come the context of our discourse will show precisely how Gold or the Sun, in one of its main practical senses, expresses what we can call the *ego principle;* whether it manifest itself in "earthy," "vulgar" form, (where it is only a mirror of the *true* Sun projected by the fortuitous Waters of the "Current"), or whether it unites only to itself, or is pure, in the form of noble, living metal, and then acquires effectively the value of "center" as in the primordial state. Such is the key to understanding the operations of the Art according to the central meaning of the work of palingenesis.

We should mention again that, in this context, the choice of the symbol of the Stone for the human body acquires a complementary justification: the body, as a completed, organized, and stable Nature is a "fixed" thing as opposed to the instability of psychic principles and the volatility attributed to "spirits"; so not only is the relation of Sun, Gold, and Fire with the body (directly or through the equivalent symbols) very frequent, but when the same spiritual interior being has acquired the supernatural stability of the regenerated, the corporeal principles are elevated to a higher plain, and the "two are made one" in a "spiritual corporeality"; and the word that serves once again to express that corporeality will be this same Stone: the Philosopher's Stone. The hermetic imperative is: "Transform yourselves, ye dead stones into living philosophical

---

[1] Boehme, *Aurora*, 13, §§55, 57: ["*Die ganze Gottheit hat in ihrer innersten oder anfänglichen Geburt im Kern gar eine scharfe, erschreckliche Shärfe, indem die herbe Qualität gar ein erschrecklich herb, hart, finster und kalt Zusammenziehen ist, gleich dem Winter, wann es grimmig kalt ist, daß aus dem Wasser Eis wird.*"—Trans.]

stones"—*transmutamini de lapidibus mortuis in vivos lapides philosophicos.*[2]

In this aspect of its symbolism an influence on hermetism is rather apparent on the part of the spirit of the classical tradition. The value attributed in the classical world to all that has form, that is completed according to a limit and a measure—πέρας; the contempt antimystically given, on the other hand, to that which is indeterminate and indefinite—ἄπειρον—is reflected in the connection that hermetism establishes between the principle of corporeality and the signature of Gold (Sun), the most *noble* of nature's elements. "To treat the Fire of Mercury [the fire-desire] with Fire, and unite Spirit to Spirit, with the aim of tying the hands of the *Virgin*, of this fleeting demon," is, in this regard, an enigmatic expression, but then full of significance for the Greek alchemists.[3] Its sense will be seen with greater clarity in what follows; and we shall also see that in every tradition of which we speak "heaven" is used as a symbol for all the invisible, spiritual, and impersonal states and principles. It has the feminine function with respect to the masculine one of corporeality, with respect to the "dragon without wings" that contains the germ of the Gold—or of the personality in a superior sense (the hermetic King).[4]

---

[2] Dorn, *Speculativae philosophiae* in *Theatrum chemicum*, 1:265-67.

[3] *CAG*, 2:206.

[4] The wingless dragon is one that cannot rise up from the earth, that is, it finds itself joined to the body.

Ten

SALT
AND the CROSS

◆

in a Greek alchemical text we read "One becomes Two and Two become Three; and by means of the Third, the Fourth achieves Unity. Thus the two create nothing but One."[1] The thoughts already expressed about the hermetic quality—☉ and ☾—lead us to the understanding of the "Third."

If as we have suggested the law of "desire" and of self-absorption is expressed by the descending direction of the symbol for water ▽, everything in the "one thing" that is on the contrary oriented toward the principle of the Sun can be expressed by the ascending opposite direction, that is, flame: whence the alchemical sign of Fire.[2]

Water ▽   Fire △

But there is an even more schematic symbolism. The passive water nature of the feminine principle as compared to the masculine can be expressed by a horizontal line —, which conveys the idea of "lying flat"; whereas the rising direction of fire can be expressed by the vertical |, which comprises both the idea

---

[1] *Philosophus Christianus*, CAG, 2:404. The analogy can be corroborated in an expression of Lao-tzu, in the *Tao te Ching*, 42.

[2] To this, incidentally, there is a strong resemblance of hermetic water and fire to the Hindu tradition's *tamas* and *sattva*.

of virility and of stability—ὁ στάς, "that which is standing." The "two" that become "three" are the two in their joining. And ideographically, that can be expressed by the cross ✛, equivalent from this point of view to the seal of Solomon (overlapping of △ and ▽). Having said this, we can proceed with the hermetico-alchemical symbolism.

The point of intersection, which is the "third" represented by the cross, can have a double meaning: first the point of the "fall" and neutralization; second, the active synthesis of both as male and female powers creatively united.

The first case defines the hermetic idea of the *fixed* (as opposed to volatile) taken in a negative sense. This is the state of petrification, arrest, suspension, and stagnation devoid of life. It is the "body" element in the widest sense where the Gold, although present, is as restricted in its power as the opposite principle to which it has reacted. It is the negative side of individuation with roots in a state of contrast between the two: the "two enemies," the two dragons that devour one another in turn, the eagle fighting the serpent, etc., according to the variations of the ciphered language. It is that which we find in the ideogram of *salt* ⊖, "materia prima" ○ qualified in the sense of stagnation as indicated by the horizontal. In its more generally accepted sense, salt expresses the physical state or world interpreted as a state or world in which the "corpses" of invisible battles, of cosmic interferences between powers are precipitated.[3] Here the body is equivalent to "sepulchre" and "prison," the symbolic rock to which Prometheus has been chained in order to purge the unfortunate failure of the titanic audacity—equivalent to the act of possession, to the primordial individuation that did violence to the "goddess."

Adding to the "Third" the Two that have engendered it, we obtain the metaphysical Triad, the hermetic notion that proceeds from the traditional general teaching: Sun, Moon, and Earth—world of pure spiritual virility, world of plasmic forces and becoming, and world of bodies—and, *sub specie interioritatis*, three corresponding conditions of the spirit. Three crowned serpents or three serpents rising from three hearts express the triad of Basil Valentine; the three ears and three "vapors"—αἰθαλαι—of Ouroboros; three serpents that emerge from the cup that the androgyne holds in one hand, while with the other she squeezes a single serpent, in the *Rosarium philosophorum* and in the *Viatorum spagiricum;* a serpent with three heads in the German edition of the *Crede mihi* of Norton; and thus we have established the provenance of the triple dignity of the first master of this tradition, Hermes Trismegistus.

---

[3] Cf. *Introduzione alla magia*, 1:129-34; and reference could also be made to the Simonian teaching (*Philosophumena*, 5.19) that explains the particular beings as the result of crisscrossing interferences of spiritual powers: their "types" (τύπος, ἰδέα) would be "seals" or "imprints" engraved by one on another.

Eleven

ChE FOUR
ELEMENTS
AND SULFUR

◆

In another of its aspects, however, the cross also leads us from the "Two" to the "Four" by way of the beams and quarters that result from the intersection. The cross, then, is the cross of the four Elements: Fire above, Earth below, Air to the right, and Water to the left.[1] The state of arrest and petrification, which is the mystery of Salt, leads us beyond itself from Fire and Water to the signs that give the hermetic sense of the other two Elements: Earth ▽ is a stoppage or syncope in the direction of the "fall" that is characteristic of the waters ▽; and analogously, Air ▲ is a stoppage or break in the ascending direction of fire △. So that from the Two, through the Third (Salt), proceed the Four: the tetrad of the Elements.[2]

Fire △   Water ▽   Earth ▽   Air ▲

---

[1] Cf. G. Kremmerz, *Fasciculo D della Miryam* ([Pamphlet D], part of the secret teachings of this contemporary group that upholds the hermetic tradition).

[2] For the analysis of the elements contained in the complete symbol of the cross, cf. Della Riviera, *Mondo magico* 24-28, 40-44; and J. Dee, *Monas hieroglyphica*, passim. For the signs of the four hermetic elements, cf. also O. Wirth, *Le symbolisme hermétique*.

According to this aspect of the symbol, the central point of the cross expresses the point of unity of the four Elements, the originating superior and anterior to their four differentiations given by the four directions. Thereby it expresses the *Quintessence*, the incorruptible and simple principle that, according to the tradition, is the substratum, the principle of life and the nexus of reciprocal union formed by the four elements.

Here we must point out that, like the elements, the hermetic Quintessence—the equivalent of the Pythagorean ὀλκάς, the Hindu *ākāsha*, the Qabalistic *avír*, Taoist *ch'i*, etc.—is not considered a speculative abstraction or some contrivance of the "physics" of yesteryear, but a reality to which corresponds a specific spiritual experience. And the symbolic central point of the cross, as soon as it is "known to the magical hero and understood," says Della Riviera,[3] "becomes the root and origin of all magical marvels."

In accord with the more operative than speculative orientation of hermetic alchemy, the sign ✝ is rarely encountered in isolation. More often it forms part of other symbols expressing the principles and powers that stand over the four Elements, although it also enters into elemental combinations. Thus, for example:

Sulfur ♄   Mercury ☿

This Mercury must not be confused, of course, with Original Mercury. It is a Mercury that is still impure and "terrestrial." Its symbol ☿ expresses the state of the elements ✝ in a nature ♉ subject to the lunar law of transformations (superior position of the Moon ☽ with respect to the symbol of undifferentiated substance ☉).

The symbol for Sulfur ♄ gives us, on the contrary, the condition of a Fire △ in domination over the elements (△ over +). Sulfur ♄ should not be confused, however, with Sulfur in a pure or "native" state, which in the beginnings of alchemy was given a different symbol ♈, the same as Aries, symbol of the masculine principle of every generation and direct manifestation of the power of Gold. Only to such a principle are expressions referred like this of Zacharias: "The *Agent*, whose nature shows the power and strength over matter to that which it is united, is Sulfur";[4] or again, "Sulfur is the principle that gives form."[5] The true Sulfur "of the wise" is an *incombustible* Sulfur. And another impressive alchemical expression that indicates the unalterable quality of "not catching fire" is this celestial and royal barrier: "Our sulfur is a sulfur that does not burn and that Fire

---

[3] Della Riviera, *Mondo magico*, 39

[4] *Philosophie naturelle des métaux*, BPC, 2:512.

[5] Pernety, *Dictionnaire*, 270.

[understood as an equivalent of "Poison"] cannot devour."[6] The expression "θεῖον ἄπυρον" is seen in Pseudo-Democritus in connection with the formula: "Nature dominates nature,"[7] and the Syrian texts also speak of a noncombustible sulfur that "arrests the fugitive";[8] it is a dominating activity, exempt from every instinctive element or inner principle (*spiritual* Sulfur, says Philalethes) of action and life, but proceeding from the superiority and fixity of the solar center. On the other hand, when Sulfur is designated by ♀, it expresses, strictly speaking, the same power, but already in an impure state, because it is chained to matter and a form that it still animates and in which it constitutes potentially the "divine" principle (the double meaning of θεῖον, "Sulfur" and "divine"). And in addition, it is the teaching of the whole tradition that "the perfection or imperfection of metals [that is, of the individualized essences extracted from the symbolic 'mineral' or Earth] is determined by the withdrawal or [by the state of] participation of their *Agent*, that is, the Sulfur."[9]

---

[6] Text in *CMA*, 3:52; cf. Pernety (*Dictionnaire*, 469): the "Sulfur of the Sages" is "the incombustible, the seed *fixed* in matter, the true internal agent."

[7] *CAG*, 3:47, 373.

[8] *CMA*, 2:28

[9] Zacharias, *Philosophie naturelle des métaux*, BPC, 2:513

Twelve

SOUL, SPIRIT, AND BODY

Before proceeding we should pause a moment in our correspondence of human nature to the principles we have been contemplating in accordance with the pronouncement: "Everything that exists in the macrocosmos, man also possesses." Sulfur, Mercury, and Salt are found in the (trimundial) universe and in man, in whom the three "worlds" are manifested as soul, spirit, and body. It should be noted henceforth that *soul* and *spirit* do not possess the same meaning here that they do in our time.

In this context the "Soul" is the supernatural element peculiar to the personality. The "Spirit," on the other hand, is to be taken as the whole package of psychobiological energies constituting something between the corporeal and the noncorporeal and that together may properly be said to constitute life, that is, the animating principle of the organism. Having said this, let us declare that man carries hermetically in his *soul*, the presence of the solar and golden force ☉; in his *spirit* he carries that of the lunar and mercurial force ☿; and finally, in the *body*, the force of Salt ⊖ is expressed—that is to say, directly linked to the "Fall" are crucifixion and imprisonment, while with the "resurrection" comes subjugated power, "burning water," fixed by spiritual law. This is why Bernard of Treviso says in *Parole délaissée*: "There is a trinity in unity and a unity in trinity, and there we find Body, Spirit, and Soul. And Mercury and Arsenic as well." And Boehme writes: "Everything that grows, lives, and moves in this world is in Sulfur, and

Mercury is its life. And Salt is the corporeal essence of Mercury's hunger."[1]

Such correspondences can easily be found in the texts; it suffices to bear in mind the symbolic equivalences so far assigned and some others that can be intuited, and to be on the lookout for those contexts where, under some other point of view, the same symbols acquire a meaning that can sometimes take the direct opposite of their usual ones.[2]

From the ternary correspondences in man we can pass on to the quaternary, which refer to the Elements. First of all we must mention the power of the Earth element. Here, to understand completely, we need to recall everything that has been said about those neutralizations of opposing principles that create the "body" aspect of beings. In one of its aspects, the opposition takes place between the universal and the individual and causes a blockage of the consciousness resulting in the perception of an exterior, material world.

In the "petrification" of the spiritual world created by the bodily senses, in the breaking of contacts, in perception conditioned by the dualistic law of I–not-I (which, as we have said, is the main obstacle to modern understanding of the traditional sciences), it is the power of Salt that operates. But Salt, Body, Stone, and Earth, in the aspect of the hermetic symbolism we are discussing, are equivalents. So the power of Earth in man will be that which forces on him, via the physical body, the materialistic vision of the world.[3]

---

[1] Boehme, De signatura, 4, §19: ["Alles, was da wächst, lebet und webet in dieser Welt, das stehet im Sulphur, und im Sulphur ist der Mercurius das Leben, und das Salz ist im Mercurio das leibliche Wesen seines Hunger."–Trans.]

[2] In one of the Azoth figures that shows a man in the act of taking upon himself the whole universe, Basil Valentine reveals the true "material of the Opus," and another figure in the same document labeled with the familiar command, Visita interiora terrae rectificando invenies occultum lapidem, gives the explicit correspondences Sun-Fire-Soul, Moon-Spirit, Body-Stone. Cf. also Bernard of Treviso, Parole délaissée (BPC, 2:432), where Sulfur is indicated as the Soul, the simple element of the Stone (of the human composite) separated from all corporeal burden; also in De pharmaco catholico (3, §16): "The Philosophers, when speaking of Earth, meant by that nothing more than the body, and by the body nothing more than Salt"; and (5, fl1): "This [Mercury] invades and penetrates, as spirit, the other two principles, Salt and Sulphur [read body and soul], which it unites and controls constantly, by natural heat." In the Triomphe Hermétique (BPC, 3:302): "There are three different substances and three principles of all bodies—Salt, Sulphur and Mercury, which are Spirit, Soul and Body." The same expression is in the Salterio di Ermofilo. Cf. also Sendivogius (De sulphure, 173): "The body is Earth, the Spirit Water, the Soul is Fire, i.e., the sulfur of Gold." See also Flamel, Désir désiré, §6, and Pernety, Dictionnaire, viii. The texts, as can plainly be seen, are quite explicit. It would be interesting to know what those who reduce alchemy to "infantile chemistry" make of such statements.

[3] Cf. R. Fludd (Utriusque cosmi historia 2 [Oppenheim, 1619] and de Givry, 5:204): The earth is represented as the center of the sensible world. The five human senses which are the basis of sensorial perception therefore correspond to it. We might also recall that in a manuscript of the fourteenth century, attributed to Hortulanus, the figura terrae is given by the opposition of the two directions, ∇ and Δ that are neutralized in the sign of the seal of Solomon (see CMA, 1:74).

From this there follows a fundamental point: the ordinary man does not know the other three Elements—Air, Water, and Fire—*as they actually are in themselves* —the common man knows only the ability to perceive what these Elements undergo when they manifest *through* the Earth element—that is to say, as they are translated in the processes of the corporeal perception. Water, Air, and Fire, as everyone knows them (that is, as states of physical matter), are no more than correspondences—so to speak—tangibly *symbolic* of the true elements called "living" by the hermetic masters. In themselves, they are other existential states, other modalities of consciousness, quite separate from the body, that can transpose all the principles of things according to their noncorporeal nature, just as in the corporeal existence, in the terrestrial body, all principles are analogously transposed and known by their manifestations in the Earth element. In the most universal sense, this *earthing* of the metals (i.e., the individualized principles) is sometimes called *impurity, dross,* or *shadow*.

The other elements beyond Earth, which together constitute the "Philosopher's Heaven,"[4] can only be apprehended by a consciousness different from that which comes from the body, even if such consciousness has been perfected by all the expedients of modern science. The principle of this other knowledge is "Like is known by like," and here again the premise is that in the essentiality of man are also contained the essences of all the other elements, that is, the potentiality of other states of consciousness apart from that under the spell of the Earth element. And here we arrive at the quaternary classification of man in the wholeness of his being.

[4] Cf. *Zohar*, 1.39b, where the statement that "The visible is the reflection of the invisible" means that the symbolic "Earth" is the visible part of "Heaven," that is, the visibility of the invisible. Pernety (*Fables*, 1:60), defines Earth as "the material principle of everything that exists," which implies also the physical state of the other three elements as well.

⊂ɦᴇ "ꜰᴏᴜʀ" iɴ ᴍᴀɴ

he quaternary division derives directly from the already explained ternary division, but within the middle term *Spirit*, which is the source of the subtle life-giving energies, we can distinguish between two aspects. The first refers to a group of forces undergoing the ascent of the "Body" principle, which are stuck to the Body as to their lodestone and nourished by the Body as the flame is nourished by the firewood from which it comes forth and which, little by little, it consumes. The second aspect refers to a group of forces conforming, on the other hand, to the idea of the "Soul" principle, which to a certain degree, transmits to them its "solar" quality.

Alchemically speaking, the Spirit is Mercury. Thus, we shall also encounter within the sign of this symbolic substance a bipartite division into ☿ and ☿. The second of these symbols corresponds to the Double Mercury or Androgyne, possessing the nature of *fiery* or *burning* *Water*, expressions that betray their identity with the Fire or Soul principle. And in fact its symbol is obtained from that of ordinary Mercury ☿ by the substitution of the sign of Aries ♈, or Sulfur in the pure state, for that of the rising Moon ☽. Thus life forces are interpenetrated by a masculine spiritual quality, which reveals the rising of ☉, the Gold or Soul. Having said this we can proceed to explain the quartering as follows:

In man, before everything else, there is a *terrestrial* being, also called a Saturnian being, or simply Saturn. It is through him the "Earth" force acts, which determines and maintains the density or heaviness ("our lead"—μόλιβος ἡμέτερος[1]—in a quite specific sense). This is the hard and tangible animal body and manifests itself principally through the element of calcium (bones), and also through horny material, cartilage, tendons, etc. *Sub specie interioritatis* this entity is seen as the power of devouring and yearning (the voracious *desiccation* and greedy *aridity* of "dry land," in the alchemical jargon), the root of all thirst and desire. The titanic, tellurian element that is spoken of in Orphism refers to this entity, which is also the primordial principle of individuation. It is the "fixed" par excellence: and even though it is the eternal matrix of individual bodies, at the same time, since they are so ephemeral, it appears as the God who after having created them, devours them. It is the hermetic exegesis of Saturn's double aspect, king of the "Golden Age" (we shall see that this is related, among other things, to the primordial spiritual state of corporeality) and devourer of his own sons.

In the second place we have an *aquatic* ("fluid") or *Lunar* entity: that is, of Mercury, or Mercury in a limited sense ☿, and Moon. Here we must refer to the general notion of the *double:* the Egyptian *Ka*, the "wind of the bones" and the *Ob* of Hebrew esotericism, the Etruscan *lasa*, the Hindu "subtle form" (*sūkshmasārira*) and *prāna*, etc. It is the life of the Saturn-body entity, by virtue of which, it is considered as the carrier of the various racial energies, the genetic inheritance of our "primordial forefathers" (the relationship between the "double" and the totem among primitives).[2] That for which the first entity is the skeleton, for this second entity is the *white* nervous and glandular system through which a plasmodic influence is exercised. With regard to consciousness it represents the treshhold over which the exterior penetrates into the interior: Mercury is the seat of the senses, the mirror in which are illuminated the phantasms of things (whence its connection to the power of the *imagination*),[3] both when they are produced through the first being (normal physical perception) and when they are produced directly (paranormal psychic perception).

Then we have the Mercury united with the Fire, a more subtle "fluid" entity, less corporeal, more specialized by an intimate interpenetration with the *soul* principle, as we explained in discussing the ☿ symbol. On the other hand, as fire on contact with water results in the gaseous or airy state, so this entity, which the ancients frequently designated as body or igneous form, we must recognize as the correspondence to the Air element ▲, understood as a blockage of the pure Fire power △. The latter, represented by *red* blood, provides the vital or animal heat

---

[1] For the Black Lead of which "the ancients speak as the foundation that underlies substance," cf. Zosimos, *CAG*, 2:223.

[2] Cf. Lévy-Bruhl, *L'âme primitive* (Paris, 1927), 238–49.

[3] Whence Agrippa (*De occulta philosophia* 2:28), has the imagination correspond to Water and simple Earth feelings.

and all power of movement, just as the preceding ☿ is the principle of "etheric light" diffused in the senses and vitalizing the *white* nerves.

Finally, we have the *intellectual* entity, which is the Sun and Gold in man. It is the center ☉, the principle of spiritual stability, radiant and not inert, primary origin of everything that through ☿ and ☿ arrives at the telluric union, to move it and make it alive in a higher sense. In itself supra-individual, it gives rise to individuality, the ego-function. It is the νοῦς, according to the Hellenic mystery conception; the first power of Fire (the "Fire of the Stone" of the Arab alchemical texts); the "stable and not falling soul" of Agrippa.[4] In the *Corpus Hermeticum* it is called "incorporeal essence, neither moved by anything, nor in anything, nor towards anything, nor for anything, because it is a primary force, and what precedes has no need of anything following"; "an essence that possesses its own end in itself"[5] is identified with this same principle.[6]

Such are the Four in man—and such are the seats wherein knowledge of the hermetic Elements can take place. They have different forms, but they are present and active in man simultaneously, the first in a spatial way, the other three in a nonspatial way, like different states of the body (in the ordinary sense) and of physical matter. The normal man does not have any distinct knowledge of them: in him they are experienced in a confused way in a general sensation (coenesthesis), which is illuminated in the form of sensory phantasms and reflected images and very rarely in *actions* of the igneous principle or of *concentric* (cyclopedic) solar vision (referring to the "third eye" of Oriental tradition). It is the impure state of the "mixed," the obscurity of the "tomb of Osiris" (Osiris = ☉) and according to the expressions of the texts, the indistinguishable quality of "our philosophic chaos," in which, whoever surrenders himself to the hermetic Art, must extract the individual natures spagyrically. Only then emerge the four possibilities as glimpses and reintegrations in metaphysical contact with the Elements. It goes without saying that the organic systems (skeletal, nervous, and blood) brought into contact with the different entities, *are not* these entities, but manifestations, apparitions of them in the heart of the saturnian terrestrial being. In alchemical terms this last is the "thickened" (or gross); the conjunction of the rest is the "subtle" or "volatile" (in the broad sense): Earth and Heaven.

So, "Like knows like." Thus, as long as man is amalgamated with the Earth entity, he will know nothing more than the Earth aspect of things and beings—their physical and sense aspect. Likewise, in the lunar entity taken from the "tomb,"

---

[4] Ibid., 3:44.

[5] Treated under *The Virgin of the World*, 3 (text in Mead, 239, 245).

[6] The lines of this four-part division follow Kremmerz, *Fascicolo D della Miryam* and *I dialoghi sull'ermetismo* (Spoleto, 1929), 6-7, 11, 116. We have chosen to give them directly, to make it easier for the reader to find the best way to explain the meanderings of symbolism in the texts.

naked, he would know Water, not the vulgar water, but the luminous and permanent Water of the Sages, and everything would be conceived as a kind of "Water" (subtle perception); and the Air and things ruled by Air—"Eagles"—would be known in the ☿ entity; and finally, in its own center, reintegrated in the solar purity of ⊙, "soul standing and not falling," a simple and universal vision, the "cyclical" or "cyclopic" vision would be enclosed in the interior of the "Fire Spheres." There the Homeric "Staff of Hermes" would be in operation, at whose contact everything is transmuted into the state of symbolic Gold (in this context, this is the passage from the common perception of the world to that of the—κόσμος νοητός—intelligible world).[7]

A final point regarding the hermetic symbolism of colors. After black, which is appropriate for Earth, the obscure Lead, and Saturn, we have the white of ☿ the Moon or Venus,[8] the red of ☿, and the golden color of ⊙. As we shall see, to each one of these colors corresponds a phase of the hermetic work that focuses precisely on the principle in question. Moreover, the symbol also encompasses the four kingdoms of Nature, considered as symbols and manifestations of corresponding forces. In the telluric entity man contains in himself the mineral kingdom; in the lunar, "our Water" entity he contains the vegetable kingdom (whence the reason for the permutation of the white color for the green of vegetability); in the igneous,

---

[7] In the literature the differentiation between ☿ and ☿ is often shown by the symbol of two "fumes" or "vapors," one white and the other red, or quite simply by two stones, one red and the other white, which are liberated from the stone (the body), by the two trees, one lunar, the other solar (cf. the Cosmopolite; Braccesco, *Clef de la grande science*, etc.), by the two Mercuries, occidental and oriental, one of them Spirit and the other corresponding to the Soul. The last is *poison*, unless mitigated—"chilled"—by the other Mercury ☿ (*CMA*, 3:208); poison, devouring fire, and also (Promethean) vulture are equivalents in the tradition, for which, cf. *Corpus Hermeticum* (10.17-18): "When the intellectual principle [νοῦς, ⊙] is liberated from the body of *Earth*, it is immediately reclothed in its tunic of Fire, which it could not save [integrally], while inhabiting this *Earth* body, since the *Earth* does not support Fire . . . with the result that Water [☿] surrounds the Earth and forms a bulwark to protect it from the Fire." Cf. also Agrippa (*De occulta philosophia*, 3:37): "The soul in its descent reclothes itself in a celestial and aerial corpuscle, which some call the etheric vehicle, and others the chariot of the soul—by means of which the Soul is infused first in the central point of the heart, which is the center of the human body, and from there expands into every part and member; which it does by uniting its chariot with the natural heat [☿] by means of the heat of the Spirit generated by the heart; and by means of this heat it is immersed in the humors [☿] through which it accedes to the members, in the same way that the heat of the Fire attaches itself to the Air and Water, although reaching the Water [☿] by the Air [☿]." For other references of correspondences with the blood, etc., cf. *CMA* (Syrian text) 2:315; *Livre d'Ostanes, CMA*, 3:120; *Corpus Hermeticum*, 10.13; Zosimos, *CAG*, 2:133; *De signatura* 11, §10; *Livre du mercure oriental, CMA*, 3:212, etc. In Boehme we can point out a very expressive symbolism: the etheric body ☿ is compared to an "oil," in which burns the igneous quality ♣ becoming splendor, light of life, "life of joy that exalts everything." Every sickness is but a "venemous corruption" of this oil—upon extinguishing its light, the body decomposes. Concerning the "aqueous" alteration of this oil by the "Fall," about which Boehme also speaks (*De signatura*, 6, §§3, 23, 25, 28; 7, §2); see below.

[8] On occasion, instead of white we find green by chromatic analogy to the energies of vegetable life.

the animal kingdom; and finally in order to represent himself and nothing but himself there is the intellectual or "incombustible Sulfur" entity ☉.

Within the framework of the world vision to which hermetism pertains, there are *simultaneously* real, magical, and symbolic correspondences; kingdoms of nature, states of matter, systems of corporeality, and human consciousness considered as different manifestations of the same metaphysical principles.

. . . .
Fourteen
. . . .

Che PLANECS

The same metaphysical correspondences apply to another teaching that hermetism also shares with the most ancient traditions: that of the Seven—which prevails in the symbolism of the seven planets.

Metaphysically, Seven expresses the Three added to the Four. According to the established meaning of these numeric symbols, Seven is the manifestation of the creative principles (triad) in relation to the world made up of the four elements (3 + 4): the full expression of nature creating nature (*natura naturans*) in action.[1] These seven principles are simultaneously internal and external,[2] residing in man and the world in the visible and invisible aspect of both. Sometimes in the teaching they undergo a duplication, which expresses the duality existing between the Sun ("being") aspect and the Moon ("energy") aspect of each individual power (whence the hermetic symbolism of the two trees each with seven braches or seven fruits, *arbor solis et arbor lunae*); or else the duplication is that existing between the septenary as it is in itself, and what the septenary becomes upon the intervention of the "Fall" and the domination of the Earth element.

As for references, we can start with this from the *Corpus Hermeticum:* "The intellectual entity, male and female god [the primordial androgyne composed of ☉

---

[1] Cf. *Livre de la miséricorde* (*CMA*, 3:168): "The Opus is wrought through *seven things:* the spiritual, the corporeal [☉ and ☾] and their combination, determined in Air, Water, Fire and Earth."

[2] Boehme, *De signatura*, 9, §8: "In eternal nature as in external nature there are seven forms, which the ancient sages indicated by the names of the planets." [*Es sind vornehmlich sieben Gestalten in der Natur, beides in der ewigen äußeren, dann die äußeren gehen aus der ewigen. Die alten Weisen haben den sieben Planeten Namen gegeben, nach den sieben Gestalten der Natur.*—Trans.]

and ☾], which is Life and Light, engenders by means of the Logos, another creative intelligence, God of Fire and Fluid, who in turn creates *seven* ministers, who enclose within their circles the sense-perceived world. Their dominion is called εἱμαρμένη [Fate].[3] Here the last phrase sends us back to the tradition referred to by Plato as the Wheel of Fate composed of *seven* spinning spheres, ruled by the "daughters of necessity." The preceding distinction makes this necessity the work of a second god, beyond whose realm, however, exists an even higher intellectual androgynous entity. And in the function of this higher region can be seen the same seven principles.

Besides, in that gnostic, mystery ambience in which the Greek alchemical texts took form, it was customary to teach the existence of two septenaries, a lower, called the "sevenfold serpent, daughter of Ialdabaoth" (a name for the "second god") and the other, higher and celestial, which in its totality could be made to correspond to the *eighth sphere* (that "beyond the Seven") or *ogdoad*,[4] also placed by Plato above those of "necessity."[5] The gnostic Valentinus calls it the "Heavenly Jerusalem."[6] A gnostic-hermetic papyrus conceives of it as the "Holy Name," being the seven Greek vowels taken as symbols for the "Seven Heavens," while the Eighth is the "Monad" or unity "of *another* kind," which repeats them on a higher plane; we can then establish a connection with the schematic of the eight-rayed stars in the *Chrysopoeia of Cleopatra*.[7] And vice versa we can consider, above all, the higher septenary, and see in the last of the seven forms the substratum of the inferior septenary, which is born through the symbolic "Earth." It is in this way that Boehme sees in the seventh principle, "Nature," the expansion (exteriorization) of the other six—the "body" being the seventh, and the others being its "life" (in a transcendent sense): "The seventh spirit is the spirit-fountain of nature. Once engendered, it becomes the mother of the other seven. It comprises in itself the other six, and generates them in turn [that is, manifests them in her own form by making them manifestations in visible nature; for example, the seven visible planets, which are the sense-perceived symbols of the invisible]: since in the seventh exists the natural and corporeal essence . . . In this, one of the seven forms of nature dominates the others, and each one collaborates according to its own

---

[3] *Corpus Hermeticum*, 1.9. For the sense of the Fluid and of the Fire, which is the substance of this passage, cf. Hippolytus (*Philosophumena*, 6, §§7, 8: "Rivers have been designated as the moist element of generation, and Fire the impetuous desire for generation." For the higher state, in this text as well as in the *Corpus Hermeticum*, "a new man, who is androgynous" is also mentioned.

[4] In Irenaeus, *Adversus haereses*, 1.30.5.

[5] Plato, *Republic*, 10.614C.

[6] In Hippolytus, *Philosophumena*, 6, §32; cf. §49 where the teaching of Marcus the Gnostic sets forth the correspondences to the seven Greek vowels.

[7] Leiden papyrus W, in Berthelot, *Introduction à l'étude de la Chimie*, 17; cf. *CAG*, 3:302.

essential strength, naturalizing itself in the body according to its rank."[8] "Body," here, of course, has to be understood in the broadest sense, in which the tangible human body is merely a particular case of its own.

These same doctrines, presented in the form of myths and descriptions of cosmic entities, must be related to the meanings and possibilities of inner experience, especially with regard to the differentiation between the two septenaries. We can thus return to the hermetic text cited above[9] wherein it is said that man, once awakened to a will to create, wants to bypass the limits of the circles of necessity and master the power residing in Fire. This is clearly a variation on the Promethean myth, which also ends in a "fall": the man who is "superior to harmony [that is, to the universal order, the unity of the various laws and natural conditions], to harmony becomes a slave. Although hermaphrodite like the Father and above *sleep*, he remains dominated by sleep."[10] But *sleep* is an esoteric word traditionally meaning consciousness weighed down by the conditions of the animal body, in antithesis to the symbol of the *awakening* of the initiate with the work of *destroying sleep* (*nidrābhanga* in the Hindu texts), by the "sleepless" intellectual nature—ἡ φύσις ἄγρυπνος—of which Plotinus speaks. As Buddhistic *avidya*, so this symbolic "sleep" can be considered equivalent as well to "oblivion," the Greek λήθη, "lethe." Macrobius[11] transmits the tradition of the division of the "materia"—ὕλη—into two parts, of which one, as ambrosia, is the sustenance of the gods, and the other, as drink of the souls, constitutes the waters of the river Lethe, the water of forgetfulness; and this tradition clarifies the meaning of the teaching of the two septenaries.

It is not a question of two really different orders, but of the same reality with two different modes of manifestation.[12] That which leads from one mode to the other is the event referred to in the *Corpus Hermeticum*, the epilogue of which is the "state of sleep," "forgetting," the loss of spiritual consciousness, the alteration of the most profound principle.

This teaching is explained by a disciple of Boehme, Georg Gichtel, who speaks of a fire (that is, an ego-power) that, when separated from the Light (that is, from the diffuse vitality), is turned into *desire*; this fire hotly devours all "oily wetness," by which the light is extinguished[13] and a black precipitation is produced (the color

---

[8] Boehme, *Aurora*, 11, §46; 16, §§5, 8; *De signatura*, 13, §1.

[9] *Corpus Hermeticum*, 1.12.

[10] Ibid., 12–15

[11] Macrobius, *Commentarium in somnium Scipionis*, Eyssenhardt, ed. (Leipzig, 1893), 531ff.

[12] In the traditions of Assyrian stock, the seven gods of the Abyss are distinguished with some difficulty from the celestial deities. Cf. Hubert-Mauss, *Mélanges d'histoire de la religion* (Paris, 1929), 114, which demonstrates that it is a question here as well of a single order with two different kinds of appearance.

[13] See note 3 above.

of Saturn, whose dark point, in an engraving of Basil Valentine, is precisely directed toward the *corpus* principle). It is the "corruption of the luminous paradisiacal body" that in *sleep* (Gichtel uses exactly this word) is replaced by the black terrestrial body, "seat of an insatiable appetite, of sickness and death." Gichtel continues: inwardly dead, the Soul (that original Fire) is converted into "Hell," where eternal corruption takes place. "And then appear *seven* forms, daughters of the Fire Dragon, Spirit-of-this-world, who are the seals that keep the non-regenerated from perceiving the Divine Fire."[14]

Transmitted as motifs in fairy tales and fables are dragons with seven heads who guard "caverns" (that is to say, the accesses to the interior of the "Earth," to the depths locked in the corporeal) or "treasures" (Gold, or precious stones—in alchemy and before that in Gnosticism, gems frequently signified "powers"). According to Mithraism the soul, in order to free itself, must go through seven spheres marked by seven gates, each one of which is guarded by an angel of the "God of Light," an equivalence to the seals that bar the spiritual ascent to the higher septenary (the seven "heavens").[15] To each gate corresponds a degree of the Mithraic initiation, however, which confirms that it is not a question of theological abstractions but of allusions to transcendental forms of consciousness, which have been paralyzed by the power that acts on those who have been conquered by symbolic sleep.[16]

---

[14] G. Gichtel, *Theosophia practica*, (1736), 2:50, 18, introd., 3:6; cf. Boehme, (*De signatura*, 12, §30): "The Tree is divided into *seven* branches: it is life. The curse of God has been cast over the seven forms."

[15] As for the two aspects of the higher septenary, to the ☉ or ☿ aspect of each one of the seven principles, the two choruses of gods can be made to correspond—the first motionless and fixed (☉) and the others in movement (☿) with whom, according to the *Corpus Hermeticum* (10.7), the souls that have reached immortality enter into contact—and the first will constitute "the highest grade of the glorious initiation of the soul."

[16] We might mention an illustration in the German edition of the *Crede mihi* of Norton, in which is shown an androgyne *sleeping* in a locked garden and Mercury standing nearby. The opposite spiritual condition is shown in a figure in the *Rosarium philosophorum* (*Artis auriferae*, 2:291), in which the androgyne is shown over the Moon (that is, Mercury) with a tree in his hand and two pairs of *seven* fruits.

···········
Fifteen
···········

the centers
of Life

Let us move on to the "Seven" in man. What the hermetists call Spirit (☿ and ☿, the "life body")—corresponding analogically to the planetary region intermediary between Earth and Heaven—also presents forces and structures corresponding to each of the planets. Plotinus himself taught: "There are within us forces analogous to the powers of the different planets."[1] And thus we come to the esoteric doctrine of the seven points through which the higher powers enter into the corporeal context, whereupon they become vital currents and energies specific to man.[2] But because of the two-way direction that each point of passage or "portal" affords, these seven centers, which normally serve to convey nonhuman forces into human channels, can be taken in an opposite direction. That is, the flow may be turned back from the

---

[1] Plotinus, *Enneads*, 3.4.6.

[2] On this basis a distinction must be made between the energies that, though always immortal whatever may be the body in which they act, are still universal or particular depending on whether they are exercised in "divine bodies" or in "mortals," in which latter case they acquire the aspect of sensations (*Corpus Hermeticum*, κόρη κόσμου, 214–15). Della Riviera (*Mondo magico*, 19) says that "Upon instilling itself in the individuals of each species, the divine virtue, to those it has given life, being, form and permanence, at the same moment loses its universal nature. . . . Wherefore, it will search uselessly and vainly outside the Center contained in the Center."

human to the nonhuman—which is equivalent to the aforementioned passing through the seven gates, breaking the seven seals, ascending through the seven heavens, and so forth.

To see this teaching in more complete and explicit terms, we have to go back to the Hindu tradition where the centers are called *chakras* or "wheels" (because of the spinning movement of the vitalizing energies that radiate from them), and also *padma*, or "lotuses." The lotus, however, like the rose in hermetism (or "flower," less specifically), is a symbol that we also find in the Chaldeo-Egyptian and Minoan traditions, where often enough it is associated with the "key of life" and has the meaning of resurrection, palingenesis, awakening; the "flowering" of the seven higher forms freed from the obstruction that the human Earth (the body) entails is the reconquest of the integral and primordial being of Gold.[3]

The varieties of hermetico-alchemical symbolism in which, one way or the other, the Seven figure, can be interpreted at the microcosmic level on the basis of such a teaching. The references to specific points of the body so rigorously followed in the Orient (references not crudely spatial, but of "functional correspondence"), are rarely encountered in hermetism. We encounter the most explicit reference—conforming quite closely to the Hindu teaching in this matter—in the fourth illustration annexed to Georg Gichtel's *Theosophia practica*. In this illustration the coronal, frontal, laryngeal, cardiac, lumbar, umbilical, and sacral regions are indicated by means of the hermetico-astrological ideograms of the planets affixed at given points in each of these regions. Since the illustration shows "the dark and terrestrial nature of man," it represents the inferior septenary. In this same depiction, a spiral extends from Saturn (symbol of the basic corporeal and "terrestrial" condition in which the other planets or principles are manifested) in an enveloping movement passing through all the other centers until it arrives at the heart, where a serpent can be seen coiled around the solar ☉ principle. This is a representation of the process of "falling," which unwinds down to the restriction where the power of the ego, far from the living Gold or Sun of the Wise, manifests only in its vulgar form of the human personality. In each one of the other centers an equivalent loss of power occurs and, in fact, to each of the centers in the chart there is given the name of a *passion*.

An equivalence to the Hellenistic doctrine is evident in the symbolic descent of the soul through the planetary spheres, from each of which the soul

---

[3] This meaning is hidden in the Jewish rite of the lighting of the candelabra with seven branches, while the Seven Sleepers of the fable may signify the opposite meaning.

takes on the garment of a given passion or the quality of the energies according to its degree. The inner meaning is the same: the debasing of the powers of the primordial man to dark, repressed, corporeal energies contained in the subconscious and peripheral psychologisms—passive, broken off from cosmic spirituality to the point where it is said: "This miserable soul, ignorant of what it is, is turned into a slave of bodies of strange form, in sorrow, bearing the body like a weight, not as one who dominates, but as one dominated."[4]

But now we can see what the return journey should be, described in clear words by the *Corpus Hermeticum:*[5] once separated from the irrational nature the Soul passes back up through the planetary spheres, "divesting itself" of whatever pertains to each of them, surmounting them, renewing the audacity of transcending the Lords of Destiny who had brought it to its fall in the first place; and so arriving, "cloaked in its sole power," at the *eighth* stage, whose symbol is the region of the fixed stars, called the sphere of "identity" or "being in itself"—κάθ' εάυθó—in contrast to the spheres overcome, which are called those of "alteration" or "difference"—κατά τò έτηρον. There, beyond the Seven, is the place of "those who are,"[6] those who have stopped "becoming." It is at that point that we reach the possession of the transcendent Knowledge. It is the moment of "birth according to essence"—ή ούσιώδες γένεσις—and "becoming a god." One is transformed into those beings—becomes them. Once "necessity," which rules the lower spheres, has been identified with the current of the Waters, the symbols of this realization will be the figures of those who have been "saved from the waters," those who can "walk on the water,"[7] those who have crossed the "sea" or the "stream" (and

---

[4] Cf. J. Evola, *The Yoga of Power*, 140ff.

[5] *Corpus Hermeticum*, 10.8.

[6] Ibid., 1.22–26, 43.

[7] In some texts the seventh sphere, instead of the eighth, expresses the same meaning; in relation to the aforementioned in the introduction (pp. 15–16), the definition of the seventh state has a special meaning and should be taken in the same sense as that of "the one standing, who keeps standing and who will go on standing" (Hippolytus, *Philosophumena*, 6.13). Some concurrences: an esoteric meaning of the biblical *seventh* day of "rest" (the Initiatic *pax*) after the other six of work; Horus, the God who succeeded in definitively conquering the dragon Typhon is the *eighth* son of Isis, who sought the virile parts (the power of Osiris), dressed in *seven* black "garments." Osiris, the "primordial masculine," quartered or mutilated by the dragon and put back together again by Horus, can then compare himself to the Vedic Prajapati, who after having created the Waters (Waters = Dragon) was assimilated by them (dissolution) and then came out of them in the form of a golden seed (*Rig-Veda*, 10.121; 1.7).

for this we can also call up all the varieties of navigational symbolism), and that of swimming upstream against the current. This last, according to the *Corpus Hermeticum*, is the means of reaching the state of "those who have attained Gnosis"—*οἱ ἐν γνώσει ὄντες*—"where one is no longer inebriated,"[8] where inebriation signifies, obviously, symbolic sleep, forgetting, the power of the Lethean waters.[9]

---

[8] Cf. G. Postel, *Clavis absconditus*, 15, f116, which speaks of the "law of grace which extracted men from the Waters of the world," and refers to the symbol of Christ, who "walks on the sea *sustained by his own power*," an identical expression to that used in the *Corpus Hermeticum* for those who reach the eighth level.

[9] *Corpus Hermeticum*, 7.2. The same symbolism is quite frequent in the Orient: cf. *Dhammapada* (86, 348, 370) where crossing the stream is explained as crossing and passing beyond the kingdom of death, and where the ascetic who has overcome the five obstacles is identified with the one who has crossed the ocean; *Suttanipata*, 3.6.36; *Katha-Upanishad*, 1.3.2. The "upstream-swimmer" is a technical expression for that "purity" of the heart that has arrived at the formless states—*arupa*—(cf. *Dhammapada*, 218). From the Gnostic point of view, Jesus was considered one of those who "have raised themselves against the stream" (*Philosophumena*, 5.7-8). Cf. plate on p. 192 of the *Chymica vannus*: a man is preparing to cross a river and on the other bank are seen "winged" beings (Air states); there is also a ship en route to a *litus secretus*. The two symbolic directions of the Waters are revealed in a Gnostic commentary to Homer (*Odyssey*, 24.9-12). Oceanus, father of the gods and of men, ebbs and flows back again; in falling he gives way to the generation of men and in rising, to the *white stone* (leucasia); he brings in the gods, referred to as the "Seven Gods" and "the Androgyne Man in everyone" (in Hippolytus, *Philosophumena*, 5.7-8).

Sixteen

Che seven,
Che operacions,
and Che mirror

ow that we have outlined the doctrine we can begin to
cut a path through the complex symbolism of the
technical alchemical literature, which otherwise would
be almost impenetrable. We shall accompany the reader through a part of this
literary labyrinth in order to familiarize him with the secret language.

Ostanes[1] speaks of seven distillations necessary for obtaining from the serpents
of Mount Olympus and other mountains[2] the "Divine Water" that kills the living
and revives the dead (the deep stages of consciousness buried in terrestrial form).[3]

---

[1] *CAG*, 2:261; 3:250

[2] Concerning "mountain," see page 130, note 3. The "serpents" here symbolize the powers residing
within "Earth's breast." The same symbolism can be seen in an illustration of Abraham the Jew (de
Givry, *Musée des sorciers*, 397): a mountain, seven caves, seven serpents; below, two griffons mutually
devouring one another indicate the antagonism of the powers, about which we have previously spoken
(p. 40), and give origin to the body as petrifying neutralization; above, at the summit, is a tree with
branches of golden, red and white flowers (awakenings in ☿ and ☿).

[3] Boehme (*De signatura*, 12, §31) says that the seven forms of human life are first killed and then aroused
to a new life. In the images of Abraham the Jew (de Givry, 297), this killing is expressed symbolically
by "the massacre of the innocents:" seven children have been killed and their blood serves as the bath
("washing") of the king and queen, ☉ and ☾. Also in Hindu alchemy one is instructed to "kill"

And Raymond Lully also speaks of the preparation of the water of life, which is the "solvent" to be used in the work: "This menstruum is *rectified* [— is replaced by | , which = resurrection][4] seven times, each time removing the residue."[5] Flamel[6] advises that in order to purify the "leprous head of the raven" it is necessary to enter the regenerating flow of the Jordan seven times. And Pernety[7] speaks no differently of a *bathing*, adding that it is a question of passing through the seven planets, realized by means of seven successive operations that conduct us through different stages of Mercury, symbolized by the various alchemical metals, up to the stage of Gold (the plane of "those-who-are," beyond the spheres of change and becoming).

In the *Great Book of Nature* a dyke is mentioned that holds back the waters from flowing into a garden. The dyke is overcome upon the instruction of an infant guide, "not the son of man," who commands: "Strip off your robes," which is explained in the seven grades of "expiation" to be discussed later.[8] And similarly, in the *Chemical Wedding of Christian Rosenkreuz* by J. V. Andreae, we see that the bridal candidates have to pass the test of the seven burdens, and then seven are the stories of the tower of the royal palace where the resurrection of the King and Queen (☉ and ☾)[9] takes place. According to Philalethes, seven are the times that the doves of Venus must circle because "all perfection resides in the number seven"; and elsewhere he mentions "the Mercury must be purified at least seven times. Only then is the 'Bath of the King'[10] ready." And with the image of the bath we return to the symbol of washing, to which is submitted the one who, being King by nature, must rule again.

In the *Book of El Habir* it is said: "Wash ye seven times the lime that is not yet exhausted" (symbolizing the thirsty "dryness" of Water)"; I direct you to work over the ashes [that which remains after the action of the purifying Fire] subjecting them to heat and irrigation seven times [here we are dealing with the

---

the Mercury six times in order to transform the Copper into Gold. See P. C. Ray, *History of Hindu Chemistry* (London-Calcutta, 1902), 1, pref., 46; 2, pref., 39-44.

[4] See page 90ff.

[5] R. Lully, *Clavicula*, §16; cf. *Theatrum chemicum*, 4.334.

[6] *Livre de Synesius, BPC*, 2.190; Flamel, *Figures hiéroglyphiques*, (chap. 4), in *BPC*, 2:243.

[7] *Dictionnaire*, 301.

[8] Italian edition, trans. Todi (1921) 7-8, 13, 20. Concerning the dam we can return to the cited tradition (*Philosophumena*, 5.7) that speaks of a wall behind which is found the "inner Man," who proceeds "from the primordial celestial Man, Adam," fallen into a work of mere clay and mud in which "he has forgotten everything" (sleep, forgetting, etc.).

[9] *Chemische Hochzeit von Christian Rosenkreuz* (Paris, 1928), 36; Boehme (*De signatura*, 10, §63) calls the other septenary the "diabolical castle," which "the knight will destroy in the seven kingdoms.

[10] Philalethes, *Epist. de Ripley*, §51; *Regulae*, §5.

other, celestial modality of water, which is used in 'resurrections']. Out of this the ashes will be sweet, good and fair. *And ye will no longer see death.*"[11] Sometimes the seven indicates symbolic periods of time (days, years, etc.), which often refer to the same order of ideas.

The seven gates of the Mysteries of Mithras are encountered in the Arabic edition of the *Book of Ostanes:* in a vision occasioned by asceticism, fasting, and prayer, there appears to the author a being who conducts him to seven doors where, guarding the treasures of knowledge, is an animal whose own parts are being devoured among themselves[12] (as mentioned on page 34). This clearly symbolizes the desire that feeds on itself, establishing by its presence the obstacle to the realization of the transcendent states.[13] And the seven initiations are seen in the symbol of the seven steps in the Stairway of the Wise in an illustration of the *Amphitheatrum sapientiae* of Khunrath, a work in which is also encountered the symbol of a "philosophical citadel" with seven towers, corresponding to the seven operations of the Art, with a dragon in the center, symbol of the prima materia.

In a mystical Syrian alchemical text, the usual veil of enigmas almost completely falls away when we come to the Mirror contained within a temple appropriately called the "Seven Doors":

> The purpose of the mirror was not to allow a person to contemplate himself physically, because scarcely was the mirror put down, when the person lost memory of his own image. The Mirror represents the Divine Spirit. When the soul sees itself in it, it observes the shameful things in itself and rejects them. . . . Once purified, it imitates and takes as model the Holy Ghost; it becomes spirit itself; calm possesses it and it turns continuously to this superior state in which it knows [the divine] and is known [by it]. *Then having become without shadow,* it divests itself of the chains that are its own and those it has in common with the body. And what is the word of the philosophers? *Know thyself.* With these words is conveyed the spritual and intellectual mirror. And what is this mirror if not the primordial divine spirit itself? When a man looks into it and sees himself, he turns away from everything bearing the names of gods and demons, and uniting himself with the Holy Ghost, he becomes a perfect man. . . . He sees the God that is in him. . . . This mirror is situated

---

[11] *CMA*, 3:95, 114.

[12] Cf. also *CAG* 2:287–88, 315, 337; *CMA*, 2:37, 38; *Livre de El Habir, CMA*, 3:88.

[13] *CMA*, 3:119–20; Cf. d'Espagnet (*Arcanum hermeticae, BCC*, 2, §52): "The garden of the Hesperides is guarded by a horrible dragon; at the entrance there is a fountain of the clearest living-Water, issuing from seven sources and pouring out in all directions. Have the dragon drink this water according to the magic number of three times seven (the seven referring to the three principles) until, inebriated, he divests himself of his soiled garment."

over *seven* doors . . . corresponding to the *seven* heavens, over the sensory world, over the twelve houses [the zodiac or forces of animal vitality]. . . . And over them rises the Eye of the invisible senses, the Eye of the Spirit, which is present and in all places. This perfect Spirit is seen in the power of which everything is comprised.[14]

In sum: in hermetism, the number seven, according to traditional esoteric teaching, expresses transcendent forms, nonhuman forms of consciousness and energy that stand at the foundation of "elemental" things. The possibility of a double relationship to these forms explains the doctrine of the two septenaries, one bound to necessity and the other opening to freedom.[15] The state of physical embodiment in which man finds himself is tied to the mystery of this septenary differentiation and, through the "centers of life," also contains the double power of the keys of "locking" and "unlocking," of the hermetic *solve* and *coagula*. Purifications, distillations, circulations, divestments, calcinations, solutions, ablutions, killings, baths, rectifications, etc., all relate more or less directly to the number seven. In the technical hermetic literature they express the work assigned to the powers through their transition from one mode of being to another, which is "nonhuman."

And so we have moved from the doctrinal part of hermetism and entered the terrain of practice. But before proceeding we shall set down a series of ideas and symbols that will allow us to clarify the essence of the hermetic work.

---

[14] *CMA*, 2:262–63.

[15] Cf. *The Virgin of the World*, 3 (Mead, 255): "The difference between corruptible things and eternal things, between physical and non-physical, is that the ones are subject to necessity and the others exist freely."

The Seven, the Operations, and the Mirror · · · · · · · · · · · · · · · · · 63

....

Seventeen

....

GOLD
in the ART

One view that is central to the Royal Art is that the hermetist performs certain operations by which he actualizes and brings to perfection a symbolic "Matter," one that Nature has left imperfect and potential and which, without this assistance of the Art, would never be able to improve itself. This view refers to everything the common man finds here below, but particularly to the importance of that which, "unknown to earlier races," we have mentioned in connection to the specific spirit of the "heroic cycles."

Concerning the first point we can cite, speaking for all sources, the *De pharmaco catholico*: "Nature rests and suspends the work on the Gold [in the sense of vulgar Gold, interpretable as the state according to which the solar force is found in the common man]. . . . This is the highest goal of all metals [of all the other natures differentiated by the 'matrix'], higher and beyond which, Nature cannot by itself bring any metal."[1] But "men can aid nature and *oblige* it to undertake something beyond that attainable by its ordinary activity"[2] to reach that goal Geber calls "the extreme limit" and "the difficult thing" and "the highest that man can desire."[3] The

---

[1] *De pharmaco*, 4, §2.

[2] Salmon, introduction to *BPC*, iii; cf. *Triomphe Hermétique, BPC*, 3:243.

[3] *Livre de la miséricorde, CMA*, 3:188, 185.

. . . .

alchemists thus establish a distinction between that Gold which is a *natural* production, and the other which is prepared by the help of the *Art* and receives the mark and sign of "the Masters of Power."[4] Concerning this, Philalethes says allegorically that if Mercury is found among merchants, the Sun or Gold, on the other hand, is "*a consequence of our work and our operation*"; and who does not know this "*still does not understand the purpose of our secret work.*"[5] As we said at the beginning, the purpose of the hermetic Art is not the *discovery* of Gold, but its *fabrication*.

Having fixed this general point, we can understand the meaning of such expressions as "death and resurrection," "killing the living and reviving the dead," and others that constitute a leitmotiv of hermetism.

---

[4] Syrian texts, *CMA*, 2:121.

[5] *Introitus apertus*, §18.

shADOWl, AShES, AND REMAINS

In order to return to life, the dead must die. The symbolism of death, in general, can be referred to "sleep" as we have shown, and since sleep or dreaming is the state of ordinary consciousness within the body, that would seem to affirm the idea of—in a more soteriologico-religious sense than initiatic—the body as evil, the fall and negation of the spirit.

References to this are not lacking, to be sure. In the *Corpus Hermeticum*—to begin with that—the body acquires the label of burden or prison. And every soul does find itself so laden and enchained: "But even underneath this burden, the soul struggles and thinks, though these are not the same kinds of thoughts that it would have if it were detached from the body"; instead of "energies" it knows only sensations and *passions* that proceed from the body. It is for this reason that as a prerequisite for the acquisition of illumination or Gnosis, hatred for the body is recommended. And it is said: "But first thou must tear off from thee this cloak which thou wearest, this cloak of ignorance, origin of every evil, chain of corruption, tangle of *darkness*, living *death*, sensation's corpse, the *tomb* that thou draggest along with thee, the robber in thine own house who through the things he loveth, hateth thee, and through the things he hateth bears thee malice."[1] Here,

---

[1] *The Virgin of the World*, 2 (Mead, 214-15); *Corpus Hermeticum* 4.5; 7.2.

in any case, the symbols of garment, cloak, tomb, death, and darkness (shadow) are clearly employed in the same sense that they must be given when they appear in the enigmas of technical alchemical literature.

Here are some "shadow" correspondences: "The bodies [in the sense of the subjects over which the Opus will be exercised] all have a *shadow* and a *black* substance that must be extracted."[2] Speaking of the symbolical Copper—the reddish yellow "metal" nearest to being transmuted into Gold—Agathodaimon says: "The soul is the most subtle part, that is, the tinctural spirit [which acts in the same way a tint or tincture diffuses its 'color' into all parts]; the body is that heavy, earthy thing pledged to darkness."[3] Zosimos counsels to work it through until the copper has no more darkness:[4] "Expel the *shadow* of the Copper," repeat the Arabs.[5] "The Copper has passed to *white*" [stage of ☿ consciousness] and has been liberated from the dark . . . stripped of its *black* color, *it has abandoned its opaque and heavy body.*"[6] Comarius, speaking of a "dark spirit" that oppresses bodies repeats almost verbatim what is said in the *Corpus Hermeticum*. He says: "Body [in the primordial sense], Spirit and Soul are all debilitated because of the *shadow* that falls over them."[7] Pelagius adds that only when the Copper *has become shadowless* can it "color" all kinds of bodies, something which, as we shall see, coincides more or less with the goal of the Art.[8] Even more explicitly, the Cosmpolite says that it is a question of clearing up the *darkness* and coming to see that Light of Nature that has escaped our notice; because in our eyes, *the body is the shadow of nature.*[9]

If these allusions were not subject to any deeper meaning, they would have a suspicious character from the initiate's point of view. Since the body, in a wide sense, is the expression and at the same time the basis of individuation, it is a question of overcoming an escapist and mystical-pantheistic tendency pertaining more to the world of religions than to that of the initiates. But a series of expressions of very different spirit are regularly found in the hermetic doctrine.

For example, for those of us who know what "Salt" is—what does an expression

---

[2] *Livre de Cratès, CMA*, 3:55.

[3] Stephanius (*CMA*, 1.261); cf. note in B. Treviso, *Philosophie des métaux*, (*BPC*, 2:389): "The shadow of the Sun is the *embodiment* of the Gold."

[4] *CAG*, 3:133; cf. Pseudodemocritean texts, *CAG*, 3:45, 49; and Pelagius, *CAG*, 3:246-47.

[5] *CMA*, 2:141.

[6] *CAG*, 3:454, 459.

[7] *CAG*, 2:296.

[8] *CAG*, 2:257.

[9] *Novum lumen chemicum*, 65.

like this, from the *De pharmaco catholico* mean: "Without Salt we could not make the Philosopher's Stone," or this: "Metallic Salt is the Philosopher's Stone"? According to the symbolism of "distillations," the *dregs* are what remains after the spirit has been extracted, that is to say, they are the *body*, from which is also taken, among other possible meanings, the symbol of the "ashes"—by analogy, that is, as residue without any more Fire. But the surprising thing is that "dregs," "ashes," and "remains" alike are valued as something precious that the "Son of the Art" must guard against underestimating and throwing away, because it is precisely from them— it is declared—that the Gold is made, or rather, the ashes are the Gold, the true Gold, not the vulgar Gold, but the "Philosopher's Gold." "In the ashes remaining in the bottom of the tomb," Artephius[10] says, for instance, "are found the diadem of our King." And d'Espagnet says: "The earth at the bottom of the cup is the true mine of the Philosophers' Gold, the Fire of Nature and Heaven."[11] Zosimos ascribes to the residue of the burnt matters, the dross, the "power of everything [$\pi\alpha\nu\tau\grave{o}\varsigma$ $\acute{\varepsilon}\nu\varepsilon\rho\gamma\varepsilon\iota\alpha$]" and adds, "Know that the ashes constitute all the mystery, which is why the Ancients speak of the black Lead, which is the basis of substance."[12] As we know, such lead corresponds to the "sacred black Stone" which, according to John the Alchemist,[13] confers "skill" on the masters; it corresponds to Saturn, about which Boehme says: "Paradise is still in this world, but man is very far from it, so long as he fails to regenerate himself. *And this is the Gold hidden in Saturn*";[14] it corresponds to Earth, about which the *Hermetic Triumph* says: "When by distillation, we extract the Water, which is the Soul and the Spirit [here Water is an all-inclusive symbol for everything that is not Earth],[15] the body remains at the bottom of the vessel, as a dead Earth, black and vile, which nevertheless must not be disdained . . . the remains of Earth are converted into a true essence, and who would take anything away from our subject, knows nothing of [hermetic] Philosophy."[16]. And we also quote the words of the Emerald Tablet: "The power of the Telesma is not complete if it is not converted into Earth." We might also recall Olympiodorus: "Dregs and ashes are the oracle revealed by the demons"; in the *Book of El Habir*:[17] "The Redness [which is the final stage of the process, equivalent to ☉ and ♀] neither appears nor seems to exist outside these precious cinders," and so on.

[10] *Livre d'Artephius, BPC,* 2:169.

[11] *Arcanum hermeticae (BCC,* 2), §§22, 23.

[12] *CAG,* 2:99, 213, 223.

[13] Ibid., 265

[14] *De signatura,* 8, §§47, 48.

[15] *BPC,* 3:302.

[16] *CMA,* 3:96, 114.

[17] [That is, the shapes and forms and movements of matter apart from substance.—Trans.]

68 · **C**he **S**ymbols and **C**eachings

Other symbols have this same meaning. When the body is associated with Gold, there will also be attributed to the body a *masculine* value.[18] And also: "Who would become Master of the Work, and seeks anything other than this *Stone*, will be as one who wants to climb a ladder without rungs, and who, as that is impossible, would dash his head to the ground."[19] In the same way, Della Riviera has the "magical hero" derive from "Hera," out of the Earth, which the *Chymica vannus* describes as "the egg of the Phoenix."[20]

Alongside the idea that this individuation that is sustained by the body (the black Stone is the *basis of the substance*) must be dissolved indiscriminately into the All, there are also other kinds of evidence. It is said of the divine Water that it "dissolves and returns the metals to this crude state, *but conserving them always in their own specie* [that is, in their own individuality] . . . without these bodies being destroyed in any way, except to receive a regeneration and new form, nobler and more excellent than they possessed before."[21] It is not a question of "destroying but of improving," says *The Thread of Ariadne*.[22] "It is incorrect to call this the transmutation of metals, because in truth it is a matter of the purgation, fixation, coloration and perfection of imperfect metals." And "even if our Gold is not the vulgar Gold, it is nevertheless found in the vulgar Gold"; the fruit of "our work is extracted from ordinary Gold and Silver."[23] And in Pelagius and the *Letter from Isis to Horus* it is said that Gold is the seed of Gold: as who sows wheat, has wheat come up and harvests wheat,[24] and so the "species" is preserved. There is a continuity. The central modality of ☉ remains (which in its vulgar form is manifested by the human personality), and the operation does not "alter" it.

We meet the same idea again in the symbolism of the *circulations*. The "vessel" in which the work is completed—the aludel, the athanor—must remain hermetically sealed until the completion of the Great Work. This has been laid down by all the authors. But it follows then that the subtle part of the "compound," also called "angel,"[25] is separated from the dense and corporeal under the heat of the fire,

---

[18] Cf. Philalethes (*Regulae*, chap. 3): "Aside from Gold, *which is the body* and which acts as the *male* in our Work" we need the Spirit, etc.

[19] *Entretiens, BPC*, 1:85.

[20] *Chymica vannus*, 279, 281; cf. Braccesco, (*Espositione*, fol. 79a): "The rays of the heavenly bodies are concentrated in no Element with such virtue and power as in *Earth*, precisely because Earth is the true and solid receptacle of the celestial virtues and the center of their spheres."

[21] *Livre d'Artephius, BPC*, 121.

[22] *Filum Ariadnae*, 38, 46.

[23] Philalethes, *Introitus apertus*, §§18, 19.

[24] Cf. *CAG*, 3:34, 258; *Livre de El Habir, CMA*, 3:115.

[25] Cf. Pernety, *Dictionnaire*, 33.

affording it no power to escape. Pressing against the upper wall of the closed container, it is obliged to condense anew and return below, as a distillation that will act on the residue to transform it. *It is a fundamental principle of the Art that the spirit must not fly out and escape, under pain of losing what was supposed to be achieved.* Artephius says: "Do not let the spirit exhale, because if it escapes from the vessel, your work will be completely destroyed."[26]

That is the reason why Fires that are too violent are ill-advised: because the force of the spirits would break the vessel and every benefit would be lost;[27] because of this, others insist likewise on the thickness of the glass of the flask and on the perfectly "hermetic" seal. And it is advisable to rush immediately to the aid of the Body when the Soul is stretched by having loosened its bond: otherwise "the Soul will abandon its terrestrial company to resolve into another element,[28] which is not the objective that is being pursued. This is expressed in similar fashion by Zacharias: "It is necessary to remain attentive and vigilant in order not to miss the precise moment of the birth of our Mercurial Water, with the end of reuniting it with its body, that until now we have called yeast or leavening and which from now on we shall call *Venom*."[29] The word *venom* refers to the point at which the principle of the work is manifested as a transcendent and dissolving power with respect to the personalized individual states. And Boehme says: "If the spirit flees from its prison, lock it back in again."[30]

---

[26] *BPC*, 2:157; cf. Philalethes, *Introitus apertus, chap. 17.*

[27] *Filum Ariadnae*, 82–83; *Livre de El Habir*, 104.

[28] *De pharmaco catholico* 2, §§3, 4; cf. 3, fl4. Equivalent teaching: "Take special care that the diluvian Waters do not suffocate the Fire of Earth" (*Triomphe Hermétique*, 306). Cf. *Dialogue de Marie et Aros, BPC*, 1:79.

[29] Zacharias, *Philosophie naturelle des métaux*, 2.534. Cf. *Turba, BPC*, 2:7.

[30] *Aurora*, 10, §50.

Nineteen

PHILOSOPHICAL INCEST

From all that has been said up to this point we can now define the full intent of the hermetic enterprise in the following way:

It is possible to cause consciousness to pass from an individualized state (which is the condition of the body = ego ☉ as "vulgar Gold") to a nonindividualized, unshaped state (Waters, Solvents, Mercury, etc.). The symbols of this process are liquefaction, fusion, dissolution, solution, separation, and so on.[1] It is also possible to confront this transformation in two distinct ways: actively or passively, as dominator or dominated, either according to ♀ or to ☾.

This alternative underscores the main differences between mysticism and initiation. In the first case a kind of indiscriminate, ecstatic nondifference appears as the goal, the point of arrival, and salvation. In the second case, conversely, the goal is a state in which an individualizing power, the same ☉ principle already manifested in the human body as the "I" hidden in the shadows, is reborn and reaffirmed.

In order to confirm definitely that the spirit of the hermetic achievement corresponds fully to this second possibility, an examination of the group of allegories in the literature that is concerned with symbolic connections between Mother and Son, Feminine and Masculine, will be decisive. We shall begin with the

---

[1] These last terms in the alchemical jargon should be taken in a double sense, including that which obtains in expressions like "solving a problem" and "dissolving a bond."

maxim of Philalethes that "the fixed becomes volatile for a while in order to acquire a nobler quality the better to fix the same volatile again."[2] In this case the "volatile"—equivalent to Mother, Woman, the Waters, the Moon, etc.—signifies the Spiritus Mundi, the universal life-force. The "fixed"—which is the Son, the Male, Fire, Sun, Red Stone, etc.—on the other hand, signifies the ego, the personality, the Soul.[3]

In general it is the unanimous opinion of all the hermetic philosophers that a "mortification" must intervene: a dissolving in the Waters, a disappearance into the Mother's womb that devours or kills the son, a domination of the Female over the Male, of the Moon over the Sun, the volatile over the fixed, and so on; but all that is simply a provisional condition for returning potentiality to the son, to enable him to reaffirm himself again over what has previously dominated and "dissolved" him, to make himself "more perfect and greater than his parents."

And it is here that d'Espagnet says, "The Female at first is stronger than the Male and dominates him, in order to transmute him into her own nature. But then the Male recovers his vigor and in turn gains ascendancy, dominates the Female and makes her like himself."[4] And the *Turba philosophorum*: "The Mother engenders the Son and the Son engenders the Mother and kills her."[5] In other texts we encounter analogous expressions: "When I find myself in the arms of my Mother, united with her substance, I control her, I detain her and fix her."[6] "The Water or Mercury is the Mother who is taken and sealed within the womb of the Son, that is, of the Sun, which came forth from this Water."[7] The Female must first be allowed to surmount the Male, and then the Male the Female."[8] And Flamel adds, "Once the infant [created by the Art] becomes strong and robust, to the point where it can do battle against Water and Fire [the force must be understood as that which manifests in the awakenings of ☿ and ♀; see further, pages 113-114 and 168-169], it will insert into its own belly the Mother that had given it birth";[9] and so forth.

---

[2] *Introitus apertus*, chap. 1.

[3] The thing to understand about symbols is that they sometimes have very different meanings, which are not necessarily contradictory but may derive from quite different points of view. So the "fixed" can symbolize the body in relation to "volatility" and to the subtlety of the vital principles, but at the same time, as in this case, it can also symbolize the Soul considered in its stability and identity, in the fact of its constituting a stable point and a center confronting the universal Life and its undetermined possibilities and also the becoming of the elements.

[4] In Pernety, *Dictionnaire*, 220.

[5] *Turba philosophorum*, BPC, 2.19. Cf. the appendix known as *L'épître à Aristé*.

[6] *Sette capitoli d'Ermete*, §4.

[7] *Livre d'Artephius*, BPC, 2:131.

[8] *Livre de Synesius*, BPC, 2:180.

[9] *Figures hiéroglyphiques*, BPC, 2:244.

Of particular importance are the forms of this cycle of allegories wherein the Mother—primary substance of every metal or individual being—becomes the *wife* of her son. These forms speak clearly to us about the role and meaning attributed by the hermetic tradition to the masculine dignity of the one who seeks realization. But the other forms of the allegory are also interesting, those that show us what the expression of the mystico-religious or pantheistic solution in the symbol of relationships against nature can be: the states in which the universal power-substance, the "One Life," dominates the personality are equivalent to the Woman who possesses the Man, the Son who returns to the womb of his Mother, the servant raised over his master, "Superior to him in all ways,"[10] and so on.

In hermetism these states do not consitute anything more than passing phases; immediately afterward the correct relations, those sanctioned by nature (after the *solve*, after the "contact," the *coagula*), are established. For all that, they confirm in so many ways the affirmative and "magic" spirit of hermetism, for whomever follows the work.

Still, the central question has not been sufficiently addressed. This "fixing" of the Female or possessing of the Mother by every creature in order to return to "Nature that takes joy in itself" to "Nature dominated by itself," which is peculiar to the male, may it not express, in the final analysis—as the equivalent symbol of the theft of the Tree of Life does—the same act of personalization, whose result, as we have seen, is the Body? And will we not find ourselves then in a vicious circle? In fact, the texts consider the body to be the center of vulgar life shrouded in darkness and death, something that must be overcome; yet the body returns to present itself as a necessary result of the *coagula* which, paradoxically, is the terminus of the Opus Magnus. It cannot be the same thing. Obviously corporeality cannot mean the same thing in the one case as it does in the other, and so the problem is to determine where the difference lies.

---

[10] Pernety, *Dictionnaire*, 449.

the tomb and thirst

For this problem as well, we shall find the best key in a previously cited text from the *Corpus Hermeticum* to the adventure of the one who wishes to go beyond the seven circles of necessity (see chapter 14).

What justifies the prior negative expressions, from a mystico-soteriological coloration that we encounter in the hermetic tradition, is not so much the fact of "individuation" or "body" per se—that is to say, the qualification and organization of what is undifferentiated and indistinct, as the work of an active principle, ♀ or or ☉ or ♈, reacting on the Mercurial Moistness and coagulating in an image, sign of its power—but a *distinct relationship* to individuation and the body. Such a relationship will be that which corresponds to a state of "love"—in the sense of "identification" and "amalgamation" (that is, in the same sense as the power, which according to Hindu teaching, "thirst" and "desire" have)—precisely with regard to the body and individuation. Such a state is one in which the Waters penetrate the solar principle with a "superfluous moisture" to injure it, intoxicate it, darken it, and carry it away. They lead it to submersion and absorption into that which already has received the impression of the form of its dominion, to attach itself to it and no longer distinguish itself, degenerating from its own nature and participating in everything and through everything of its nature. It converts itself, so to speak, into the image of itself, an image that, as such, suffers the condition of the thing in which it is manifested. Such a development immediately presents itself to us internally in the myth of Narcissus. Narcissus is lured to "death" in the "Waters" by an awakened passion for his own image reflected in these same waters, and this "death" is the substance of that which men who are bound by desire to the world of bodies and becoming call life.

In the introduction (see pages 11-12) we quoted a gnostic text in which we recognize these same symbols: in the intermediate stage, prior to his reintegration, it is said of Primordial Man that "He stands upright here below, having been engendered by the image [reflection] in the current of the Waters." In a similar text we read, "Recast in *watery form*, it [the soul] suffers . . . as the slave of Death."[1] We have seen finally that Water, either as itself or as Mercury, is in a certain sense understood in hermetism as hunger, desire, or burning thirst. And it is clear that the myth of Narcissus also forms part of the hermetic tradition, and we have pointed out the metaphysical meaning that it contains. The *Corpus Hermeticum* (1.12-15) speaks of "a form of marvelous beauty in which all the energies of the seven powers were united with the divine form." There is an allusion to a vision of this form in the *Water* and in the *Shadow* over the *Earth*, and a love that is manifested in "Nature"; we are told how the same Primordial Man "upon perceiving in the water the reflection of his own form, was seized by desire for it and wanted to possess it. The act followed the desire and so irrational form was conceived. Nature possessed herself of her lover, embracing him tightly, and they were united in mutual love." Hence the "fall," the origin of the "sleep," the submission to the tyranny of cosmic law—άρμονία—on the part of whomever was placed under it by dint of his own nature (see page 54). It is precisely to this situation that we referred when we spoke of the bewitchment of the terrestrial:[2] petrification, transformation of the energies into passions and sensations, "Metalness," the veil of "darkness" and "leprosy," the state of silence or the "vulgar" state of profound powers and principles in man, external consciousness tied down to the physical world through the brain, etc.

"Man," says Boehme,[3] "died to the divine celestial essence [about which he

---

[1] In Hippolytus, *Philosophumena*, 5.10; cf. Heraclitus (frag. 68 Diels) "For souls, to become water is death."

[2] A passage from Plotinus (*Enneads* 6.4.14) explains the teaching: "It has occurred to the Higher Man to want to be in addition someone else, and on encountering us . . . he has united himself to us and us to him . . . As with one voice and with a single word, the ear that hears and receives makes another elsewhere, because from that active power [of the spoken word] is born a hearing that has present in itself this power in [its] action; so we have become two together, and no longer what we were apart or what we have added, only that the higher man is "asleep and as though not present." For the corresponding myth in Buddhist teaching, cf. our work *The Doctrine of the Awakening* (London, 1951).

[3] *De signatura*, 14, §6; 15, §§6-8; 4, §28; 5, §15.

speaks elsewhere as the 'noble *Gold* of celestial corporeality'], because the *inner desire,* having arisen from the fiery center[4] . . . inclined toward external temporal birth. So in man the divine essence, or inner corporeality, is converted into death." The same author then speaks of the alchemical symbolism of Saturn, to which we shall return presently, and says that the body from that time on remains in Saturn, clad in miserable rags; the Golden Child is hidden by Saturn behind a black cape. It is the "tomb of Osiris," the body turned into the Sepulchre of the Living. The primordial violence done to the Tree constitutes the corporeality, in a transcendental sense, according to which the body is identified or associated with Sulfur, Fire, and divine Gold. The symbol of transcendental man refers to that: he is the Absolute Individual. But when the passion of the Primordial Waters rises again, arresting the process, then he is Attis, the "ear of corn cut while yet green"; it is premature death, the mutilation that causes Attis to be sterile—ἄκαρπος. This is the mystery of the body in which man is found here on earth. The angels fell not because they wanted to possess "women," but because they had "desired" them: it was the burning, fiery desire imprisoned in Adam, according to Gichtel,[5] which deprived him of his spouse Sophia, that is to say, which separated him from Life and power.[6]

The difficulty, then, is explained: In hermetism it is never a question of separating from the Body in order to escape (the "spirits" must not flee, the soul must not escape into the Air, etc.), but of separating in order to reestablish a causal and dominating relationship of the solar principle, free of passion, with that to which it has given form and which is now offered to it in its greater nonhuman powers so that it can itself undergo a rebirth. From this is derived, in hermetism, a

---

[4] In Adam, says Boehme (*Aurora,* 11, §62), it was Nitre, or the active force of personalization, which struggled with the "Fountain of Life."

[5] Gichtel, *Theosophia practica* 1, §§19–20; 3, §§66–70; 6, §§45–46. The symbolism of the *magnet* in some cases can be applied to the power of the Body that has attracted the soul, tying it to itself. The resultant state is equivalent to the *ahamkara* in Hindu tradition, by means of which the ego makes its own the characteristics that come to it from the Body.

[6] A correlation between "thirst" or "desire" and the failure of a "Titanic" adventure can be found in Orphism. The inscription of the *Lamina Turii II* reads: "I am of your blessed race [Uranian—ἐμοὶ γένος οὐράνιον, Lamina Petelia]. But Moira and the flashing lightning bolt struck me and withered me." The sudden fulmination hurled at the Titans on the part of Zeus as well as the "aridity" causes the "thirst that parches and consumes me" from the *Lamina Petelia,* which can be quenched only by the Waters of Mnemosyne, reserved for initiates. Metaphysically to interpret such thirst as desire, however, one would have had to recognize that it is not so much the effect as the cause of the Titans being crushed by lightning. But it must be noted that the hermetic "purification" that fetches the primordial states back from those it has degenerated is also sometimes called "fulmination" (cf. for example, Pernety, *Dictionnaire,* 175); the awakening of the central power that acts in the Opus Magnus is often compared to a "lightning flash" that suddenly destroys every "imperfect metal," i.e., every individual essence not qualified to pass the test that it confronts now for the second time.

"transcendental realism" wherein the reversal of values peculiar to the mystical language acquires a different and very special sense.

In the "image generated by the Waters" Primordial Man "stands on his own feet," but this is nothing more than spectral support. Once identifying himself with his body, man finds himself defined by it. All his faculties of watchfulness, instead of looking *ahead* of the body, are looking *back* on it. And this is why only exterior reflections arise from everything he comes into contact with. From this point of view, Boehme rightly says "in that faltering Angel," man, the body *engenders the soul;* the flesh, despite not being spirit, is the *mother* of the spirit.[7] It is a question here of the Soul and Spirit of the "dead" and regarding which—from the modern, materialist point of view—is the truer.

The "spirituality" of "psychological man" is nonessential, contingent, and there are only too many circumstances that speak to us of this contingency, of the dependency of the "superior faculties" and individual consciousness itself on the body. The body is truly the root and origin of the soul and its faculties, but without producing them directly; the situation is almost analogous to a drum that without producing the sound itself, is the necessary condition for the sound to be manifested. And so also life, consciousness and self-consciousness cannot be manifested in man except *through* corporeal reality.

Occultly and hermetically considered, this reality is the place in which the metals that seem noble but are vile, in which the elements that seem alive but are really dead and sterile and disdained by the wise, are found in their true nature—primordial corporeality—except for a certain impurity, darkness, and moistness, which it is possible to get rid of.

Such is the key to all those alchemical expressions that proclaim through symbols the superiority of the Body and present it as the true materia of the work and the vein of the Gold. This is the reason that the *De pharmaco catholico* exhorts the alchemist not to fly off into the heavens but to search here below, in the *humus,* in "Earth." Here is where the Stone addresses the personifications of the vulgar faculties: "Thou art not that Gold of which the philosophers speak, on the contrary, that Gold is hidden within me. . . . Thy soul [that is, the living principle] constantly resides in me, and is more stable and fixed than it could ever be in thee . . . without me it is not possible to make perfect Gold and Silver . . . nor could ye elevate yourselves beyond the state in which Nature has put you."[8]

And Zacharias says: "The Body has a greater power than that of the two brothers we call Soul and Spirit," and adds that when "what was hidden is

---

[7] *Aurora*, 16, §5; 21, §69.

[8] *Triomphe Hermétique, BPC*, 3:185, 201. Cf. also the dialogue following the text, where the three kinds of Gold are mentioned (3:231 ff.).

revealed," the Body has the power to fixate and reduce the Soul to the Soul's nature, "wherein it is to be made into Gold."[9] "It is necessary to animate the dead body and resuscitate it," says Albertus Magnus,[10] "in order to multiply its power to the infinite." There are so any possible quotations in the same spirit that we would have difficulty choosing among them.[11] "Osiris is Lead and Sulfur"—Ὄσιρίς ἐστιν μολύβδος καὶ θεῖον, says an Alexandrine text.[12] Black Lead—the fallen body—called the "tomb of Osiris," is associated besides with the Egg that is the ἐν τὸ πᾶν. It is fixed in the "spheres of Fire" and attracts a new soul to itself. And in this, say the texts, consists the Great Mystery.[13]

---

[9] *Philosophie naturelle des métaux*, 4.531, 532.

[10] *Compositum de compositis*, §5.

[11] Cf. Cosmopolite, *Novum lumen chemicum*, 10, 50-51; *Livre d'Artephius*, BPC, 2:144. 117; Pernety, *Dictionnaire*, 354ff.

[12] *CAG*, 2:88.

[13] Ibid., 98, 192, 169ff.; 93, 95.

Twenty-One

SATURN:
INVERTED GOLD

To bestow on these symbols a more concrete meaning, we have to fall back on the quadripartite division (discussed on pages 47-49). Magical Lead more exactly corresponds to the terrestrial element, to the *minerality* of the body, to that which in the body is obedient to the forces of the mineral kingdom (the skeleton). And that is just where the primordial state of the individual, Osiris, lies sleeping—and Saturn also, who was the king of the Golden Age: the metaphysical kingdom corresponding to the state of *being* in the absolute sense.[1] And if we remember that the calcareous element is expressed by the skeleton, the correspondences established by certain ancient texts, via pseudo-homonyms, the *titanic* element, the *earth* element, and the calcareous element are all very interesting. In one anonymous Greek text, Earth appears at the end, and the operation pertaining to it is called *the almighty limestone*.[2] And Agathodaimon adds: "Such is the Word on lime, the omnipotent [or 'titanic'— τίτανος] lime, the *invincible body*, the only useful thing. . . . Whoever finds

---

[1] P. Negri (*Introduzione alla magia*, 2:76ff.) has also indicated such a correspondence etymologically, breaking it into *Sat-urnus* and conferring on the *urnus* terminal the same value that di-urnus and noct-urnus possess, the root *sat* coinciding with the Sanskrit word that means "being" and which figures in the Hindu designation of the corresponding "Golden Age" of Hesiod: *Satya-Yuga* or *Krita-Yuga*.

[2] *Oeuvre des quatre éléments* in *CAG*, 2:340.

it, will triumph over the incurable sickness of poverty—τὴν ἀνίατον πενίαν νόσος.[3] But Plutarch informs us *penia*, "privation" or "misery," is the materia that "in and by itself is full of need; it is satisfied in full by the Good, ever inclining to it, tending to participate in its nature."[4] Poverty, the "incurable sickness" is then the same state of privation that in "the matter" is the need, "thirst," the "aqueous form"; and the Good is the actuality of the Absolute Individual bound to the "ominipotent lime," to the resurrecton and transfiguration of the Titans. Once again we return to the same meaning.

Now that said correspondence has been clarified, let us turn briefly to the myth of Saturn. Saturn also suffered emasculation, after which he hid in Latium but Latium (from *latere*) is nothing more than a duplication of the idea of hiding oneself,[5] of passing to a state of latency or silence (nonmanifestation); we have explained the emasculation as the deprivation of the power, which is equivalent to the premature reaping of the corn and the biblical prohibition concerning the Tree of Life. Other possible meanings of the myth might be seen here in an allusion to the transformation of connections that refer to Lead in the sense of a corruptible body, which Saturn himself devoured and destroyed.

Thus in alchemy we encounter a duplication: Saturn is the "ancient" and the "divine" (or sulfurous) and at the same time it is *inverted Gold*—Lead—as the vulgar body;[6] it is the father of *our* Stone and that of the Philosophers[7]—in which, according to *De pharmaco catholico*, it is manifested as "cosmic spirit" with a "body and spirit-nature comparable to Arsenic," that is, to the virile power par excellence. Boehme explains that Lead and Gold are produced in Saturn by the same

---

[3] Ibid., 285.

[4] *De Iside et Osiris* §56. We must understand "good" in the sense of Platonic philosophy, that is, as completion, as nature complete and perfect in itself.

[5] "*Latium a latere*," Virgil, Aeneid, 1.8. [Latium, an ancient country in Italy, is etymologically a place of "concealment" or "retirement."—Trans.]

[6] Syrian texts, *CMA*, 2:158.

[7] "*Hic est Pater et Mater eius, sive lapis noster et Philosophorum*" (Codex plumbeum, reproduced in *Introduzione alla magia*, 1:298). In the same codex is found the expression "leprous Gold," referring to Saturn, in which leprosy, the sickness that consumes, represents the sudden infection suffered by the Sun in the terrestrial body (cf. vulture that *consumes*, thirst that *consumes*, etc.). In a text of Isaac the Hollander (reproduced by *Revue Théosophique*, [1927], 379–91) we read: "From Saturn proceeds, and from Saturn is made, the Philosopher's Stone. . . . There is no greater secret than this: that this is found in Saturn, since in the Sun [the vulgar Sun, that is to say, in the intellectual faculties of external consciousness] we do not find the perfection that we find in Saturn. In its interior, and in this all the Philosophers agree, it is a most excellent Sun. . . . In truth, Saturn is the stone that the ancient philosophers did not want to name." "Nothing does it lack, but to be cleaned of its impurity; its *interior must be made exterior* that is to say, its *Redness* must be brought out and then it will be an excellent Sun." (§§1, 4, 5, 16–17).

power, and adds: "It is not death, *but an enclosure that represents the divine celestial essence.*"[8]

A hieroglyphic appearing on the cover of the *Twelve Keys* of Basil Valentine expresses the same idea: in this we see a Saturn crowned with sickle and compass (symbols of the two powers: the sickle is dissolution and the compass is the power "to measure," to set limits, the *coagula*) at the top of a symbol that comprises the different elements (or phases) of the Work. Immediately below Saturn, that is, *latent* (Latium), is ♀, the symbol of Sulfur, which contains the Phoenix bird within itself; it concerns the "Primordial Fires," of the first inextinguishable, ubiquitous, superpersonal powers of animation and individuation.

However, whenever the texts speak of the Sulfurs of Saturn or the like, it is an alluson to these forces (or "Gods")[9] hidden within the organs that they themselves have formed in the "Earth"; uniting with which (as with their original members) the power conferred by will—Telesma—what "is here," will be made perfect. Wherefore it has been said: "Let descend and everything will be fulfilled"—εἴ κάτω καὶ γενήσεται,[10] and in the *Book of Mercy:* "Return the Soul to the Bodies: make your Souls perish in the Bodies and purify the Souls and Bodies cleansing and washing them together. Submit the volatized Souls to the Bodies from which they have escaped."[11]

The reason is thus clear for the importance attributed to the alchemical "ashes," the "sediment," the *caput mortuum* or "precipitate," to the terrestriality remaining in the bottom of the vessel when separation is worked; which is why it is called "the diadem of the king," and why it is said that in the residue of "combustion" is revealed the "energy of everything"—παντὸς ἐνέργεια. What in appearance is the most worthless of the four entities (see pages 47-48)—Saturn—is actually the most precious, because it bears within itself the "traces" or "memories" or "signatures" of "the state of being" (the Golden Age), while the other more subtle modes of the human entity correspond to states already derived from a disempowered condition. They are allegorized in the hermetic interpretation by the myth of the Ages of Silver, Bronze, and Iron that succeeded the *Saturnia Regna* ("Saturnian realm").[12] "Paradise is still on this earth, but man is so far from it that he cannot regenerate it unless he can reenter

---

[8] Boehme, *De signatura*, 4, §§22-23.

[9] Cf. Della Riviera (*Mondo magico*, 207-8): "Now this Lead or Saturn, is called Father of the other Gods, that is of the other magic metals; given that all of them in the beginning were hidden in him: but they come to light during the construction of the magic world, being rendered manifest and visible by the spagyric Art of the Hero."

[10] Berthelot, *Introduction à l'étude de la chimie*, 294.

[11] Arab texts, *CMA*, 3:169.

[12] One particular meaning of "ashes" is that they can be destroyed no further—they are the absolute residue after the purifying action of Fire. Rosinus says: "This is the earth of your body, the limit of that which is permanent" (*Ad Sarratantam*, in *Artis auriferae*, 2:183). From this point begins the resurrection.

it through his own reintegration. *And it is there that the Gold is hidden in Saturn* in despised shapes and colors and very different from its normal state."[13]

On the basis of such ideas we can now offer a synthesis of the condition of the human being by means of the ideogram ☿, found in Della Riviera,[14] if we may so interpret it. The vulgar Moon and Sun (☽ and ☉)—that is, the exteriorizations of ordinary waking consciousness—are in ascendance (above) with regard to the elemental forces of the Body (symbolized by the cross ✛), which, however, in their depths (♈ in turn is found under ✛), are recapitulated by the primordial virile form, ♈, the sign already explained as θεῖον—Sulfur or Divine Energy—in a "pure state." With these three parts of the hieroglyph (♉, ✛, ♈) we can convey three systems of the human entity, hermetically speaking. To the vulgar ☉ and ☽ (Sun and Moon) correspond the head, with its cerebral organ that plays the role of a center of transformation of all perceptions into sensations and material images, with corresponding subjective, emotional states.[15] The waking consciousness does not usually illuminate anything but what appears in this site.[16]

As for the elementary Cross, ✛, it corresponds to the middle zone of the human organism with the center in the heart, which is equivalent to the center of said cross and thence to the Quintessence, to the secret Heaven, the Water of Life, and all the other symbols referring to the "Spirit" principle. In a special sense, elemental "life" is bound to this zone as vibrating or rhythmic life in communication with the rhythms of the cosmic forces expressed in different ways within the physical body, above all in the respiratory and circulatory systems. From this region is now excluded the ordinary consciousness; the processes that take place within it, it does not know except through the "signals" given in the function of the higher zone (images-emotions).[17] The contents of this region are essentially made up of *translations* of processes that at first are produced nonmaterially in the mid-region, manifesting forces still deeper.[18]

---

[13] Boehme, *De signatura*, 8, §§47, 48.

[14] *Mondo magico*, 24. The same symbol is in J. Dee, *Monas hieroglyphica*.

[15] Particularly, to the moon ☽ corresponds the "image" aspect and to the sun ☉ the "emotional" aspect of waking life.

[16] Cf. Boehme, (*Aurora*, 25, §109): "The brain is certainly under the corporeal rule of this world, from which sense and instinct have been generated. . . . But the holy and true Spirit of man is generated in the secret Heaven, in the Water of Life."

[17] From here another variant of the symbolism proceeds (cf., for example, Pernety, *Dictionnaire*, 322), according to which the central site and the heart correspond to the Sun, whose light is reflected in the Moon, that is to say, in the reflective faculties of the brain and in emotional repercussions. The Moon then becomes an inclusive symbol for all the "vulgar" forms of the faculties. Cf. *Zohar*, 3.253b: "The brain is the emblem of Water (= Moon) and the heart of Fire."

[18] Cf. Boehme, *Aurora*, 25, §§101-2: "The brain that is in the head is a power of the heart: because all the powers rise from the heart to the brain. The brain in the head has its roots in the heart."

So attest the ancient teachings, both Oriental and Occidental, concerning the relation between the heart and the intellect: the dependence of the brain on the heart is not one of "sentiment" (the heart associated with "sentiment" is a profane notion), but of "nobler" forms of the intellective faculties that precede hierarchically their sense-perception through the brain. Hence Geber says: "The intelligence has its seat in the heart, because that is what precedes all the other organs;[19] it supervises everything brought to man's brain. Without it the brain could never be awakened."[20]

From the center of the Cross, which is the equivalent of the central and immobile hub out of which the "wheel of the elements" rolls, we rejoin the third region, the inferior region corresponding to Υ. This is the site of the nonhuman creative forces that in the corporeal structure crop up from the power of sexual generation, whose organs are situated precisely in the center of that which physically corresponds to this region. It is the foundation, the first root out of which everything springs into action through elemental processes to be manifested in the energies and internal and external forms of the particularized consciousness of the individual. This is the dark world in an illustration of Gichtel's, called the "root of Souls in the center of Nature"[21]—dark insofar as it hierarchically precedes every manifestaton (light). Here is the end point of the *visita interiora terrae rectificando.*[22]

We feel it has been apposite to add to the quaternaries these ternary correspondences, because they help us understand certain special and technically important aspects of the hermetico-alchemical teaching.

---

[19] It follows from this that it is a question of the deep intelligence, from that which presides at the same processes of the organism, of which the waking cerebral consciousness knows nothing by direct experience. This was intuited by Nietzsche, when he spoke of "the great intelligence of the body" as distinguished from the merely individual faculties.

[20] Geber, *Livre des balances, CMA*, 3:140.

[21] Also in the engravings of Fludd (*Utriusque cosmi historia*) in the genitals appears the inscription *Centrum.* In other illustrations in the same work (de Givry, 5:200, 201, 203), where man appears inscribed in circles that give prominence to his macrocosmic correspondences, the center of such circles remains also within those organs. Cf. Agrippa, *De occulta philosophia,* 2.27, figs. 2 and 3. According to esoteric Hindu teaching the seat of the root power—*kundalini*—called *mūlādhāra,* is located in the same region.

[22] In *De pharmaco catholico,* 3, §17, one of the consequences of the *visita* is the knowledge of the genesis of the "metals," and the power to distinguish by experience "the perishable and elusive from the imperishable and the permanent." This is precisely the knowledge of the deep processes that contain, as reality, what seems accidental and phenomenal to the exterior consciousness.

Twenty-Two

The Field
And the Seed

Before passing on to the practice section, we shall discuss the hermetic symbols referred to as Seed, Field, and Flowering.

The "Field" as Earth generally stands for the group of conditions and possibilities contained within corporeality that is understood in an all-embracing sense. The Seed is, first of all, vulgar Gold, which "separated from the Mine (Universal Life) is as dead"; but when thrust into Earth, or the Field, and after putrefying, it is reborn and brings to full flower the principle whose potentiality it held—whence is drawn a further symbolism taken from the vegetable kingdom, which is born in and rises up out of the "depths" of the Earth: trees, flowers, gardens, et cetera.

Upon this foundation there appears to us, first of all, the inner meaning of the correspondence between Saturn and the cultivation of the Earth and the Fields, for which he was established as the god in the ancient Italic myths: in the sense that that context of analogous traditions cannot but confirm.[1] Concerning the symbol

---

[1] This symbolism is also found in the *Laws of Manu* (12.12ff.) and in the *Bhagavad Gita* (13.1–2) and is explained in the following terms: "This body [or *kaunteya*], is called the Field . . . by the one who knows it, and is called by the sages the Connoisseur of the Field. . . . The wisdom concerning the Field and the knower of the Field I believe to be the true wisdom." In the qabalistic tradition the initiates ("those alone to whom the mysteries are confided"), are called "cultivators of the fields" (*Zohar*, 3.141b, 127b, etc.). There is no need to refer here to evangelical symbolism or to the Eleusinian rite in which resurrection was represented by an ear of corn.

in general we can cite the *Hermetic Triumph*: "The Stone is a Field that the Wise cultivate, into which Nature and Art have planted the seed that must produce its fruit."[2] We may also consider the eighth key of Basil Valentine, in which is seen a sower, a cadaver stretched over ears of corn, and a man rising out of the grave, with the legend: "A creature of heaven . . . dies and rots. Then the stars, by means of the elements, will give life again to this putrid corpse, so that from it may rise a new celestial body. Once this is done, thou shalt see the terrestrial completely consumed by the celestial and the earthly body forever in a heavenly crown of honor and glory."[3]

Alongside Boehme's words: "Sulphur is the material womb *to which we must return*," because "Everything that is embodied, whether spiritually or materially, consists of a sulphurous property," we must add these two passages: "The grain of wheat will not germinate if it is not thrust into the earth," and "Wherever the seed, which is your Soul, is sown, there will the Body be lifted up."[4] Flamel, after saying that the "Earth of the philosophers is their imperfect body, and is called the Mother, because it contains and comprises all the Elements,"[5] also speaks of a sowing of Gold in the white tilled Earth.[6]

After the sowing comes the growing, symbolized by the seasons: after the *black* winter follow the *clear* spring, *red* summer, and *golden* autumn, whereupon the fruit is ripe and can be picked. These are the four traditional hermetic colors used to designate the phases of the Great Work. The three last correspond respectively to the resurrection of the states of consciousness or of nonterrestrial entities—☿, ♀, and ☉—enclosed in the human Earth; and said resurrection in turn is equivalent to the backward movement *sub specie interioritatis* through the three eras that preceded the "Age of Iron" until we arrive at the golden age of Saturn.

In order for the seed to bear fruit, as we have seen, the seed must die, break, and *be opened*. Regarding this moment of crisis, the process is articulated by different aspects, to which we will refer in a theoretical and symbolical scheme to be continued in the section devoted to praxis.

---

[2] *Triomphe Hermétique*, 285, 287.

[3] *Dodici chiavi*, 55. The same symbol is in the eighth key of Michael Maier.

[4] Boehme, *De signatura*, 10, §56; 8, §1; 10, §50. *Aurora*, 21, §49.

[5] *Désir désiré*, BPC, 2:317, 315.

[6] The tilled *white* earth corresponds more exactly to the body in the ☿ state. See below, chapter 40.

the sworð anð
the rose

We know now that "seed" and "vulgar Gold" represent the ordinary personality. This is the "King that is not king," because "standing upright" is precarious in face of the strong forces of the body upon which—after identifying with a particular form and the "Fall"—the law of the hermetic "Rulers of Destiny" goes into effect. This principle, also called "*exterior* Sulfur," continues in its way, however, to express the principle of virility; in Boehme's terms, it is the "property of Mars" united to the "sulfurous furor" in the "elemental [earthly] body." To this can be referred the Iron (= Mars) of the last of Hesiod's ages and the general ideogram of virility and erect position, created by verticality.

But in the state of the fall we must also consider the instinctive and ardent force of the animal nature transfused into the same soul. This is one of the meanings of the Red Lion, or fiery Dragon, often justly associated with terrestrial man. The hermetic "Kill the living"[1] refers as much to this same force as to the Mars element, and to the Gold locked in the prison of the sense of self imposed by the body. To this we must add the metaphor of beating, striking, and knocking down; and the Fire of the Art that acts in this phase takes as symbol whatever instrument is capable of inflicting a wound: sword, spear, scissors, hammer, sickle, etc.

---

[1] Cf. *Rosarium philosphorum* (in *Artis auriferae* 2:233), in which it is said that Mercury triumphs even over Gold, because it is what kills and what brings to life.

From the state of activity normal to the ordinary waking state, we then pass on to the passive: the masculine Ⅰ, knocked down as ▬, which is also one of the Water ("dissolving") symbols. This is the sowing of the seed and its "death" in the Earth. We might also observe that the horizontal that cuts the vertical makes a cross with it ✚, which is why some hermetic authors actually took the Christian crucifixion itself as a symbol for the Work. And the more so since in this there occurs a spearing in the side, that is, in the place where, according to Gichtel, the serpent of the "Spiritus Mundi" imprisons the Sun (ego principle) in its encircling coil; and since the side wound exudes *white* water and *red* blood, which hermetically designate the two successive phases of the Work; and since before his crucifixion, Christ, according to the tradition, suffered insults while dressed in a mocking *purple* robe,[2] which Herod replaced with a *white* robe; and finally, the crucifixion is followed by the "descent to hell," to the bosom of the Earth, and then the resurrection and ascension.

Out of the negative state ▬, the principle of virility rises anew in a third phase in the form of pure and transcendent activity, capable of inducing a rebirth in all the elements a metaphor for the exaltation, elevation, standing up that can be expressed by a return to verticality Ⅰ. This same is the ascendent direction of the forces of growth in the vegetable kingdom, which—after breaking the Earth apart—are uplifted to the Sun as grasses and plants.[3] The Flower is produced in the Air—when we are in the other "philosophical seasons"—after the *black* winter. The ripe fruit of autumn will signify the *fixation* of the resurrected solar principle.

The Rosicrucian symbol of the Rose that blossoms at the center of the cross (transformation of the interference of the two principles Ⅰ and ▬ from the point of a fall and neutralization to a living and radiant point at the center of the four elements) reveals the whole meaning. On the other hand, it also pertains to hermetism: the Porta Ermetica of Rome leads directly to the "*Ad Rosam per Crucem*,"[4] and the Rose or Flower, a symbol also common to

---

[2] We must recall here the alchemical allegory of Bernard of Treviso, of a King cloaked in the "purple of a false royalty"; and that of Zosimos (*CAG*, 2:112, 116, 207) of the Man also dressed in red who suffers the bath in a black solution together with "the burning of the blood and bones of the dragon." The red in this case is the color of the vulgar human Gold.

[3] On this cf. A. Reghini, *Le parole sacre e di passo*, 85–92; J. J. Bachofen, *Urreligion und antike Symbole*, 1:279, 372, etc. Let us emphasize, in passing, that the myths of emasculation may also be considered from another viewpoint, wherein the virile parts signify vulgar Mars, the material aspect of force. Cut and fallen to earth or into the sea, they produce, as a seed, a plant (the almond tree of Attis) or a goddess—Venus—under whose footsteps over the Earth, the flowers spring up afresh. Likewise, the Earth produces vegetation from the blood of the bull stricken by Mithras, etc.

[4] P. Bornia, *La Porta Magica* (Rome, 1915), 31.

other esoteric traditions,[5] is encountered in the technical texts of alchemy.[6]

Continuing with the vegetable symbolism, the development of initiation had a characteristic expression in the lotus, a flower whose corolla ◯ opens on a vertical stalk | that rises up to and above the water level ▬, while its roots have grown out of the abyssal mud of the Moist Earth.[7] Thus, together, we get the hieroglyph ♀ which in Egyptian hermetism signified "the key of life," "living," "to live," with regard to resurrection and immortalization: in a bas-relief of the Twelfth Dynasty the "key of life" is delivered to a king by a goddess, accompanied by the following words: "I give thee life, stability, purity, like Ra [the solar god], eternally."

We can also cite in the hermetic work Arab alchemical texts concerning this virtue of the *stem* | . In these is mentioned a "green thing, called myrtle, which grows out in shoots from a base, called "*stem* of myrtle," and it is said: "Mix ye the stem with the Stone. . . . This stem will *burn* the soul and consume the combustible imperfections of the Stone. It liberates it from all corrupting principles; *it returns life to the dead;* and Fire has no further power over it."[8] Turning to Boehme: "The liberation-quality passes through the astringent quality [by being assimilated by the contraction of the hard Earth], lacerates the body and moves out of the body, outside and over the Earth and thus advances, tenaciously, to the sprouting of a large *stalk*. . . . The qualities burst into flames on the stalk and enter it:[9] they generate colors, in accordance with their kind." Then on the stem a spadix or "bud" appears, "which is a new [state of the] Body in the bud or spathe, similar

---

[5] In Apuleius, one who has degenerated into an animal is restored to his original state by means of a rose; in Catholicism, María, *Janua Coeli*, is called the Rosa Mystica; in a medieval poem, *Il Fiore* (Cf. Valli, *Il linguaggio segreto dei Fideli d'Amore* [Rome, 1928], 49, 119) there is mention of a kiss to the rose given with arms forming a cross. In this work of Valli's, (p. 249) is the drawing of Francesco da Barberino, wherein among the personages ascending in pairs (men and women) the seven steps leading to the Androgyne, the first couples are represented as being stung by arrows, while the last bear roses. And "Amor" in his flight to the Androgyne, also bears roses. Cf. *The Mystery of the Grail*, and also Charbonneau-Lassay, "Le symbolisme de la rose" in *Regnabit*, no. 10, (1926).

[6] Cf., for example, B. Treviso, *Philosophie des métaux, BPC*, 2:428; Zacharias, *Philosophie naturelle des métaux*, 536, 537; *Livre de Cratès in CMA*, 3:56; Boehme (*De signatura*, 8, §52; 7, §36; 15, §35): "The outer Body is nothing more than a clump of brambles in the center of which, however, roses could blossom"; "roses that bloom after winter"; "In the same way that the flower rises out of the earth, the image of light rises after death"; "Subjugate the Ego and prosper like a flower in the divine spirit"; etc.

[7] In the well-known Hindu mantra, *Om mani padme*, "Om, the jewel in the lotus," the jewel is a mineral symbol that may well be likened to the Philosopher's Stone. Cf. also *Brihadāranyaka-Upanishad*, 2.3.6: "The aspect of the *incorporeal spirit* is like a tongue of fire or like a *lotus flower*, or like a sudden *flash of lightning*."

[8] *Livre du mercure occidental, CMA*, 3:215.

[9] Corresponding to the esoteric Hindu teaching is the blossoming of the lotuses (*sphota*), that is, of the "centers of life" (cf. p. 56ff.) in the vertical dimension via the path that the ascending current of regeneration (the stem) takes. Cf. J. Evola, *The Yoga of Power*, chapter 10.

to that which plunged its roots into the Earth in the first place, but which now has taken a subtler form."[10]

For more general associations with flowers, resurrection, or alchemical spring-time, we can but repeat the impressive words of Ostanes referring to the "strange and terrible Mystery"; "When the highest descends to the lowest, and the lowest rises to the highest; when the blessed waters descend to visit the dead stretched out, enchained, cast into the *darkness* and *gloom* of Hades; when the Pharmakon of Life reaches them and *awakens* them, taking them out of *sleep*, right where they are; when the New Waters penetrate . . . , rising in the midst of Fire. . . . The waters, on reaching them, awaken the chained and impotent bodies and spirits . . . , little by little they are unfolded, ascend, redressed and are seen in living and glorious colors, like *flowers* in *spring*."[11]

These are the variations of a primordial symbolism linked to the vegetable kingdom, in which the Tree also appears, though understood in a different way; primordial, we say, because in the Hyperborean and Nordic-Atlantic tradition the rune, Y that is, "Cosmic-man-with-upraised arms" (see page 11, note 39), and the Hermes (of Cyllene)—which also had the value of "resurrection," "opening mouth," "rising sun," "Light of the *Fields*"—is ideographically equivalent to the symbol of the "Tree." This "Tree" is born of the Stone or "Rock" and in one of its variants gives rise to the hieroglyph that in Egyptian signifies the "double," that is to say, the subtle states of corporeality, the hieroglyph, *Ka*, rendered by the two raised arms ᙀ.[12] To hermetism, the convergence of all these elements organized into a single understanding and transmitted across the centuries is perfect.[13]

---

[10] *Aurora*, 8, §48, 52, 56.

[11] *CAG*, 2:292-95; cf. Zosimos, *CAG*, 2:122-3.

[12] Cf. H. Wirth, *Der Aufgang der Menschheit*, 99, 206, etc.

[13] Let us note in passing that the vegetable symbolism of the Tree can be extended to the "garden" and the "forest." The first, whose importance in the biblical and koranic scriptures surely escapes no one, is frequently encountered in hermetism as the "garden of the Philosophers" and "garden of the Hesperides," concerning which and speaking for all we can cite Pernety and d'Espagnet (*Dictionnaire*, 207 and *Arcanum hermeticae*, §§52, 53), for the important references to the dragon who guards it, to the symbolical colors of the flowers to which the "Fire of Nature" gives birth assisted by the Art, and finally, to a Fountain of the clearest waters gushing out of seven springs. In the Koran (2:25), the garden, under which streams run, still contains the fruits "by which it was nourished in the beginning," and the worthy who will dwell in it eternally will find therein "immaculate, *untouched* wives," which meaning will be understood if we return, for example, to the "Women" for which the angels descended.

Twenty-Four

STEM, VIRUS, AND IRON

T he Greek alchemists have a technical term that expresses the power of the "stem," that is, *ióς* (*ios*). And
ἴωσις (*iosis*), therefore, is the result of the action of the
ióς. The *ióς* in itself has the same sense as *virus*, and *iosis* is the state of *virulence*,
understood as the active and specific property that leads in certain metals to their
oxidation. On the other hand, oxidation is usually accompanied by a rusting in
metals, and the reddish color of the rust provides an allusion to the solar virile
nature of the new force manifesting in the metal.[1] This is why *iosis* has been
assigned the sense of "purification" via "separation,"[2] that is to say, of an energy
that recovers its orginal power by separating from the corporeal amalgams. The
violent aspect of transcendental force that emerges at the moment of separation is
given the value of "poison" or "dissolving acid," which at times goes by the same
term, *iosis*. Having alluded to rust and oxidation, we wish to turn to another
variation on the vegetable symbolism: upon being oxidized and experiencing iosis,
certain flowers are produced in the metals, the equivalent of symbolical corollas
that blossom on the "stem."

In this sense, iosis is a "virulence," that is, virility. Note, however, that if *ióς*

---

[1] The symbol of rust was kept alive in all the successive alchemical literature and, in general, must be
interpreted precisely on the strength of its reddish color.

[2] Cf. *CAG*, 2:176, 196, 198.

is the equivalent of *virus*, from the root *vir* (cf. Latin: *vis, virtus*), it is identical to the Sanskrit *vīrya*, a technical term of the Hindu doctrine of regeneration whose sense corresponds entirely to what is hidden in alchemical iosis. In reality, *vīrya*, in the Hindu doctrine, and especially in Buddhism, is that purely spiritual energy that, once isolated, is capable of reacting on the habitual functioning of the elements, setting in motion an action that is no longer a part of nature and that is a result of the "unnatural Fire" and the "Fire against Nature," whose meaning attributed by the hermetic texts we shall explain below. In order to isolate the *vīrya*, an energy is necessary that is capable of suspending desire (*canda riddhipādah*), after which is awakened the spiritually virile power that brings the elements of the human being to a state no longer in flux (*vīrya riddhipādah*).[3] The rising of the stalk over the Water and the Earth, and its blossoming hermetically adumbrate these same meanings.

The virile character of the power at work in the resurrections (*virus, virtus, vīrya, vis, vir*) suggests that in hermetism the elements, although in their vulgar, dead, or terrestrial state, constitute an approximation or a transposition, often felt to be most apt for the preparation of the Philosophical Gold. By that we are told that Mars (god of iron and war) is a metal from whose "tincture" (or tint)—if its extraction be obtained (that is, if one manages to separate the virile-warrior element of man from its corporeal condition)—one could obtain Gold.[4] Braccesco returns time and again to iron: "Iron is called man [*vir*], because he has a flexible soul and a healthy spirit, because his root is pure; he is young and strong because he is hard and strong." "On Mars," he says, "depends the perfection of the elixir," given that it possesses "the power nearest to conversion into Elixir"; it is a "fixed Sulfur";[5] its property is not found in any other substance. "In its *lime, it dominates Fire, and is not dominated by it* . . . , but, admirably, it reposes in it, rejoicing in it."

Senior also has the symbolic Iron say: "I am Iron, the strong one, hammer and hammered, all good comes through me; and *Light*, the secret of secrets, by me is generated." Because it possesses a stronger will than other bodies, it has been chosen by the Wise.[6]

Naturally, as encountered in man, Mars has impure parts: it is prone to "combustion," resists "fusion" too much, and "lacks lustre" (Francis Bacon, Geber); it must be washed and "subtly triturated." Nevertheless, the "heroic" power, the spiritual-warrior virtue hidden in the symbol of this metal and god, is recognized

---

[3] Cf. T. Stcherbatsky, *The Central Conception of Buddhism* (London, 1923), 50; C. Puini, *Introduction to the "Mahaparinirvana-Sutra"* (Lanciano, 1919), 11–13.

[4] Boehme, *De signatura*, 8, §32.

[5] For the meaning of this expression see pages 42-43.

[6] Braccesco, *Espositione*, fols. 65a, 58a, 58b, 59a; cf. 63a.

as one of the best principles and "prime matters" for the Work; it can do no less than confirm the sprit of that tradition to which this same Work pertains and about which we have already spoken.

In conclusion we must add that in more recent times, the symbolism of the philosophers has particularly turned to the hardness and infrangibility acquired by iron when treated by Water and Fire: we refer to *steel*. The Cosmpolite compares the "Steel of the Wise" to the symbolic virtue of the Magnet, which here is understood as the transcendent "hardness" of the dominating Spirit and incombustible Sulfur to which the mercurial forces in a state of freedom are attracted and submit, as the female to the male. And Philalethes says: "Our steel is, in the end, the true key of the Work, without which it is completely useless to try to light the lamp or the philosophical furnace. It is the vein of Gold, it is the purest spirit of all, an infernal and secret fire, and it is, also, in its way, extraordinarily volatile. It is, in sum, the wonder of the world and the focus of the higher virtues by inferior beings."[7]

Now it only remains for us to see in detail the operations on which the foundation of such power must be completed in order to attain that prodigious existence, which beyond all the allegories and enigmas, the hermetic masters promise us as "heirs of the wisdom of the centuries."

---

[7] *Introitus apertus*, §3.

Part Two

the

hermetic

royal

art

che reality
of palingenesis

Before we engage ourselves in the practical details of the "Royal Art," we need to decide on the most exact terms to convey the character of its *reality*.

It would be very far from understanding the essence of the Art if, misled by the analogy of mystical and religious expressions, such as "death and resurrection," "rebirth," "mortification," and so on, one were to believe that it all comes down to something "moralistic," vaguely spiritualistic, or merely mystical.

And in fact, to some degree, almost everyone tends to adopt such a view, because of such expressions. But we have said from the beginning that the very fact that the hermetic doctrine has always and continuously been disguised, even in periods when to speak of palingenesis "mystically" did not constitute a heresy, indicates that in reality something quite different has been involved: something that in itself again demanded that law of *silence*, which had been so rigorously observed in the pagan mysteries.

To indicate (see the preface) the derivation of the hermetic tradition from a primordial "royal" and "heroic" vein is itself enough to explain its concealment in the period when Christianity dominated. But the fact is, there is also another reason encapsulated in the maxim, "The Sage, in his wisdom, should not disturb the mind of the ignorant." This is a maxim that had to be observed even more rigorously in a time when the number of "ignorant" had come to be almost total.

To account for this, we must go back to a fundamental traditional teaching already cited: that of the *two natures*.

There is the nature of the immortals and the nature of the mortals; the higher region of "those who are" and the lower region of "becoming." The idea that these two branches could have originally been one single thing (according to Hesiod's thinking, by which "one is the lineage of men and the other of the Gods, both proceeding from a single matrix") and that the duality is simply the consequence of the fall of the one and the ascension of the other (according to the hermetico-Heraclitean conception of the god as an "immortal man" and of man as a "mortal god"), did not keep the differentiation from being intrinsic and essentially twofold.

Passage from one to the other was considered possible, but exceptional and on condition of an essential, effective, and positive transformation from one mode of being into the other. This transformation was acquired by *initiation*, in the strictest sense of the word. By initiation some men could escape from one nature and achieve the other, ceasing thereby to be men any longer. Their arrival at the plane of another form of existence, constituted an event on the new plane exactly equivalent to generation and physical birth.

So those who were reborn, were regenerated. In the same way that physical birth involves the loss of the consciousness of the higher state, so death implies the loss of the consciousness of the lower state, with the result that, to the degree to which all consciousness of the higher state is lost (that is, and according to the terms we already know), to the degree in which the "identification" (the "self-absorption") occurs, to that same degree the loss of consciousness of the inferior (human) state caused by death and the disintegration of the support of such consciousness (the body) results in the loss of *all* consciousness in the personal sense. In the eternal sleep, in the larval existence of Hades, in the dissolution—which is thought to be the destiny of all those for whom this life and the forms it takes constitute the beginning and end of everything human—in all this only those will escape who, while still in life, have learned how to focus their consciousness upon the higher world. The Initiates, the Adepts, find themselves at the end of this road. Memory—ἀνάμνεσις—according to Plutarch, having been acquired, they have freed themselves, they have broken their chains, and wearing crowns, celebrate the "mysteries" and consider the masses of uninitiated and "impure" men on earth to be asleep, all crammed together and stuck in mire and darkness.[1]

To tell the truth, the traditional *post mortem* teaching has always emphasized a difference between survival and immortality. Various forms of survival can be

---

[1] In Stobaeus, *Flor.*, 4.107. According to the *Corpus Hermeticum* (22.3), man has the hope of immortality. It is said that not all human souls are immortal, but only those that become *daimons* (10.7, 19). The decisive thing is their level of identification with the latter. Pythagoras would have admitted that "the soul in some cases can become mortal, when it allows itself to be dominated by the Erinyes, that is, by the passions—and makes itself immortal again when freed of the same—which are passions again" (Hippolytus, *Philosophumena*, 6.26).

conceived that are more or less contingent, passive, and conditional survival for this or that human principle or complex. But this has nothing to do with immortality, which can only be thought of as "Olympian" immortality, as "becoming a god." Such a conception prevailed in the West up to Hellenic antiquity. But directly out of the doctrine of the "two natures" proceeded the knowedge of the destiny of a death, or of a larval and precarious survival for some, and a conditional (on the condition of initiation) immortality for others.

It was the vulgarization and abusive generalization of a truth valid exclusively for initiates—a vulgarization that began in some degenerate forms of Orphism and was soon fully developed by Christianity) that was to give birth to the strange idea of an "immortality of the soul," and then extended unconditionally to the same for all souls. From that moment until today, that illusion has been perpetuated in diverse forms of religious and "spiritual" thought: the chimera that the soul of a mortal is immortal; that immortality is a *certainty*, not a problematical possibility.[2]

Once the false notion was established and the truth perverted in this way, initiation could no longer be presented as necessary; from that moment its value as a real and effective operation ceased to be understood. Little by little, all truly transcendental possibility was forgotten, and now when men spoke of "rebirth," it had dwindled into a sentimental fact with merely a moral and religous meaning, into a more or less undefinable "mystical" state.

From then on it would have been futile to try to suggest, during the centuries dominated by such an error, that "something different" was possible; that that which some considered a sure thing and others an arbitrary hope was actually a privilege bestowed by a secret and sacred Art; and it would have been useless to try to explain—just as in the deterministic world of matter and energy, so in the operations of this Art—that morality, faith, devotion and all the rest are ineffectual weapons against human frailty. "As the gods must one be, not as good men. It is not that one must free oneself from sin, but that one must transform oneself into a god—that is the goal," Plotinus had already said.[3] To declare the relativity of everything that is religion, speculation, and human morality from the standpoint

---

[2] As for Christianity in its less popular forms, it presents an aspect of the tragic doctrine of salvation, which to some extent preserves an echo of the ancient truth: the idea—pushed to extremes by Luther and Calvin—that man on earth stands at the crossroads between Salvation and eternal damnation. This point of view, if lived intensely and coherently, could create the conditions for liberation at the moment of death or in *post-mortem* states. (Cf. Evola, *The Yoga of Power* and *The Doctrine of the Awakening*.) Among authentically traditional forms, there is an especially esoteric Taoism, which has professed most clearly the doctrine of conditional immortality and the only one possible. See the introductory essay to our edition of the *Tao te Ching* of Lao-tzu, *I libro del principio della sua azione* (Milan, 1959).

[3] *Enneads*, 1.2.7; 1.2.6.

of *reality* in its transcendence of all mortal construction;[4] to speak of the divine as of a symbol for *the other* state of consciousness; of the coming of a Messiah as of the *melior spes* nourished by those seeking initiation; or to speak of the "resurrection of the flesh" as of just another symbol for the regeneration of the same principles of the organism that can be realized while we are still in life—to make such attempts would henceforth prove to be utterly useless.

And how would it have been possible to avoid the most tragic misunderstandings if these same words and primordial symbols now degraded by religion had been employed? Much better then to speak of Mercury and Sulfur, of metals and puzzling things and impossible operations, better to attract the greedy attention and curiosity of the "puffers" and "charcoal burners," of those who then gave birth to modern chemistry; and best of all, in order to keep others from suspecting that the rare and enigmatic allusions were actually metallurgical symbolism referring to things of the spirit, to pretend, on the contrary (as those positive souls who write the history of science still believe to this day), that it was nothing more than a mystical allegory for metallurgical questions and the workings of natural and profane science, standing in opposition to the supernatural terrain of faith and dogma.

As far as we are concerned, on such grounds, we can understand the occultation and even deplore the fact that it doesn't go far enough to impede, in our time, certain "spiritualistic" interpretations of alchemy which, while not lessening the naive incomprehenson of historians of science one bit, have raised it to a mystical-moralistic plane—and even to psychoanalysis[5]—and thereby simply made it worse for those who do not want to jump from the skillet into the fire.

On the contrary (and perhaps we have said as much already [p. 77] about the faculties or "vulgar" metals that have presaged it), perhaps the very ones who positively believe that every psychic and spiritual faculty is conditioned and

---

[4] From the point of view of the profane disciplines it is expressed thusly in an Arab alchemical text: "He who knows this [our] Science, even superficially, and who deserves to be one of its adepts, is superior even to those spirits who are the most distinguished in all the other sciences. In fact, any man instructed in any science whatsoever, who has never consecrated a part of his time to the study of even one of the principles of the Work, in theory or in practice, possesses an absolutely inferior intellectual education. The most he can do is to align words, combine phrases and definitions from his imagination, and to investigate things that have no existence of their own, but which he still believes exist outside himself" (*Livre du mercure occidental, CMA*, 3:214). Even Aristotle, although considered "the most brilliant of nonluminous beings," could not have compared himself to those beings who have reached the incorporeal state (Syrian texts, *CMA*, 2:264). And in the *Corpus Hermeticum* (16.2) it is said: "The Greeks, O King, have new kinds of language to carry on arguments, and their philosophy is a buzz of words. We, however, do not use words, but the great voice of things."

[5] This is what the psychoanalyst C. G. Jung has done systematically in his work, *Psychology and Alchemy*, on the basis of the "unconscious," of "projections of the unconscious" and the like.

determined by empirical factors (organic, hereditary, environmental, etc.) and who since Nietzschean nihilism have been led to the idea of the relativity of all values, as well as that greatest of renunciations, the "renunciation of belief"—perhaps such persons are better situated today to understand the effective reach of the hermetic and initiatic work.

Here "rebirth" is neither a sentiment nor an allegory, but a concrete fact that no one can understand who has not passed through the Mystery. Its true meaning—as Macchioro justly points out[6]—might just be glimpsed today, if at all, by abandoning mystico-religious conceptions and turning to whatever remains among the primitive peoples of the world, as a degenerated residue of a superior primordial teaching. "For them," writes Macchioro, "palingenesis is not an allegory, but a reality so real that frequently it is considered a physical and material fact. The mystery does not aim to teach but to renew the individual. There is no need to justify or impose the renewal: palingenesis occurs and that is that."[7]

And in the same way that if the necessary circumstances were present to produce some physical phenomenon, the phenomenon would reliably be produced; so, when the necessary conditions to produce an initiation are provided, the rebirth is just as reliably produced—independently of any question of worthiness. It is as though in Eleusis, if it could have been affirmed, coherently, that a bandit was an initiate, then he participated in immortality, while an Agesilaus or an Epaminondas, if not an initiate, would after death find no better destiny than any other mortal. If already, in those days, a Diogenes could be scandalized by such an idea, how many more today would be prepared to agree with him!

Those who have, instead, abandoned the unrealistic conception of the noncorporeal and who at the same time are capable of considering the spirit as an objective force—an active force, reacting, necessitating, determined, and determining—would not find the thing to be more against nature than if today we were to submit a bandit, Agesilaus, or Epaminondas to a high-tension wire and find that the current would certainly not forgive Epaminondas and Agesilaus for their virtue and electrocute only the bandit, because of his crimes.

It is proper, then, for the hermetic Art, as for any other initiation—whether oriental or occidental—to turn the individual from "human values" to the problem of the spirit in terms of reality. But then the individual finds himself confronting his body, which is the fundamental nexus of all the conditions of his state. The consideraton of the connection between the ego principle in its double form of thought and deed, and corporeality (in the complete sense of this term), and the

---

[6] V. Macchioro, *Heraclitus* (Bari, 1922), 119–20.

[7] Ibid.

transformation of said connection by means of well-defined, practical, and necessary acts, even though they are essentially interior, constitutes the essential core of the Royal Art of the hermetic masters. The latter will be directed first of all to the conquest of the principle of immortality, and then to the total stable nature, no longer transitory or deteriorating the elements and functions by which the human manifestation is established within the realm of becoming. Flamel says: "Our Work is the conversion and change of one being into another being, as from one thing into another thing, from debility to strength . . . from corporeality to spirituality."[8] And Hermes adds, "Convert and change the natures, and you will find that which you are seeking."[9]

All that remains is to study the single operations themselves that technically comprise this Great Work.

---

[8] Flamel, *Désir désiré*, §6.

[9] Ibid.

Twenty-Five

ȼhe

SEPARAȼion

The testimony of the literature agrees that the first step in the hermetic Art is the *separation*. In the ciphered language it is designated by a great number of expressions, sometimes with the intention of confusing the profane and sometimes to indicate the various aspects that comprise it. We shall have an opportunity to see for ourselves why terms like separation, dissolution, extraction, preparation of the Mercury of the Sages, preparation of the Corrosive Waters, Death, reduction of the prima materia, washing, *coniunctio*, denudation, etc., are all equivalent.

We shall establish the technical problem in Sendivogius's terms, according to which the arcanum of the Work is contained in the Sulfur of the Philosophers, which, however, is found in a "darkest prison" whose keys are guarded by Mercury.[1] Mercury, in turn, is under the custody of Saturn. In order to understand this we have only to relate such symbols to the meanings of the various entities within man.

The task is to emancipate the subtle form of life (Mercury) that unites Soul and Body from Saturn, which is the physical body itself, and which in the process of identification with form attracts and *fixes* to itself the Mercury in its individual character designated by ☿ (as opposed to ☿). Among the various meanings of the hermetic allegory, Saturn amputating the feet of Mercury (this is found, for example, in Abraham the Jew) is just this. Mercury is thus converted into an

---

[1] Sendivogius, *De sulphure*, 157, 171, 196, 219.

individualized Mercury, not free to choose his own individuality, but bound and hobbled against the possibility of taking any other form of life than that of a particular designated life. This is the sense in which Mercury is under the custody of Saturn.

The bondage of ☿ is transmitted to ☿, and so the activity that now provides a glimpse of the influence of a higher principle ♈ remains channeled in the pathways of the body and submitted to conditions the latter dictates. This is how the "ego" principle, or Sulfur, continues to be controlled as well, to the point of being permanently housed in the form of a given individuality, that is, the individuality of that particular physical body. Mercury then, possesses the keys of this prison, subject to Saturn.[2]

Hermetically speaking, *separation* means the extraction of the Mercury from the Body. Once the action of the animal organism on the vital force has been suspended, the other principles are virtually free as well. For this reason it is said that Mercury is the only key "capable of opening the locked Palace of the King" or as Philalethes also says, "breaking the barriers of the Gold."[3] Thanks to the separation Mercury is again liberated, returned to the state of vital, unlimited possibility (it is this that is known as "conversion in the First Matter"). And now the internal Sulfur finds the way open to every transcendent activity or transformation.

Such, then, is the blueprint, which a few texts will confirm. And now we are in a position to understand better what it means to "purify and animate the common Mercury." In terms similar to Sendivogius, Pernety speaks to us of a hidden Fire burning inside the natural Fire (this is the deepest stage of the ego force) that is to be reanimated by liberating it from the prison in which it has been locked up: "The Body is the principle of fixation and deprives the other two principles [Spirit and Soul] of volatility [the possibility of freedom that is characteristic of all noncorporeal states]; the Spirit [i.e., Mercury] provides the *entrance* by opening the Body; and Water, with the help of the Spirit [by Water, here, we need to

---

[2] Cf. the passage of Della Riviera, (*Mondo magico*, 19) wherein it is said that the divine virtue, on being diffused into individuals, "loses at that very moment its universal nature . . . wherefore it is useless to look for it outside the [true] Center within the limited [consequently human] Center. This Center is that which has been called the Cavern of Mercury; and the Spirit is no other than the gift hidden therein: and ultimately this same Mercury is the son of Maya, identified, in the ancient theology, with the earth itself." Cf. Boehme, *De signatura*, 8, §34: [*"Der Künstler soll recht verstehen, wo die Möglichkeit leige als im Sulphur (der die Grundlage aller Operationen ist). Saturnus halt ihn und den Merkur in sich zu hart gefangen; so ihm aber der Künstler zu Hilfe kommt . . . so wird er stark und wirft Saturnum weg und offenbart das Kind."* (The artist must know sulfur well. It is the basis of his operations, and he must liberate it and the Mercury, who are prisoners of Saturn. Only then can the Child be manifested.)— Trans.]

[3] Salmon, introduction to *BPC*, cxvii.

understand that which by 'dissolving' the Spirit, returns it to freedom] fetches the Fire from its prison, and is the Soul."[4] The same author says specifically, "The whole secret of Hermetic Philosophy lies in keeping the Mercury pure [so to speak], in the state in which it was found before being mixed with any other metal [before being specialized as life bound necessarily to an individual being]. This is the Mercury-principle, which must be distiguished from vulgar Mercury, which is lifeless outside the Mine [outside the universal possibility, now that it has been arrested by Saturn], because its inner Fire is dormant and cannot act [in any supernatural way] if it has not been put into action by the Mercury principle."[5]

We have seen that *desire* is what has bound life to a body in the sense of having "fallen." And we have also spoken of the traditionally established connection between the desire principle and one of the meanings of the Water symbol. So now we are in a position to understand what Flamel means when he exhorts us to *drain off* the Water (Mercury): which means to remove the symbolic *humidity* which represents the desire-force, "until it has taken root in its own element [reintegration into its original state through the suspension of desire]."[6] Similarly, other authors speak of a preliminary realm of Fire bent on destroying the "superfluous humidity" and seeking the dessication and "calcination" of the whole substance. The *Livre de l'Alun et du Sel* says that the process consists essentially in extracting (from the body) the pernicious humidity and infusing into it, a contrary fiery wetness— *humiditas ignea*. "Then the Water will be spiritual and have the power to trans- form one Nature into another Nature."[7]

Again our system runs straight into Philalethes who speaks of a "Passive sulfur, occurring in Mercury [the ego-force left wanting behind by the vital principle when it is fixated in the Body] which should be active and effective . . . thence it is clearly necessary to introduce a life principle—but of the same nature—which resuscitates the life that is hidden within it and which is as dead at the core." At this point the Magi "mixed life with Life [that is, after separating the vital principle, they re- united it to its original trunk], moistening the dry, animating the passive by the active, and finally, resuscitating life by means of death."[8]

In the next chapter we shall clarify the proper meaning of this "death." But for

---

[4] Pernety, *Dictionnaire*, 403.

[5] Ibid., 294; cf. 296.

[6] Flamel, *Désir désiré*, 313. We can now also cite d'Espagnet (*Arcanum hermeticae*, BCC 2, §50ff.) who says that Mercury has two inherent defects, one deriving from earthiness, which was mixed in with congelation (that is, individuation), and the other from hydropesis, involving an impure and crude Water (that is, which is still in its primary state of chaos and thirst) and which has entered into the flesh.

[7] Flamel, *Désir désiré*, 313.

[8] Philalethes, *Introitus apertus*, §11.

now let us note again the complementary symbol of "moistening the dry," which is contrary only in appearance to the draining of the Matter. It is still a question of the desire principle that in one case is considered under the symbolic aspect of Water, of Chaos, of "Nature taking pleasure in itself" and "fascinated by its own elements"; and in the other case, on the contrary, it is taken as the dryness inherent in thirst, as the desiccation and contraction that the impure and devouring Fire produces in the Life principle. This is why it is also prescribed "to irrigate the Earth, rendered dry by the action of the Fire, by means of a Water of the same nature [that is, which has been purified by separation]." Thus the pores of this symbolic Earth are opened, and the "Thief will be obliged to flee with his artifices of iniquity." Here the "Thief" stands for the gnostic "counterfeit spirit," the Hindu "ego of the elements," that ego which is but a creature of the body. "The Water will be purged in this way of its leprosy and dropsical or superfluous humor [this is the excess of the moist principle over the golden, an excess that constitutes the consuming state of—leprosy—of desire] by adding the true Sulfur. Thus wilt thou obtain the Fountain of Bernard of Treviso."[9]

We shall return to this fountain later. In it we can recognize the fons perennis of the classical Mysteries, the fountain of that Water which, evangelically, quenches all thirst and confers the life eternal. But here we now perceive the symbolism of the Two Waters, corresponding to the two regions, that of being and of becoming. This is the life-force as it manifests according to the requirements of one framework or the other. The separation, says Arnold of Villanova,[10] produces the "Divine and Immutable Water" (the "permanent" or "eternal" as opposed to the law of the lower region of changes): an operation that simultaneously is brought into contact with the thawing of the ice to the fluid state of the water, that is, in the alchemical "solution."

Here then is the explanation of the convergence of the various symbols: to separate from the body means to cause the life-principle (Water or Mercury) to pass on to the unindividuated state; as passage from the "fixed" stage to the "unfixed" there is the "solution"; as liberation of that which the body has locked up, hidden from itself, there is "extraction"; as returning to the original state there is "conversion into the prima materia" and "concocting the Mercury of the Wise";[11] and, finally, coniunctio, when the two states are hypostatized and in the transformation one sees the unification of the specialized life with the immutable life which, however, is not external to it but stunned and inebriated in the root of the former.

---

[9] Ibid., §6

[10] Arnold of Villanova, Semita semitae, 18; cf. Flamel, Désir désiré, §1

[11] Cf. Triomphe Hermétique (BPC, 3:141): "Mercury is called Spirit of the Philosophers because only the wise know the secret of converting it into spirit liberating it from the prison of the body, in which nature had locked it."

Twenty-Six

DEATH AND THE
BLACK WORK

O nce the influence of the physical body on ☿ has been suspended, its influence on the psychic and mental principles of the person, having their foundation in ☿, is also suspended at the same time. At this moment we come to that crisis to which we referred when we spoke of the symbolism of the seed, which "must die in the Earth, in order to come to fruition." All the common faculties—even the sense of the ego itself—are affected by it. Here appear all the symbols already assigned to philosophical Mercury as a weapon that wounds, stuns, and kills: dissolving water, poison, philosopher's vinegar, viper. Then the *nigredo* appears, the "blacker than black" color of putrefaction or hermetic "mortification," sign of the first effective change in the entirety of the symbolical "substance," which passes to the horizontal position ⎯, corresponding naturally to that which has been struck down.

To explain this experience in general terms without resorting to esoteric teachings, the simple fact itself suffices that when the activities of the external waking consciousness in the ordinary person have been reduced, the collective consciousness is likewise reduced. Said reduction, in its successive stages, is parallel to the progressive separation of the Mercury principle, which when disengaged, ceases to perceive images from the exterior world. If the normal man is able to orient himself at all without the direct support of these images, he finds himself in a state of reverie, and then in the dream state, in which the energization of the imaginary activity, dissociated from the external senses, is accompanied further by a reduction and emptying of the consciousness of self. When that alienation increases, sleep comes and then consciousness is abolished. Farther beyond lie trance, lethargy, and the cataleptic state. Farther still, when the separation is complete, he enters into a state of apparent death, and finally into the state of the dissociation of the organism no longer held together by the vital force, which is to say: death.

Such is the phenomenology of the "separation" and the dissolution when it appears spontaneously, passively, and negatively whether in man's ordinary night or in the great night, or when it is invoked by special substances, such as drugs, anesthetics, and poisons. These are all genuine states and conditions of being.

Now the whole secret of the first phase of the hermetic Opus consists in this: in working in such a way that the consciousness is not reduced and then suspended at the threshold of sleep, but instead can accompany this process through all its phases, in complete awareness, up to a condition equivalent to death. The "dissolution" is then made into a living, intense, indelible experience, and this is the alchemical "death," the "blacker than black," the entrance into the "tomb of Osiris," the knowledge of the dark land, the realm of Saturn, of which the texts speak.

The sense of the secret operation in the classical mystery initiation that assured the mutation of nature and immortality is no different.

"Man's soul at the moment of death," says Plutarch,[1] "experiences the same passion [πάθος] as those who have been initiated in the Great Mysteries; the word corresponding to the word, the deed to the deed [τελευτᾶν and τελεῖσθαι]." Initiation is celebrated as a voluntary death and as a gratuitous salvation, according to Apuleius.[2] Boehme would say: "Death is the only way by which the spirit can change form," specifying that by means of a *willing* spirit it can traverse the "fiery death."[3] The whole difference is that the "philosophal death"—*mors philosophorum*— is *active:* it is not a question of a body which, upon disintegrating loses its soul, but of a soul so concentrated in its power, that it unmakes the body. Porphyry says it in the clearest possible terms, adding that it is not absolutely true that one death follows the other; that is to say, that the common death must be followed by liberation and transfiguration (the "spiritualist" theory) or that initiatic death must follow physical death.[4] None of this has anything to do with mystico-sentimental states nor with "mortification" in the ascetic or religious sense. It is a question of a state of spirit, but not separable from any real modification of the bonds between the different elements of human wholeness.

---

[1] In Stobaeus, *Flor.*, 4.107; cf. Porphyry, *Sententiae*, 9.

[2] Apuleius, *Metamorphoses*, 11.21.

[3] Boehme, *De signatura*, 14, §73; 15, §51.

[4] The Latin text of Porphyry (*Sententiae* 9) is: "*Mors duplex: altera quidem aeque omnibus nota, ubi corpus solvitur ab anima; altera vero philosophorum, quum anima solvitur a corpore: nec semper altera alteram sequitur.*"

But the adventure is not without risks. It can happen that any alteration, the process of which is not completely under one's control or is influenced, for example, by an ill-timed ego reaction, establishes between said elements abnormal or fragmentary connections, to which—if the ordeal is not mastered—there cannot less than correspond diminished or abnormal forms of the faculties of awareness. Artephius says that along with the "solution" and the "black color," there is produced a "discontinuity of the parts." In effect, the disintegration of the "composition" or "mixture" of its elements is provoked, with the result that whoever confronts the experience and during the whole time it lasts, is in constant danger of death, or at least in danger of all those disorders (schizophrenia, amnesia, stupefaction, confusion, epilepsy) that can result from the relentless separation of the vital energies from the organs and bodily functions to which they correspond.[5]

When, however, all the changes of state have been carried out and maintained without losing control or consciousness, and the separation has actually been made, the beginnings of the new birth have been set in motion. "The [initiatory] generation is realized when the Materia is in complete dissolution, which [the Philosphers] call putrefaction or blackest black."[6]

Among the many references to "mortification" we can cite the words of Basil Valentine's *Azoth,* plate 5, the picture wherein we see an old man in decomposition locked up with a raven (the technical alchemical symbol for this state) inside the "philosophical egg" surrounded by Fire, in the act of exhaling two spirits (the subtle principles, "Spirit" and "Soul"): "My surname is Dragon. I am the runaway slave, and they have closed me in a grave in order that I might be rewarded with the royal crown and I can enrich my family . . . My Soul and my Spirit abandon me [these are the two exhaled spirits, the two clouds, one white, the other red, that must be extracted from the Stone]. . . . May they not forsake me forever, but let me see the Light of Day again, so that this Hero of Peace,[7] whom the world awaits, can come out of me."[8]

---

[5] Cf. *Introduzione alla magia* 2:305–14: Some effects of the magical discipline: the separation of the "mixture."

[6] Pernety, *Dictionnaire,* 181.

[7] *Pax,* in the sense of the ending of a symbolic "war" undertaken by the hero.

[8] In *BCC,* 2:214. For this phase the symbol of the "sepulchre" is frequently used. The "black," in connection with Saturn, Lead, and Chaos, is called the "Grave from which the spirit must exit in order to glorify its body" (Salmon, introduction to *BPC,* xv). In the *Viatorum spagiricum* is seen a coffin in which are the King and Queen (the vulgar forms of ☉ and of ☽) with a skeleton of Mercury alongside, and we find it again in the *Margarita pretiosa* and in the edition of the *Rosarium* contained in the *Artis auriferae,* in Flamel, etc. The expression is characteristic: "Here is a grave containing no corpse and a corpse not in its grave. *The corpse and the grave are the same thing.*" (in *Theatrum chemicum,* 3:744).

"The dissociation," Flamel explains,[9] "is called death, destruction and perdition because the natures are changing form: undergoing calcination and denudation." Other authors speak of a great eclipse of Sun $\odot$ and Moon$\mathbb{C}$, beyond which chaos obtains,[10] specifying that the black and dark color expresses the state of the body when the soul has been snatched away, necessitating an invasion of a "white smoke" (incorporeal aerial state) into it, which multiplies the Waters.[11] For the direct "experience" let us again turn to Boehme: "Being is liberated, or liberates itself from death with an agony experienced in the great anguish of impression [cf. Plutarch's πάθος], which is the mercurial life [lived in a free state]; and in this pain, the nitrous terror [the terror is 'that which comes from Mercury or the anguish of death,' while Saltpeter is the principle of individuation], brightens like lightning. Immediately liberty returns to itself and the being plunges into the dark and austere anguish,"[12] corresponding to the color black, which, on the other hand, Synesius calls: "The black Earth, or raven's head, called dark *Shadow*: on this, as on a tree trunk, the rest of the Magisterium has its foundation."[13]

We can say, then, that the power at work in this phase is the same as that which is called forth in the phenomenon of death. It is clearly expressed by an Arab text: "The Dragon, that produces the various colors [symbols of the successive phases of the Work], is the very one that would have been fatal to your existence *and would have separated your Soul from your Body*."[14] Here is a comparison, also found in the esoteric Hindu teachings: *Aum* is the *mantra*[15] of the serpent power (*kundalini*) used by the yogins to open the "threshold of Brahma" and to cause to flower the "centers of life" in regeneration—it is also the *mantra* of Martya, the God of Death. "Be attentive to Mercury drawn from Arsenic—warns *The Book of El Habir*—because it is an igneous venom that dissolves all things."[16] "The

---

[9] *Figures hiéroglyphiques*, 231.

[10] Philalethes, *Introitus apertus*, §20

[11] Morienus, *Entretiens, BPC*, 2:110.

[12] *De signatura*, 3, §§19, 20.["Das Wesen gehet alles aus dem Tod durch Sterben, welches geschieht in der großen Angst des Impressions, welches das merkurialische Leben ist; allda geschiehet der salnitrische Schrack als ein ausfahrender Blitz; dann die Freiheit scheidet sich allda in sich selber und ist doch das ingezogene Wesen aus der Lust der Freiheit, mit im Begriff des Inziehens in der herben, strengen, finsteren Angst blieben."—Trans.]

[13] *Livre de Synesius, BPC*, 2:186.

[14] *CMA*, 3:74.

[15] According to Hindu tradition, *mantras* are formulas which when pronounced under definite and supernatural spiritual conditions, have the power to evoke and actuate supersensual forces. Cf. Evola, *The Yoga of Power*, 108ff.

[16] *CMA*, 3:102.

Mercury burns and kills everything," is repeated by others.[17] But then we are given the prescription, "To mix the metals in their due proportion with Mercury and to continue until the result is converted into an igneous venom."[18]

And again: "the Philosophers called this tincture Sulfur, *Sulfurs,* Consuming Fire, blinding *ray,* stone of the sling that *shatters* and destroys the Stone, leaving a permanent scar of the fracture."[19]

---

[17] *BCC,* 1:458.

[18] *Livre de Cratès, CMA,* 3:54; cf. 67.

[19] *Livre du feu de la pierre, CMA,* 3:216.

Twenty-Seven

Che Crial of
Che void

"**S**eparation," according to the alchemical authors, is "a most difficult thing, a labor of Hercules," compared to which the rest of the operations are mere "woman's work" and "children's games": so strong is the irrational tie that binds all the elements together in the human "mixture." The authors exhort tenacity, constant patience, and tireless application; they counsel against haste and repeat that "any precipitousness is of the devil"; we must work, they say, without becoming discouraged, with ardor, but without letting ourselves be carried away, lest the Work that has begun be ruined.[1]

The difficulty is the breaking into and opening up of the Gold, that is, in the setting aside of the personality. For it has been said that it is harder to undo the Gold than to make it.[2] The second difficulty is to preserve, in the midst of this destructive stage, no matter what happens, a "quintessence," an active, subtle and

---

[1] Cf., for example, Pernety, *Dictionnaire*, 360; *Livre de El Habir*, *CMA*, 3:103; Paracelsus, *Thesaurus*, in Poisson, *Cinq traités*, 86; *Turba philosophorum*, *BPC*, 2:22; *Dialogue de Marie et Aros*, *BPC*, 1:80; Geber, *Summa*, *BCC*, 1:521; *Filet d'Ariadne*, 84; Sendivogius, *De sulphure*, 157. In the words of Geber (*Livre de la clémence*, *CMA*, 3:136): "I recommend you to act slowly and with precaution, not to hurry, but to follow the example of Nature." Such an example can also be interpreted as attention to those processes in which the separation is produced in natural ways (sleep, etc.; see below).

[2] *De pharmaco catholico*, 1, §8; farther on (12, §2) they speak of the Soul and Cosmic Spirit locked up in the Gold as a center in its circle ☉ and say: "The magical Elements open the solid body of the Sun, and make possible the extraction of the Soul and Clarified Body."

essential principle from within this same Gold. The vulgar Gold is found and preserved mostly in *fixed natures* and it is very difficult to reduce it to a state of "dissolution" without its losing its inner, buried principle, or "Soul," as well.

To depart from the metaphor: as long as external consciousness linked to the brain and settled in the organic individuality prevails, we feel ourselves to be a person, "I," but we are barred from the other, deeper states of being. But let the Gold be broken—"put to the sword," "crushed," "pulverized," or "flattened thin," etc., (all equivalent expressions in the ciphered language)—and one passes on to these noncorporeal and "fluid" states. It is at this time that a negative condition for the sense of the ego is encountered. And hardly have these states been encountered—the inner experience feels as if there is no ground underfoot—when there is an instinctive, irrestistible reaction, an automatic fear-response that suddenly startles and jerks us back to the point of departure—to the "fixed," to the "body" or "Earth"—and the gates are shut again.[3]

We must therefore proceed patiently, persistently, and subtly, learning the symbolic "science of balances" or "dosages," that is, the quantity of activity and passivity necessary to use and equilibrate; *filing down* little by little the "Iron"[4] in order to avoid those automatic jumps mentioned above, that would hold back the process of separation—but at the same time taking care that there remains a sufficient quantity of the solar ⊙ element in order not to end up in diminished forms of consciousness, which would lead not to the hermetic realization but to the negative states of trance, somnambulism, or mediumship.

So we can have some presentiment of what we have been told: of the weary peregrinations and running through the darkness, of the fear and trembling, sweats and horrors, before coming to see the Light described in the mystery literature;[5] and we can see what the passage through the elements would be, after reaching the confines of death and crossing the threshold of Proserpine,[6] and what might be that analogue of Earth dissolving itself in Water, Water in Fire, Fire in Air that is mentioned in a Tibetan text as the experience that comes immediately after death.[7] There are successive losses of solid support (Earth, i.e., the body) that distinguish

---

[3] I dare say, there is no reader who has never experienced those abrupt jerks at the moment of falling asleep, exactly as if the ground under him suddenly gave way. A reaction of this kind at the beginning of the separation is spontaneously produced every night in sleep.

[4] This clarifies to some extent what is meant when in the literature we read about *receptacles* in which are deposited "iron filings." The various quantities of the substances, with their dosages, etc. refer in general to the inner science of the combination of spiritual states represented by metals or other substances.

[5] In Stobaeus, *Flor.*, 4.107, cf. Aristides, *Eleusis*, 256.

[6] Apuleius, *Métamorphoses*, 11.23.

[7] In the *Bardo Thödol* (*The Tibetan Book of the Dead*) trans. by Lama K. D. Samdup (London, 1927).

the phases of the detachment: losing the sense of Earth, and suddenly feeling the Void—being precipitated or dropped—finding oneself as if dissolved in a great sea or in a dizzying expansion of the Air.[8] And the Red Lion, that is, the irresistible and savage instinct of the animal ego's self-preservation, has to be "reduced to extreme weakness," in order to pass such trials and complete the final process of "mortification" and "separation."[9]

Everything said up to now enables us to understand a wide range of symbols and alchemical allegories that disguise similar experiences: birds with wings that carry other birds without wings in order not to "lose the ground under foot"; seas through which, one is carried to and fro; currents that one must swim against; falls, aerial captures, etc. We shall leave it to the sagacity of the reader who will find all this in the texts, to take it *sub specie interioritatis* and understand

---

[8] Cf. R. Steiner, *Das Initiatenbewußtsein* (Dornach, 1927), 64-69, 114-18, etc. A mysterious correspondence of Agrippa, concerning a neophyte who also wanted "to explore his abyss," gives this instruction: "Cast him out to test space and let him be carried on the wings of Mercury from the Austral to the Boreal Heavens"; (from the introduction to the Italian translation by A. Reghini of the *De occulta philosophia*, 1:xxvi).

[9] Philalethes (*Introitus apertus*, §25) speaks of a discipline "intended to strip the King of his golden vestments [meaning vulgar Gold] and to engage the Lion in such combat as to reduce him to extreme weakness . . . then the realm of Saturn appears. . . . There is no further sign of life in the mixture. This sad spectacle and image of eternal death is all the more agreeable for the Artist."

Twenty-Eight

the flight of the dragon

n addition to the difficulty of the "opening," in retaining consciousness and suppressing the reactions that would return one to the animal body, there is the danger of being overwhelmed by the experience itself, of failing to master the use of the "seed" or "subtle essence" of Gold, which we have to know how to extract and preserve: for it is like the bursting of a dam.[1] Everything that has been in a state of slavery and suspension as Mercury or fixed life, locked in the body, now, after the separation, finds itself in absolute freedom. This freedom is a necessary intermediary experience, and is a matter of determining up to what point the consciousness can support the unexpected change of state and actively transform itself so as to maintain a continuity, and to assimilate it precisely *as* liberation.

Anyone who has always dwelt in darkness, if suddenly subjected to a very brilliant light, could well be blinded. In the same way the fully liberated power of life could prove lethal to one who knows life only as a mixture of death and sleep.

It is because of this danger that the alchemists recommend our constantly taking care that the "subtle" not escape from its "vessel" and dissolve in the Air.[2] Bernard

---

[1] Ideographically, this is earth ▽̵ that unbinds and frees itself from immobility and thus we have ▽, the Waters.

[2] Cf. *CAG*, 2:151: "The operator needs a *subtle* understanding *in order to recognize the spirit which has exited from the body* if he is to make use of it and by surveying its guardianship, reach his goal— taking care that *when the body is destroyed, the spirit is not also destroyed at the same time.*

of Treviso explains it in these words: "This Fountain has a terrible power . . . terrifying because if it should become enflamed and furious it would engulf everything and if its waters were to escape we would be lost."[3] It is necessary to possess the dignity of that "King of the Land" in whose name alone, says the author, the Fountain is reserved and who, is so strongly fortified thereby that "none can conquer him." And so the already difficult trick of closing one's eyes and fearlessly letting whatever happens, happen, is complicated by another subtle and equal necessity: one must *kill* as well as be killed, and "fix" what is fleeting.

Flamel, in commenting on the eighth of his hieroglyphic images, in which we see a Red Man planting his foot on a winged lion who wants to carry him off and ravish him, says that this is the "Lion that devours all metallic nature [all individualized nature] and changes it into its own and true substance [nonindividualized, liberated]," and that can gloriously transport the Red Man beyond the waters of Egypt—that is, from the waters of corruption and forgetting.[4] We must awaken the force but not let it unseat us. The characteristic depiction of this ability is dramatized by the myth of Mithras who seizes the bull by the horns and does not let go despite the animal's mad stampede until the bull, exhuasted, gives up and allows himself to be led back to the "cavern" (the alchemical texts speak specifically and frequently of Mercury's *cavern*), where Mithras gives it death. After its death there follows the symbolic emerging of vegetation from the earth, sprouting from the blood of the sacrificed animal.

Basil Valentine agrees, using more complicated symbolism: "One who is curious to know what this 'All-in-Everything' is [said to be the goal of the Art] must give the Earth great Wings [equivalent to the flight of the Dragon, the stampede of the bull, the arousal of the Serpent, etc.], and must rise up and fly over the mountains, up to the firmament; then he must clip his wings by dint of fire, so that he falls into the Red Sea [here, fire and Red Sea are symbols of the intervention of the principle of affirmation], and drowns."[5]

But in the reciprocal killing and being killed, both natures are changed into one another, utterly interpenetrating. So that sometimes we speak of *union* and *sepa-*

The operator has consummated his task not when it has been destroyed, but when he has penetrated into the depths of the Metal."

[3] Bernard of Treviso, *Philosophie des métaux, BPC,* 2:388–89.

[4] Flamel, *Figures hiéroglyphiques, BPC* 2:259. The waters of Egypt also represent "the routine thoughts of mortals."

[5] B. Valentine, *Dodici chiavi,* 21. Pelagius (*CAG,* 3:260) says that "the dissolution in the divine Water is called *iosis because ios*—poison, active force, *virus*—resides in it potentially and then becomes active (the awakening and flight of the dragon).

ration as though they were synonyms.[6] We now find ourselves at one of the first phases of the formation of the hermetic Androgyne, composed of Sulfur and Mercury. The "two enemies" are embracing one another. The two serpents of the caduceus are intertwining themselves (male with female) around the rod of Hermes. In the Divine Water or Mercury of the Wise begins the *state of unity*, which is the true "First Matter" from which it is possible to obtain all the "Elements" and "Kingdoms" of the Great Work. But the work is arduous: "We must understand that we are in the midst of a terrible labor, trying to reduce to a common essence—that is, to wed—the two Natures [active to passive, individual to universal]."[7]

When the "black" has reached its limit, when immobility is complete, and when everything seems deprived of life and sound as in chaos or in "Tartarus"—then the Earth is known. But in this desert of death and darkness a splendor announces itself. It is the beginning of the second Kingdom, that of Jupiter who dethrones Black Saturn and is prelude to the White Moon. Dawn ("The Light of Nature") breaks. The water of death becomes the Water of Resurrection. Once the body has been dissolved and that darkness dissipated that (according to the Cosmopolite) represents the body to the human eye, and once the "pores" (gateways) have been opened—Nature begins to operate and the Spirit manifests itself in the metallic "congealed" body.[8]

This is the "White Opus," the *albedo*.

---

[6] This is *matrimony*—the action of the wingless dragon that carries along the one who has no wings, and who in turn returns the former to Earth (Pernety, *Dictionnaire*, 219). R. Lully says that the "black" is made of Sun and Moon, indicating an immediate union of the two so complete that in future they can no longer be separated. Concerning the dragon (here conceived as especially regal and celestial) and its flight, we can note that it constitutes a frequent enough symbol in Chinese esoterism. And there are, as well, particular analogies between the allegory of the Mithraic bull and the illustrations of esoteric Buddhism (cf. Evola, *Doctrine of the Awakening*).

[7] Zosimos, text in *CAG*, 2:217.

[8] In the words of the Cosmopolite, *Novum lumen chemicum*, 10, §50.

Twenty-Nine

Che ORY PACh
AnO
Che wec PACh

Before moving on to an examination of the hermetic symbols of the *albedo* we need to say a few words about the techniques for bringing about the experience. Essentially, there are two: we can proceed by directly provoking the detachment, such that *as a consequence*, the individual faculties conditioned by the body and brain are suspended and thereby the obstacle they constitute is overcome; or, we can proceed from said faculties, submitting them to an action, such that *as a consequence*, the possiblity of detachment and resurrection into Life are virtually assured.[1]

In the first case it is primarily the force of the liberated Waters that is used. In the second, however, it is that of the "Fire" or ego that acts upon itself. We can refer to the two ways respectively as the *wet path* and the *dry path*. In the terms of the secret hermetic language, in one path one is burnt by water, in the other, washed by fire; one liberates us from slavery by freeing the life principle ("Our Mercury"); in the other the principle of life liberates itself from slavery by its own

---

[1] This is not unrelated to what has been said in the *Livre de la miséricorde* (*CMA*, 3:182): "for the subtilization some employ external procedures and others penetrating procedures."

power. Among the many possible meanings of the two hermetic paths, dry and wet, the following predominate.[2]

In his *Liber singularis de alchimia* Barchusen says, among other things, that the dry path is characterized by the direct action of the naked "Fire" and by an absence of the "black," which expresses mortification. This is also associated with the method that employs the so-called *double Mercury*, which is androgynous or counterbalanced. "Some," says Salmon,[3] "use a simple Mercury [wet path]; others, like Bernard of Treviso, a more active double Mercury, obtained by stimulation, adding a vivifying Spirit to it, a Gold artificially prepared."

Symbolism aside, the absence of the "black" of which Barchusen speaks alludes to the possibility of working in a way that avoids crises, jerks, and abrupt changes, obtaining thereby as far as possible a continuous process of transformation: that is, by the use of a principle that is not only a Mercury having the raw power of life, but a Mercury that, being animated by a certain Gold brought to a given degree of purity (its "artificial" preparation), is now ready to participate in the double Nature that is the aim of the Work.

Ideographically, the succession of | , —, and | (see chapter 23) would not be obtained, but instead, the gradation of a "double substance" +, in which predominates the active principle whose starting point is in the waking consciousness (☉). The center of action then is not ☿, which is too far from the limit that ordinary consciousness can reach directly, but rather ☿. With this Mercury, which now contains the Fire within itself, it can go on subtilizing and purifying—without reaching the "black" first and then the "white," but having from the start a much higher degree of luminosity and a certain condition on which it can be made to work without the ascending and descending phases of separation, maintaining itself instead, always in full and active consciousness within the body and corporeal systems to which the different powers correspond.

In the dry path the difficulty is the overcoming of the barrier set up by the ordinary faculties with no further help than these same faculties, which—it cannot be denied—implies a special privilege, a kind of natural "dignity," or prior initiation. In the wet path, especially when the means used are violent and external, the greatest problem is to maintain the consciousness, which has been brusquely

---

[2] Among the methods indicated by the Greek alchemists to obtain the Mercury, those that proceed by desulfurization (ἐκθείειν) of cinnabar (sulfur of mercury, whose red color expresses here, in the familiar symbolism, the active and intellectual qualities of the ordinary personality), or by heating the metals with Vinegar (dissolvent), constitute the wet path. Those, on the other hand, who resort to preparations of nitre—νιτρέλαιον—belong to the other path. (The purifying power of niter ⊕ is indicated in Jeremiah 2:22).

[3] Introduction to *BPC*, cxi. Cf. Pernety, *Dictionnaire*, 34; equivalent to the double Mercury, the *hassem* of the Arabs, symbolic alloy of Gold and Silver, which is where we are directed to begin.

deprived of "fixed" support—the body. The difficulty in the dry path is all the greater when our sense of individuality has been more developed, with that predomination of the cerebral faculties so characteristic of Occidental modern man.

For ancient man, for the Oriental, and in general for every being whose mind is still open or semi-open to the noncorporeal world, the wet path has offered and continues to offer more immediate possibilities—owing to a lesser dependence of the deeper organic circuits on the control and fine tuning of the brain. On the other hand, in this case a supreme effort must be made if the accomplishment is to remain active and not fall into passive mystico-ecstatic states.[4]

In the dry path it is a matter, above all, of destroying by means of an appropriate, rigorous inner discipline, all the infections that the amalgam with the body has evoked and fixed in the subtler principles of life, and by means of which the body exercises its power over the superior nature. This requires asceticism and purification, but in an analogous spirit to that of a person who has carefully gathered all the necessary ingredients for a physical phenomenon to take place. Asceticism in this case is the equivalent of an exercise and a *technique:* that is why certain rules of life are prescribed that if carefully observed, result indirectly (passing through ☿) in certain modifications in the subtle elements of the human being that are propitious or indispensable to the Work.[5]

Thus, a hermetic master will not say that to feed an inclination, for example, toward concupiscence or hate is something "bad" (whoever wishes is free to do so), but that it is contradictory for a person to intend to indulge that freedom and at the same time aspire to anything that the direction of the energies set by greed or hate has made impossible.

And a hermetist will ask only that what is desired and the implications of that desire be well understood. Moreover, the full waking consciousness and the direct action of the ego are to be maintained in a clearly moral discipline, and when certain conditions and qualities of the Soul have been established and reduced to a *habitus* by virtue of constant practice, the corresponding modifications are transmitted from ☿ to ☿. Then, if the right path has been taken, one can better decide what is necessary as a favorable provision for the "separation."

---

[4] Cf. *Introduzione alla magia*, 2:352ff.; 3:16ff.

[5] The correspondences established by the esoteric Hindu teaching between the seven virtues and the seven passions and the seven centers of life—like those between other groups of moral qualities, positive and negative, and the currents (*nadī*) running out of each of them—may serve to provide a basis for the practical development of these ideas.

Thirty

ḣERMETIC ASCETICISM

n Greek alchemy we find the general conditions for the practice to be purity in heart and body as well as righteousness, dispassion, and the absence of greed, envy, and selfishness. "Whoever develops these qualities," says Lippman,[1] "is worthy, and only the worthy becomes a participant in the grace of The Above, whereupon in the deepest recesses of the soul, in true dreaming and visions, his intellect opens to the comprehension of the Great Mystery of the Egyptian Priests—which they communicated only orally (or enigmatically, so as to disarm the demons)—and turns the Sacred Art into child's play. And Zosimos says: "Repose the body and calm the passions; if you yourself control yourself in this way, you will attract the divine essence to you."[2] "Be ye pure of women," a Syrian text teaches, "cleansed of every spiritual and bodily defect and make a vow of good will."[3]

Others[4] demand a wise and penetrating genius, a body in which nothing is lacking to enable one to operate with a sound judgment and subtle, though natural spirit, free of every tortuosity and impediment. In an Alexandrian papyrus one is

---

[1] E. O. Lippman, *Entstehung über Ausbreitung der Alchemie* (Berlin, 1919), 34.

[2] *CAG*, 2:84

[3] *CMA*, 2:1.

[4] Arnold of Villanova, *Rosarium*, 1, §5; R. Lully, *Theor. test.*, 31.

put on guard against the demon Ophiochus who "puts obstacles in our path . . . now producing negligence, now fear, now the unexpected, and in some cases punishments and afflictions, with the sole purpose of forcing us to abandon the Work."[5] According to Geber,[6] the obstacles arise either from the natural organic weakness of the operator or from the fact that the "spirit is too full of fantasies and passes easily from one opinion to the opposite; or because he doesn't know exactly what he wants and cannot decide." The secret chemic language also frequently expresses the duty of creating a perfect balance between all the "rectifications" (or principles of purified and strengthened being); a balance allowing the attainment of a *center* in the Self, which is the only place the operation can begin.[7]

In modern authors we can find analogous prerequisites: a great physical and intellectual equilibrium; the state of perfect neutrality such balance augurs; a healthy body, without appetites or desires, being at peace with oneself and others and with the things around one; making oneself absolute master of the animal envelope in order to make of it an obedient servant to the psychodynamic authority that must purify itself of every obstacle; to liberate whatever may be necessary.[8]

Eliphas Levi repeatedly warns that we must make use of every hour and moment; we must rid the will of any dependency and accustom it to domination; we must become absolute master of the self, learn how to deny the call of pleasure, hunger, and sleep and be unmoved by success or failure. Life must be given over to the will directed by one thought and served by the entire nature to *submit in every organ to the spirit*, and by sympathy to all universal forces corresponding to them. All the faculties and senses must participate in the Work; nothing must be left inactive. The genuine spirit must have secured itself against all danger of hallucination and terror, and so find us purified inwardly and outwardly.[9] The ancient teaching was that the Art engages the whole man—*ars totum requirit hominem*. The first condition, says Dorn, is the integration of oneself: "to become one." "Never look outside for what you need, until you have made use of the whole of yourself."[10]

---

[5] Leiden papyrus X, in Berthelot, *Introduction*, 19.

[6] Geber, *Summa*, in *BCC*, 1:520, and *BPC*, 1:90.

[7] Cf. Geber, *Livre des balances* (*CMA*, 2:147): "The balance of the natures is indispensible to the Science of Equilibrium and the practice of the Work."

[8] So Kremmerz describes the hermetic preparation in *La Porta Ermetica* (Rome, 1905); *Avviamento alla scienza dei magi* (Spoleto, 1929); *Commentarium*, nos. 4-5, 6-7 (1921).

[9] E. Levi, *Dogma and Ritual of High Magic* (1921), 243-45, 264, 271, 279-80.

[10] *Physica Trithemii* in *Theatrum chemicum*, 1:472. [This quotation from Dorn appeared in an earlier edition of *The Hermetic Tradition*: "*Ex aliis numquam usum facies quod quaeris nisi prius ex te fiat unum.*"—Trans.]

The alchemists teach that the impurities, in addition to being of Earth (the body), are also due to Fire, and that we must remove, not just the dirt, but the *combustible parts* from the substances.[11] These are the instinctive and impulsive elements of the personality: animosity, irascibility, fiery passion—all the forms of vulgar and impure Sulfur deriving from the bodily nature.[12] We have seen, in fact, that the subtle human form, the body-life mediator between Soul and Body, consists of two elements, one subject to the telluric influences ☿, and the other to the sulfurous influences ☿: purification requires the neutralization of both influences, and for that a preparation is necessary that reduces the terrestrial as well as the combustible. For amplification of these ideas we can refer to Geber and Albertus Magnus, who have more fully expressed them, although always in the usual evasive cipher language.[13]

In general two kinds of impurity, "leprosies," or infirmities of the "metals" are to be distinguished: one called original, curable only by effective separation (from the condition of the body); and the other elemental and quadripartite, is immediate material for work on the dry path. Negative qualities are to be stabilized within the spirit analogous to the four Elements; and for their treatment is prescribed a kind of conversion from one into the other. The superfluous Water will be dried and activated by the Fire; the (vulgar) Fire weakened to the point of being incapable of combustion or "viper attacks," whatever change of state may take place—then it must be congealed and reduced to the subtle and corrosive virtue of

---

[11] Geber, *Summa*, 1, §4; and in the proem: "What is cast off by imperfect bodies and without which they cannot receive perfection, is . . . useless Sulfur and impure earth."

[12] Cf. Pernety (*Dictionnaire*, 245-46): "Sulfur external, dry and separable from the true substance of the metals [i.e., of the vulgar ego] suffocates the inner and deprives it of its activity; and mixing its own impurities with those of Mercury [as ☿] produces the imperfect metals"

[13] Geber, *Summa*, 3, §§1, 2 (*BCC*, 540, 541): "Sulfur or Arsenic (bearing always in mind the [Greek] homonymy in which arsenic signifies virility), which it resembles, have in themselves the same two causes of corruption and impurity. One is the inflammable substance, and the other the *faex* (dregs) or earthly impurities." The dregs—he adds—impede the fusion and penetration (which is the solution of the fixed, in order to reach that for which the fixed constitutes an impediment); the inflammable substance cannot sustain the Fire (the emotions, the impulses, and turmoils proceeding from the depths) and in consequence cannot confer the fixation (that is, maintain the domination on the part of the ego as *incombustible Sulfur*). The Mercury also has two forms of impurity: an earthly impure substance (the body) and a superfluous and volatile humidity or fluidity (desire or instability) that is evaporated in the Fire, but without burning (it is the dissolution in the negative sense in the act of separation, where on the contrary there must intervene an active, i.e., inflammatory quality). Albertus Magnus (*Compositum de compositis*, §1) speaks of Sulfur's modes of existence, two of which constitute impurities (combustible and liquid), while that of the third is separated from the others and preserved: "*rectified* by resolution, it yields only *a pure substance containing in itself the active* [perfectable] *force* nearest to the metal." The central nucleus (☉ or ♃) of the operator is unveiled.

Water;[14] the Earth quality, made "porous" and subtilized, must be converted into Air; finally, the ungraspable, diffused and mobile Air quality must be coagulated and fixed in one solid property like that of Earth.

Geber submits, on this basis, actual details and procedures of value as "medicines" for each of the seven metals.[15] There is a whole series of suggestions that indicate adaptations, dispersals, readaptations, and transformations of psychic powers and actions that, correspondingly, the spirit must execute upon itself. The discipline is applied to the senses, the will, and thought, from top to bottom, in the dry path.

The inner and outer asceticism fortifies and simplifies the ego principle; this greater force, which has been awakened in the center, reacts on thought and imagination, subjugating them, controlling them against all the influences they endure while passing through the lower and dark side of the unconscious. This mental control acts in turn on the sufferings and appetites, tranquilizes the innermost being, cleansing, brightening, and subtilizing the perceptions. So, through ☿, the path to the I ☉ is opened as far as ☿. If no further hindrances or obstacles can be found in the mind, heart, or sensibilities, when every reason for alteration or disturbance has been removed, its action can proceed to the Mercury or life principle immediately after contact with the body ☿, and through the isolation of the peripheral sensitivity, attempt to obtain the separation and extraction. Then, beyond the progression of the aforementioned equivalent states in the common man—sleep, dream, and lethargy—at the very last the light will appear.

---

[14] Cf. *Livre de El Habir* (CMA, 3:105): "How can weakness constrain the strong? This is possible because the weakness is so only in appearance—tested, it proves strong, stronger than anything that appears strong. . . . That which resists the Fire is strong only in appearance, while the other, which is volatile and seems so weak, is actually the stronger." We should recall here what Lao-tzu said concerning the analogy with the subtle and invincible virtue of water.

[15] Geber, *Summa*, 3, §§1, 5, 9, 10, 12. The seven metals can also be interpreted as symbols of characteristic human types, to each of which is adapted, according to its own nature, a specific medicine and method.

Thirty-One

CHE PATH OF
CHE BREATH AND
CHE PATH OF
CHE BLOOD

We hesitate to mention one of the practices used in the initiatory schools as the fulcrum for making the potential separation into an actual one. The reason we avoid it is that it is not possible to draw it directly out of the hermetico-alchemical texts, which speak constantly about the regimen of Fire—that is to say, the dosage and inner conduction of the spiritual force in the Work—but are silent about the means of accomplishing this. (What might seem to allude to this refers strictly to chemical symbolism and tells us very little.) Mirrors and other objects, however, have served in magic as devices for fixating or neutralizing consciousness and objective perception by means of the visual sense for separation and contact with the ethereal light.[1] In Hindu yoga special forms of mental concentration are used, sometimes assisted by symbols or adapted magical formulas. Other schools use different methods, but we must always bear

---

[1] For the technique of the "mirror," see *Introduzione alla magia*, 1:85ff.

in mind that all of these are simply aids or stimuli for an act of the spirit.

The fact that ☿ is the point of departure for the dry path, and that therefore ☿ manifests in the organism through the respiratory and blood system, will suffice to enable us to glimpse two keys and two points of leverage for those who understand. On the other hand, we already know the importance that respiration (more directly controllable by the ego than the blood system) has in Hindu esotericism, as it did in ancient Egypt: the concentration on the subtle force hidden in the breath (*prāna*), according to the yogic teaching, constitutes a way of achieving and "purifying" the ☿. But alchemy itself is not lacking in allusions to this possibility. The *De pharmaco catholico*, for example, teaches us that Mercury is specifically supported in the lungs by means of the element of Air—which "pervades and penetrates, like the spirit, the other two principles, Salt and Sulfur, that is, Body and Soul, and that it unites both, firmly linked by natural heat";[2] after which it is not difficult to understand on what the "Fire" has to act in seeking to undo and alter said union.

Passing to the second key (which in certain methods is a further development of the first), this is acquired by concentrating on the *blood*, which can be attained by the sense of body heat. In this respect, the hermetic allusions are more frequent in expressions that are to be understood simultaneously as real and symbolical.

The Arab authors have spoken of a "decomposition that by gentle Fire transforms the nature into a *blood*."[3] And Morienus says: "The perfection of the Mastery consists in taking the united bodies . . . Now it is the *blood* that principally and strongly binds the bodies; because it vivifies and unites with them."[4] And Pernety: "The solution, dissolution and resolution are truly all one with subtilization. The means for achieving it according to the Art is a mystery that the Philosophers reveal only to those whom they judge qualified to be initiates. *It cannot be realized—they say—except in its own blood*"; blood that the same author relates to the "Aqua Nostra, which composes our own bodies."[5] "In the three solutions of which I speak," says the *Hermetic Triumph*,[6] "Male and Female, Body and Spirit, are no other than the Body and the *Blood* . . . The solution [in the sense of] the Body in its own *blood* is the solution of the masculine by the feminine and that of the Body by its Spirit. . . . You will try in vain to make the perfect solution of the body, *if you do not return the stream of its own blood back*

---

[2] *De pharmaco catholico*, 5, §1. Cf. *Introduzione alla magia*, 3:11. Still more explicit is Pernety, *Dictionnaire*, 6, and *Fables*, 1:96.

[3] *CMA*, 3:110.

[4] *Entretiens*, BPC, 2:97.

[5] Pernety, *Dictionnaire*, 467.

[6] *Triomphe Hermétique*, 283

to it, which is its natural menstruum, its Woman and its Spirit together, that to which it is united so tightly as to constitute nothing less than one and the same substance."

Dorn[7] says, "From the pale body we separate with the *blood*, this Soul, which is such a prize for us that we consider all bodies vile"; and for Braccesco, the incorruptible and quintessential Materia that we must extract from the corrupted elements is drawn from human blood;[8] and in the *Great Book of Nature*, the *tinctura microcosmi magistere* is explained as "human blood for making the lamp of life."[9] Finally, in Artephius the "Water that changes Bodies into Spirits, stripping them of their corporeal grossness," the "Sanguinary Stone" and the "power of the *Spiritual Blood*, without which nothing can be made," all go together.[10]

The symbol of the crossing of the Red Sea, likewise employed in hermetism,[11] can be introduced into this same order of allusions: especially if we recall that in some gnostic schools, whose symbols we have drawn parallels with those in hermetics on several occasions, it was taught that "to come out of Egypt means to come out of the Body" and "to cross the Red Sea is to cross the Waters of corruption, Waters that are nothing less than Chronos," explaining that "that which Moses calls Red Sea is the *Blood*," and declaring with authority that "in the blood flashes the flaming sword barring access to the Tree of Life."[12]

So we come to the idea of an operation and transformation that is found in the subtle principle of the blood by virtue of the Art, whose sense once more appears

---

[7] G. Dorn, *Clavis*, 3, §14.

[8] Braccesco, *Espositione*, fol. 77b.

[9] *Trad.*, 120; cf. 117. Here we must keep in mind the traditional initiate's symbol of light as the "life" of the body.

[10] *Livre d'Artephius*, BPC 2:128. On reading that this is also "the living Water that irrigates the Earth to make it germinate," one is spontaneously reminded by way of this spiritual blood, of that other spilled by the dead bull of Mithras, which on falling to earth produces the same effect. Cf. *Livre de El Habir* (*CMA*, 3:92): "It is important for you to know the power of this eternal water . . . because its power is that of the spiritual blood. When introduced into the body . . . it transforms the body into spirit as it is mixed with it, and both things then become one . . . The body which has given birth to the Spirit becomes spiritual and takes on the color of blood." Cf. also Della Riviera (*Mondo magico*, 60-1): "And as the blood is the seat of the vital spirits, thereby it contains in itself the spiritual life of everything. It is this blood that Orpheus is talking about in the *Lapidary*, when he says that the blood of Saturn fallen to earth, is congealed in Stone: these words contain, and perfectly embrace, both natural magics, that is, the theoretical and the practical at the same time . . . It stands to reason, we read qabalistically, that the *magical blood* provides us with the health of the vital spirits; because it contains said quintessence . . . Moreover, this blood is called the Milk of the Virgin, the Virgin being understood as the Moon."

[11] Bernard of Treviso, in his *Sogno verde* (Green Dream), speaks of a sea, red for being of *blood*. In it floats an island having seven kingdoms, whither the author is transported by a whirlwind.

[12] In Hippolytus, *Philosophumena*, 5.16; 6.15, 17.

to be a repetition of the "heroic" adventure. Boehme, after declaring that the Fire of human life resides in the blood, speaks of a second blood that must be introduced into the choleric human blood and into the fire of death (created by the "Fall") in order to extinguish it.[13] All this must be connected to the "Red Lion" who is to be brought to exhaustion; with that *ios* or *virus* that is a red *rust*, negatively speaking, that must be taken out of the copper; with the birth of the Son that in a little while will acquire form and surpass the father (the operator who has produced him), breaking the igneous essence that is the head of the Serpent, and passing through the death by fire;[14] with the liberation of the "tenebrous spirit" full of vanity and softness which, "when it dominates the bodies, prevents them from receiving the whiteness";[15] with the greed of Mercury that it is necessary to destroy and of which it has been said: "The cleansing is an appetite that feeds on itself . . . and produces in the Four Elements [of man] an *analogous spirit*, with the boiling saltpeter whose principle is the humid element."[16]

---

[13] Boehme, *De signatura*, 11, §10

[14] Ibid., 4, §24

[15] Comarius, text in *CAG*, 2:296.

[16] Boehme, *De signatura*, 13, §34; 14, §47. When it is said that all vegetative life, that is, ☿, consists of *desire* (*De signatura*, 6, §1), it refers to that infection transmitted by the lunar principle whence elemental greed is derived and the blind instinct of preserving the animal body. We may also recall by this the *eros*, which according to Plotinus (*Enneads*, 3.5.7), is engendered by the reflection of the "good" in this world, mistaken as the good in oneself.

che heart and
che Light

A s in physiology, so in hermetism: the heart and the blood are connected to one another, and the transformations and evacuations of the blood are centralized in the heart. At the center of the elemental cross as at the center of the Body in the "white" work, the heart is where the "life-bestowing light of the Quintessence" appears.

Let us attend to Gichtel: "The Work takes place in the *heart* and here the gateway to the heavens [i.e., to the occult states] is most violently attacked. The soul seeks to withdraw its will from the outer constellation in order to turn to God at its center; abandoning all senses and passing through the eighth form of Fire [which lies beyond the lower septenary and hence marks the boundary between the natural exterior world and the intelligible inner world—see chapter 15], which requires a relentless effort, the sweating of blood [the 'Herculean task' of 'separation'], because the soul must now struggle against God [in order to maintain itself and not 'be dissolved' in the light] and it must struggle at the same time against man [in order to overcome the human condition]."[1] The same author says that "the life of the Soul rises out of the eternal inner fire," which has its center in the heart and is swallowed up by "the fiery Dragon"; he speaks of a Holy Life of Light, hidden, inactive, and invisible to ordinary men, but when it is awakened it annuls

---

[1] Gichtel, *Theosophia practica*, 2 §5; introduction, §8; 1, §53

the dark Fire, producing in the innermost heart a spiritual light so bright that it breaks the chains forged by the ancient Dragon around the Solar principle.[2] This light, according to Gichtel, is ultimately related to Water and to the Woman, the Virgin, Sophia (= Wisdom), which "drags the Soul completely out of the Body and makes it cross a sea of fiery water,"[3] whose correspondence with Bernard of Treviso's Sea of Blood, and with the symbol of the Red Sea, is obvious.

Also for the Cosmopolite, Water is found in the center of the heart of the symbolic metals.[4] In the *Book of Clemency* the inner voice that manifests as a revelatory vision declares "I am the light of thy pure and dazzling heart."[5] And in the *Corpus Hermeticum* one is exhorted to be sober and "open the eyes of the heart,"[6] which can be compared to intellectual rebirth—νοεμὰ γένεσις—the equivalent of the rebirth from the Water or from the Virgin and is completed in the awakening of the consciousness belonging to the "middle place" (see pages 82-83).

In any case, the agreement of the hermetic teachings on this point with that of other initiatic teachings is clear. In the Upanishads, for example, it is said that the union of the two gods—the right-hand god, who is the flame, and the left-hand goddess, who is the light—into an androgyne is accomplished in an "ethereal space of the heart"; wherein "the spirit maintained by knowledge, all light, all immortality," by "the seer unseen, the knower unknown," shines in man at the interior of the heart. For the heart is the dwelling place of the spirit, where—at the breaking of the chains of every bodily thing in the state of sleep—it becomes light itself.[7] Purusha, the "Inner Man," vigilant over the sleepers (the "perennial guard"), the

---

[2] Ibid., 2, §§6, 12, 13, 51, 54. Cf. Boehme, (*Aurora*, 25, §98; 11, §§68, 70): "Heaven is hidden in the heart"; "The gates of Heaven are opened in my spirit; whereupon the spirit sees the divine and celestial being, not outside the body—but in the bubbling wellspring of the heart the *lightning* strikes, releasing its flash in the *sensitivity* of the brain, where the spirit contemplates . . . for the flash begins in the heart and rises up to the brain, through the seven fountain-spirits, as though it were *dawn*, and this is the goal and the enlightenment."

[3] Gichtel, *Theosophia practica*, §§98, 99. Gichtel, in describing the experience, says: "Suddenly my spirit received an impact and I fell to earth." (3, §50), which would be interesting to compare with the expressions concerning the *death of the heart* that figure in the secret language of the so-called Fideli d'Amore: in the *Vita Nuova*, "Love" awakens the sleeping "Lady" and gives her Dante's *heart* to eat—and in Lapo Gianni, when the "Woman" appears bringing "health," "the heart that was living, dies." (Cf. L. Valli, *Il linguaggio segreto*, 159, 277); cf. the hermetic maxim, "Kill the living, resuscitate the dead."

[4] *Novum lumen chemicum*, 4, §24. Dante (*Vita Nuova*, 2) speaks of "the Spirit . . . that dwells in the most secret chamber of the heart."

[5] *CMA*, 3:135.

[6] *Corpus Hermeticum*, 4.2; 7.1.

[7] *Brihadaranyaka-Upanishad*, 4.2.2-3; 2.5.10; 4.3.7-9; 2.1.15. In the final passage, the spirit that has passed into the state corresponding to sleep, and which is called "Great King Soma of the white robe," can be compared to the hermetic *albedo*.

"intelligible, sleepless nature" is the true light and ambrosia: he who has been extracted from the body like a dagger from its sheath, takes his "permanent dwelling place in the heart."[8]

The relationship established by this tradition between the seat of the heart as the Dominator and to the "dike that contains the worlds within certain limits, so they do not fall back into chaos,"[9] is reflected in the qabalistic expression: "The heart in the organism is like a king at war."[10] On the other hand, the association in the Qabalah, as in some Christian medieval manuscripts, between the heart and symbolic "palaces" or "temples,"[11] can throw light on the places wherever we find these same symbols used in the hermetic tradition.

We can also refer to the general traditional doctrine according to which at the moment of death, or mortal danger, or extreme terror, all the vital energy diffused throughout the body rushes to the heart, whose corona begins to radiate with a supernatural light, through which the spirit "escapes."[12] This said, it is enough to remember that in principle the process of initiation is the same process that in others produces death. This reconfirms the link between the center of the heart and the "place" where the new development will occur, the place wherein the initiate will reach the "triumphal death" that wins immortality and recovers the possession of the "Tree" and the "Woman." Once the chains of the heart that "keep the unregenerated from seeing the light" have been broken and contact has been established with that for which the heart is a symbolic correspondence in the physical organism, an uprooting takes place, a subtilization, a breakthrough, an illumination in the sensation of the blood by which is obtained that "spiritual blood," without which, Artephius says, nothing is possible. It is the androgynous Mercury par excellence who, on the dry path, has the power of the "Living Water to irrigate the earth and make it germinate."

---

[8] *Kathā-Upanishad*, 2.5.8; 2.6.17. Cf. *Bhagavad-Gita*, 15.15; 13.17.

[9] *Brihadaranyaka-Upanishad*, 4.4.22.

[10] Cf. for example, Bonaventura, *Vitis mystica*, chap. 3; John Chrysostom, *Homilies*, 84.9; Zohar, 1.65; and the words, as well, of Milarepa (from *Vie de Milarepa*, trans. J. Bacot, 141, 173, 226): "I kneel down . . . in the mountain monastery that is my body, in the temple of my breast, at the summit of the triangle of my heart." "In the desert grotto [cf. the cavern of Mercury" and the "cavernous" chamber of the heart], I shall transform the transmigration in liberation. In the monastery of thy body—thy strong soul will be the temple wherein are reunited the gods joined by illumination"; ". . . the holy palace that is the region of the pure idea" [cf. the "palace of the king" of Philalethes].

[11] *Sepher Yetzirah*, chap. 7.

[12] Cf. Agrippa, *De occulta philosophia*, 3:37; *Brihadaranyaka-Upanishad*, 4.3.8; 4.1.2.

Thirty-Three

DENUDATIONS AND ECLIPSES

To a certain degree, the work of asceticism and purification is also a condition for the "wet path" by way of "preparation." It so happens that every psychic element remaining after the "separation" acquires the capacity to transform the most profound powers that manifest themselves. We encounter them polarized according to their nature. So, if the appropriate preparation has not eliminated the dregs of the passions, sensations, inclinations, and irrational complexes tenaciously rooted in the penumbra below consciousness, the result will be an inordinate empowerment of all these elements, which will then be transformed into so many different channels through which will violently course elemental energies never before imagined. Hence the saying: "Fire increases the virtue of the wise and the corruption of the perverse."[1] In the field of cognition all vision will be deformed, obscured, or falsified, if not replaced by mere hallucinatory projections of subjective impulses and complexes with repercussions in the organic functions. Every danger that can overload the circuit with a high voltage that will limit resistance and the capacity for transformation is concentrated in the force field.

All this must be expected if the "mortification" has been insufficiently rigorous. For this reason, the alchemists exhort us to beware of the rosy and golden colors that may appear *after* the black but *before* the white: they indicate a residue of the

---

[1] *Livre de la clémence, CMA*, 3:136.

ego quality (in the negative sense, as human ego in the animal body), that may alter the experience to follow; the true red color (active reaffirmation) must appear *after* the white, as only in the white can the new condition of existence be reached.[2]

On this subject Della Riviera says that it could happen that, once the Vulture of the dry and arid Earth[3] has obtained a part of the "virgin's milk reserved for feeding the delicate, newborn infant," marvels and astonishments take place: "Eclipses, new darkness, furious winds, hurricanes and venemous breezes, which may cause you to think that they are neither infusion of the Soul nor an illumination of the Body, but death and destruction for both." Only after the heavens return to calm, will the earth depart from night, green and flowering: and the symbolic Child, divested of his many-colored garments, will assume a pure white attire, "symbol of celestial purity"—the *albedo*—after which will follow the royal purple and imperial sceptre.[4] Andreae also mentions an unleashed wind and a darkening of the Moon,[5] and Philalethes points out the malignity of Air (in the no-longer earthly state) and the formation of dark clouds that are cleared by the Waters (purified) up to the lunar whiteness.[6]

The Greek alchemists mention magical conjurations—δαιμονοκλησύαι—that they use for paralyzing the demons that might wish to prevent the divine Water from transmuting Copper into Gold;[7] demons that, aside from possible references to effective operations of ceremonial magic, have the same symbolic value as the onrush of unclean animals to drink the blood of the bull struck by Mithras. Only by scaring them off does the miracle of vegetation continue, which said blood causes to spring from the Earth.[8] In the hermetic interpretation of the classical myths this is the labor that Hercules must fulfill by killing the Harpies, black birds

---

[2] R. Bacon, *Speculum alchimiae*, §6; cf. Albertus Magnus (*Compositum de compositis*, §5): "Whiten ye the black earth before adding the fermentation [the active, or red, principle] . . . Sow ye your Gold in the White[ned] Earth."

[3] This *vulture*, hidden in the Earth, that is in the Body, can be compared to the Promethean myth: it is the stolen, or *infinite* Fire (in hermetism the soul is called Prometheus as often as *infinite*), converted into the principle of *thirst* that consumes man in his fall, when he finds himself chained to the rock or Stone that is "fixed" in the body, and deprived of the Living Water. The "Vulture that shrieks from the mountaintop" is a frequent allegory in alchemical texts. Symbolically, the mountain expresses the highest state that can be attained while remaining on "Earth," and the Vulture of the Mountain aspires to fly into the Air and promises the supreme prize to the one who suffers him and restores to him the "liquor" (d'Espagnet).

[4] Della Riviera, *Mondo magico*, 90-92.

[5] J. V. Andreae, *Chemical Wedding*, chap. 5.

[6] Philalethes, *Introitus appertus*, §6.

[7] *CAG*, 2:397.

[8] F. Cumont, *Les mystères de Mithra*, 137-38.

rising out of the separation, "rapacious spirits unleashed in the magical world";[9] and it is also the extermination of every last one of the armed warriors who, in the myth of Jason, are born on the Field of Mars, where the extracted teeth of the Dragon have been sown.[10]

Finally, in mystical terms, Gichtel speaks of the danger that appears at the moment when the power of the Virgin is transmitted to the "Igneous Soul," because this last may then depart from humility and equanimity and fall back in love with itself, turning thereby into an egotistic and puffed-up demon. Nor can the Virgin help because her husband (the Soul) can neither be liberated nor dissolved, but always becomes only more fiery and exalted, and repels anything that is not fire; so that Sophia retreats into her principle of Light and darkens the fire of the soul, which thereupon falls into the state of "sin."[11]

It is a matter then of allusions to what can be derived from the dregs and elements that have not been reduced to "ashes" (such that they can no longer be "rekindled") that have been left behind when the deeper forces emerge from the ☿ life, reinforcing and multiplying—and being unable to stop reinforcing and multiplying—everything they encounter. In the wet path, the separation would not take place until there is nothing left but the pure ego principle to be invested and transported. On the dry path this would be when this same principle has reduced its own nature to a "quintessence" of all the superior ☿ faculties, suitably equilibrated and purified.

We might, at this point, recall the disconcerting caveat that Andreae issues concerning the "trial of the balance"—which indicates precisely in what sense the polarization of the power, by virtue of the greater "weight," is produced. He said, "You must know that, no matter what path you have chosen, by virtue of an immutable destiny you may not abandon your decision and go back without running into the greatest peril of your life. . . . If you have not purified yourself completely, the wedding will be for ill." And in the moment of trial he warns; "If anyone now in this company is not completely sure of himself, he should quickly depart . . . because better is it to flee than to take on what is beyond one's strength."[12]

In this sense, apart from the differences between paths, the texts are in accord about the necessity for a preparation of the substances. In the Work no substances will be utilized as they are, but only prepared (whittled down) substances. A

---

[9] Della Riviera, *Mondo magico*, 105. Cf. *Filum Ariadnae*, 26.

[10] Cf. Pernety, *Fables*, 457-79. The myth also provides the remedy: we must make such soldiers fight and destroy one another, *without ourselves entering into the battle*. Cf. Evola, *The Yoga of Power*, 175.

[11] Gichtel, *Theosophia practica*, 2, §§66, 67, 70; cf. 6, §§45, 46.

[12] Andreae, *Chemical Wedding*, 1,§4; 2,§15.

recurrent theme in alchemy is "getting rid of the heterogeneous parts": everything that is not itself or that is an irrational interference of one faculty with another.

A second theme is the *denudation*, which extracts and isolates the useful elements. The initiate's use of the symbol of "nudity," on the other hand, is traditional.[13] We must, nevertheless, emphasize two different understandings of the hermetic "garments" and their "stripping": the first refers precisely to the ascetic preparation, to the innermost simplification of the soul which, while the general conditions of the human state of existence remain, must be returned to itself; the second refers to a plane of *reality* and corresponds to the separation, understood as the putting into action of the consciousness and the power underneath its garments that now represent the conditions of the same general human corporeality.

---

[13] For example, Philo of Alexandria (*Leg. alleg.* §15) calls the "naked" those who, "abandoning the life of death and participating in immortality," are the only ones who "contemplate the ineffable mysteries." The renouncing of the possession of "clothes" and "ornaments" can be equivalent to the precept of *poverty*, which then is elevated to an initiatory meaning. In a gnostic testament we find an important connection between nudity and spiritual virility—*ios* or *vīrya*—relative to the "Gate of Heaven," "reserved only for pneumatic men." "On entering, they cast off their clothes and become bridegrooms, having obtained the virility [read βαλεῖν and not λαβεῖν] of the Virgin Spirit" in which the Mercury in "white" is easily recognizable (Hippolytus, *Philosophumena*, 5.8). Cf., also, Plotinus (*Enneads*, 1.6.7): "Those who ascend by the rungs of the sacred Mysteries are purified and drop their vestments which had covered them, and go forth naked."

Thirty-Four

the thirst for god and the corrosive waters

We have said that after the preparation and whittling down, the essence of the wet path consists in directly provoking, artificially or violently, the separation so that it is not ego (Gold) that is to liberate Life (Mercury), but it is Life that must liberate the ego and cure its leprosy.

For that we may employ the technique of elevating the forces of the same desire to an abnormal intensity, but directed elsewhere. The premise in this case is set forth by Boehme, who says that "hunger" is the principle both of corporeal birth and of rebirth, being that which impels toward the body and impels toward eternity.[1]

Hence Gichtel says, "Everything comes down to the conversion of our Soul and the direction of our 'desire' inwardly, to desire and never cease desiring God until Sophia and the Holy Spirit meet the desire . . . The perpetual "hunger" of the obsolete body serves as fertilizing manure: it exhausts everything to the point of disgust and anguish until it is constrained to turn to the Father."[2] He

---

[1] Boehme, *De signatura*, 15, §51.

[2] Gichtel, *Theosophia practica*, 1, §25; 3, §26

continues with some interesting technical allusions: "The magical or magnetic desire of the soul's will is the architect and creator of what the soul has conceived in its imagination, that is, of the noble and gentle Light of God[3] . . . Under the powerful desire of prayer, the soul is enflamed with a clear light, which triumphantly causes the celestial Virgin to ascend . . . The Fire [of the inner man in desire] swallows up this celestial presence of the Light, which the soul *imagines yearningly*, attracts to itself and makes manifest—then burns clearly, producing, in the heart, a beautiful, clear Light."[4] Here images work as "transformers" in a transcendent sense, with regard to states of deep emotion concentrated in the release of the fire of desire.

In the *Book of Ostanes* we find: "When the love for the Magnum Opus penetrated my heart and the work's preoccupation drove sleep from my eyes; when its preoccupation kept me from eating and drinking to the point of emaciating my body and I appeared to be in an alarming state, prayer and fasting finally delivered me" to what followed. In the form of a vision, as the first of a series of experiences the author speaks of a being who leads the alchemist to seven doors, just as Gichtel says God introduced his spirit into the seven centers.[5]

Cyliani speaks of the state in which "one has lost everything and has no more hope" and when "life is a reproach and death a duty"[6]—in the same way *sui juris non esse* [based on some law outside oneself] the disgust for the world, death of the free will, hastiness to renounce, total submission, and faith, of which the mystics speak, can themselves be considered useful and practical elements for the Work, if one lacks the capacity to make the separation oneself (the dry path) but still longs for the supernal, having the center of self in the "Waters," in the viscous "Soul," in which the self must be used up.[7]

On the other hand, we already know that all this can be justified hermetically only by the standard of the very real effects that can follow initiation, and not by moral or religious values; so, if the results are the same, we can also turn to other methods, which to the eyes of the profane may present quite a different character.

---

[3] More technically Boehme (*De signatura*, 8, §6) writes: "The oily quality only exercises its vivifying faculty when it is compressed in the anguish of death, which agitates and exalts it. Seeking to flee, it escapes and thereby creates the vegetative life," that is, the symbolic growth of ☿ equivalent to Sophia and "Light."

[4] Gichtel, *Theosophia practica*, 4, §42; 8.

[5] Ibid., 6, §43; 3, §66; 4, §8.

[6] Cyliani, *Hermès dévoilé* (rev. ed., Paris, 1925), 23.

[7] So, if the process continues, we can grasp the idea that the subsequent change of state may be interpreted as the *grace* of the mystics.

Such may be the violent forms of orgiastic ecstasy among the Cybellenes, Dionysians, or Maenads, who, under certain conditions, are brought to self-transcendence and violence to themselves by evoking elemental forces.[8] We can refer further to what in hermetism are called Corrosive Waters (or poison), in the special sense of substances capable of artificially provoking the dissociation between different elements of the human composition. The texts, nevertheless, either advise against the use of these waters and "violent Fires," or recommend the utmost precaution because, they say, they burn rather than wash; they dissolve bodies but cannot save spirits; they work not with the "slow fire of nature" but with the "impatient haste that proceeds from the Devil." Their action is abrupt and discontinuous—so the difficulty of keeping them active in the changing state is all the greater.

In this order of things, Greek texts have indicated the use of magic herbs—βοτάναι. For the most part, we must refer to the ancient traditions concerning the "sacred" or "immortality-conferring" drinks, like the *soma* of the Vedas, the *haoma* of the Iranians, the mead of the *Eddas* and even wine itself.

Originally it was a question of symbols: the holy drink was the Ether of Life, the principle of exaltation and inner regeneration, which to come into contact with was for man a much likelier possibility in the beginning than it was in later times. For the tradition maintains that at a certain point in time, such a drink ceased to be "known" and something else was substituted for it, which was no longer just a symbol, but a real drink composed of substances adapted to produce a psychophysical state constituting a favorable condition for the spirit to be able to realize the true and immaterial *soma, haoma,* etc. In the hermetic use of the βοτάναι one of these artificial means to reach an exaltation or inebriation was probably thought to be a means of arriving at an effective ecstasy.

The same can be said of that which, in more disconcerting jargon in some alchemical texts, goes by the name of *urina vini,* meaning "urine of a drunken man."[9] "Urine" is explained by the root *ur,* which in Chaldean designated fire (Latin, *urere,* "to burn") and with the anagram *UR Inferioris NAturae,*[10] which is precisely the humid Fire agent in these methods. Specifically, "urine of a drunken man" alludes to the state of exaltation, "inebriation," or "enthusiasm"—μανία— which is linked to one of the manifestations of such Fire. When others add that the urine must be "infantile" and "prepubertal," they allude to the condition of

---

[8] Classical mystery literature speaks continually of "sacred orgies," as a designation, generally, of states of sacred enthusiasm, even frenzy, which lead to a particular type of initiation.

[9] *The Great Book of Nature,* 120.

[10] Della Riviera, *Mondo magico,* 196.

simplicity and purity (or of elementarity, the "nascent state") that must be maintained in such "combustion," that it produces that "movement or impetuosity of the spirit" and that "inspiration" that are the only things—and not reason, reading, or study—that can effect, as Geber says, the discovery of the secret.

Let us make mention at this point of the frequent references to wine in the most recent texts, starting with Raymond Lully, and repeat that here it may be either symbolic wine or actual wine, or both at the same time. We shall cite but one text: "It is a wonderful thing, and to the vulgar incredible, that the spirit of the wine extracted from its body [a question of capturing the subtle aspect of the experience provided by wine] has the power, by dint of its continuous circulating movement, to extract . . . any other spirit from its body: be it vegetable [☿], mineral [☉] or animal [☿]. . . . The *Quinta-virtus-essentia-prima* of *Vinum* attracts the *vires* [powers, virilities] of all beings infused in it; loosening them from the elements through dissolution of the natural ties; enabling the spirits, by appetence and reaction, to elevate themselves above the passive resistances."[11]

And is it not significant that the word *aquavit*, "firewater," (i.e., "brandy," *aqua ignea*) aims so directly at the experiences of the alchemists and can also signify that other ancient designation, *aqua vitae* or "Water of Life," or "burning water"?

It might be helpful to emphasize that in the use of the corrosive waters (as well as in the "Path of Venus," which we shall discuss presently) the fundamental condition is the preparation of the androgynous element: "The secret of the success of the operation is the secret double fire." This means that the operation must connect its activity, beginning with the incombustible Sulfur, for the empowerment, in some external fashion to the substances used and to maintain connection to the end. It is in this sense that we speak of the "Philosopher's Wine," as opposed to ordinary wine, also called *aqua ardens*, and in commenting on the recipe of Raymond Lully, *recipe vinum rubeum album (spiritus vini philosophorum)*, we say that the preliminary condition is the secret fire.[12] In all other cases, that is, in the case of a passive experience, the sole result will be the phenomenology, utterly

---

[11] G. Dorn. *Clavis*, BCC, 1:233, 239. Cf. R. Lully in *Theatrum chemicum*, 4:334; Arnold of Villanova, *Opera omnia* (Basel, 1585, 1699); *De pharmaco catholico*, 17, §1. For the coming together of other traditions on this theme we may recall that "vine" in Assyrian was *karana*, that is, "the tree of the drink of life" (D'Alviella, *Migration des symboles*, 184), and that the wine used in orgiastic tantric rituals (*panchatattva-pūjā*) with regard to the awakening of consciousness in the form of the Air principle, takes the name of "savior in liquid form" (*dravamayi-tārā*), but also of "semen or power of Shiva," the name also given by Hindu alchemy to Mercury (Evola, *The Yoga of Power*, 107, 120). For the technique of the "Corrosive Waters," see *Introduzione alla magia*, 2:140ff.

[12] Cf. esp., J. Seger Weidenfeld, *De secretis adeptorum sive de usu spiritus vini lulliani* (London, 1634).

devoid of any interest to us, of "artificial paradises" and of those who abuse alcohol or drugs. As Titus Burckhardt has aptly remarked,[13] a drug as such can only prepare or encourage the attainment of a spiritual state, it cannot engender it. Its action must be directed and integrated; the "qualitative" compulsion knows only how to come from another domain.[14]

---

[13] T. Burckhardt, *Alchemie: Sinn und Weltbild* (Olten, 1960), 184.

[14] [The final paragraph and notes are from the 1948 edition.—Trans.]

Thirty-Five

ϹHE PAϹH OF VEƝUS AƝ϶ ϹHE RADICAL PAϹH

In the wet path of hermetism the repetition of sexual symbols occurs too frequently not to suggest a certain foundation to the suspicion that this tradition must also have possessed knowledge about another type of "corrosive waters" related to the power of disintegration that a woman exercises over a man when she unites with him in love and the sexual act. As could be said of *soma*, so in this respect, it could be said that the "Woman" of the Philosophers (symbol of the life-force), after a certain point, had ceased to be "known"; whereupon the terrestrial woman was substituted as a means of returning to the life-force, by way of the dizzying ecstasy that *eros* can produce between two sexual beings.

Hence the idea of certain "operations using two vessels," to which we enigmatically allude in alchemy. The two vessels may also be interpreted as the bodies of two persons of different sex, which contain separately the two hermetic principles that in other alchemical practices are prepared together within a single being: the active and the passive, the golden force against the captivating and sympathetic wet force that "dissolves" the former in its own "enclosure." So it would be possible to give a concrete interpretation, alongside the symbolic one, to such expressions as: "Our coporeal gold is as though dead before it unites with its mate. Only then is the secret, interior Sulfur developed,"[1] and: "With the Sulfur of Venus, the inner Sulfur of man is rectified, reinforced and wholly perfected."[2]

On this plane the phases of the rapture produced by the extraction, then by the arrest and fixation, which we have already seen in the symbols of cutting the wings of the Dragon at the height of its flight into the ether and the felling of the Bull at the end of his raging stampede, can be recognized behind the expressions of an alchemico-qabalistic text where the lance of Phineas appears (Numbers, 25:8), which "transfixed them in the moment of their union and *in locis genitalibus*, to the solar ☉ Israelite and the lunar ☾ Midianite . . . This biting fang, or power of Iron, acting on the Materia, purges it of all filth. The Israelite ☉ is here no other than ♀ the masculine Sulfur [in its vulgar state]; and by Midianite ☾ we must understand ▽ the Dry Water [here perhaps alluding to the mopping up of the 'superfluous moistures' which by corresponding preparation the woman must have consummated in her sensitivity and faculty of sensation] duly mixed with the ore or *red* marcasite. The spear of Phineas not only cuts down the male Sulfur ♀, but also mortally wounds the ☾, his female, and both die mixing their *blood* in a single procreation [supernatural rather than physical]. Then the wonders of Phineas [who represents the operator] commence to manifest themselves."[3]

The *De pharmaco catholico* also mentions the extraction of the hot solar Mercury from the Ore of Venus by means of Tartarus (equivalent of chaos, the dissolving power of such symbolic combustions) and Sal Ammoniac, whose virtue of contraction, in contrast to the former, could have the same meaning as the aforesaid "lancing."[4] And if the hermetic texts frequently speak of a death that is

---

[1] Philalethes, *Introitus apertus*, §1.

[2] *De pharmaco catholico*, 13, §§1, 5. Braccesco (*Esposizione*, fols. 56b, 63a) also speaks of two sulfurs, one of Venus and the other of Mars. The reader will have acquired by now a certain practice in the transposition of symbols. Also corresponding to Venus (the Feminine) is a Sulfur that is likewise a vessel (body) *for itself*. Philalethes (*Introitus apertus*, §19) speaks of the other path, besides that in which only the internal heat operates, in the following terms: "The other Work is done with ordinary Gold and our Mercury, maintained *for a long time over a hot fire* that serves to cook them both, with the help of Venus, until from the two exits a substance that we call lunar [that is, ☿] juice. The impurities must be discarded and the purest part taken." By such a procedure the true sulfur will be obtained, which is then united to the Mercury (fixation of the white, see chapter 38) and then "to the blood that is peculiar to it" (the red work).

[3] *Asch Mezareph*, chap. 5 (quoted by Eliphas Levi). The Qabalah contains further reference to sexual esotericism. Cf., for example, *Zohar*, 1.55 b, "the saint—though blessed—elects to reside only where male and female are united," inasmuch as the occult sense of the sexual union is the path of the spiritual Androgyne destroyed by "sin."

[4] Cf. also the recipe of the *Great Book of Nature* (128): "To dissolve a metal, make it red hot and then submerge it in water." Plotinus (*Enneads*, 3.5.8), in an unfortunately confused text, gives an idea of how to understand ambrosia as an inebriating force that spins around itself without emptying into another. When the power of stopping (striking with the lance) acting on desire results in that, amor (eros) is transformed into a-mors (non-death, ambrosia), to use the same phonetic assimilation as employed in troubador esotericism.

the consequence of the *coniunctio*, of the "joining," perhaps it also refers to the trauma that can occur at the height of the embrace and orgasm if subjected to a deliberate control.

In reality, the life-force itself is eminently hidden in the energy of generation and here it is a matter of surprising it, arresting it, and taking possession of it at the moment it is turning to the procreation of another being. It appears naked, so to speak, in a nonindividuated state, which cannot transmit iself from one being to another, if, for a moment, it does not pass through the free and undifferentiated stage. But this stage, in itself, is the "poisonous" aspect of Mercury, the state that kills. Thus it is possible to encounter in the sexual act a condition analogous to that in which, under the guise of an active death, the initiation is completed. Hence the sense of the double aspect of Love and Death in certain ancient deities: Venus, as Libitina, is also a goddess of death—we read in a Roman inscription dedicated to Priapus: *mortis et vitae locus.*[5]

The convergence of the various meanings is finally complete in the Hindu notion of *kundalini*, which is, at the same time, the Goddess and the "serpent power," the force that has produced the organization of the body and continues to sustain it, the root of sex, the power manifested in death and separation, and the power used by the yogis to cross "the threshold of Brahma" and break onto the "Royal Path."[6]

In the alchemical texts we may find other allusions to the use of the power in man that manifests itself as sexuality: especially in the more or less direct references to Saturnal and Ammoniacal Sulfur that lies sleeping in the inferior seat ♈ (see page 83), and corresponds to the "Father" (Gichtel); and Infernal Niter ⊕ that is a "fiery magical key," an adversarial and destructive power for the other Sulfur, the exterior one (*De pharmaco catholico*). But when a similar power is found throughout a work, it is no longer the wet path, even though it still has some of those qualities, but it is now a path that, on the contrary, could be called *ultra dry*, inasmuch as it leads directly to the final "red" stage, jumping over all the intermediate phases, striking the Materia directly with the fiery lightning bolt contained in the interior of the tellurian and saturnine being, the same that brought down the Titans.

This is an extremely dangerous path! Geber calls it the "balance of Fire," and considers it "extraordinarily difficult and perilous," "a royal operation, prompt and quick," but the sages reserve it only for princes, alluding to the presupposition of an exceptional qualification and natural "dignity."[7] Of the four ways that we are told

---

[5] Bachofen, *Urreligion*, 1:263.

[6] The hermetic expression "royal path" is found again precisely in these traditions. Cf.*Hatha-yoga-pradipika*, 3.2–3 (commentary): "*Prānasya çūnya padavī tathā rājapa thāyate.*"

[7] Geber, *Livre de la royauté, CMA*, 3:126, 131. On the contrary, "balance," which is acquired by the synthesis of the balances of Water and Fire, is recommended: "If the balance of Water is united to that

about in Andreae, this is the one by which "no man reaches the palace of the King," that it is "impossible because it consumes and can only be suitable for incorruptible bodies."[8]

Perhaps it is the same thing as the direct and fiery awakening of *kundalini*, according to tantric Hatha-Yoga, only preceded by a single "heroic" preparation— *vira-krama*—without "mortification" or "solution in the white," that is to say, without passing through the middle part of the breast (see page 82). The general danger of *death*—death not simply as a physical fact—that confronts the initiate is maximal here;[9] it is said in the hermetic *Rosarium*: "*Nonnulli perierunt in opere nostrum.*"

As an attenuation of this method we can mention, finally, still another path of a certain "androgynous" style, both dry and wet at the same time, which refers to the *heroic* initiations in the strictest sense, related to the ancient sacred meaning of war, to the ancient assimilation of the warrior with the initiate, to the *mors triumphalis* as "the path to heaven," etc. A transporting and violent force is awakened, an *eros* similar to the frenetic and orgiastic forms of the wet path—but along with that is added the metallic quality of Iron or Mars.

The heroic impulse offers, technically, the same possibilities as the mystical impulse, the orgiastic ecstasy, and the subtle mortification of hermetic asceticism, but only when the Mars element, by elimination of the earthly, watery, and combustible dross, has been prepared to the point of nearing the Gold or Sun quality, and when the same impulse is so intense that it can carry itself beyond the closure constituted by the virile hardness and beyond the individual limit as well.

Also by the same path, however, one can come to "break the enchantment that holds the Gold body in bondage and would impede it from exercising its masculine functions" without having to follow the method according to which "the Fire is worked most gently and tempered from beginning to end," but following that other method in which a "violent Fire similar to the Fire used for the multiplications" is necessary.[10]

---

of Fire, everything will come out in its more complete form, though Fire by itself alone can also lead to perfection" (ibid., 132).

[8] *Chemical Wedding*, 2, §15.

[9] Cf. Evola, *The Yoga of Power*, part 2. For the practical aspect of the sexual methods, see *Introduzione alla magia*, 1:238ff.; 2:329ff. For an explanation of the techniques relative to magic, initiatic, and ecstatic usage in the different traditions, cf. Evola, *Eros and the Mysteries of Love: The Metaphysics of Sex* (Rochester, Vt., 1991).

[10] Philalethes, *Introitus apertus*, §18, and also Geber, *Summa*, BCC, 1:530. [On the heroic path, warrior initiation, and triumphal death, cf. Evola, *Revolt against the Modern World*, chaps. 18, 19, in which he also alludes to the technical side of evoking the "double" or Mercury in warrior experiences.]

. . . .
Thirty-Six
. . . .

the hermetic
fires

Before concluding these preliminary remarks about technique and getting on with it, we need to mention something about the *Fires* employed in the Work by the hermetic masters.

"Without fire," it is affirmed, "the Matter is useless and the Philosophical Mercury is a chimera that lives only in the imagination. It is on the rule of Fire that everything depends."[1] And we need hardly belabor the fact that this is not vulgar, physical fire.

Crassellame scorns those who "flutter day and night around stupid coal fires." He calls them "singed moths" and adds: "In what kind of flames do you persist? It is not violent coal, or inflammable kindling that the wise use for the hermetic Stone."[2] And many other authors mock the "charcoal-burners" and the "puffers"—Pernety would like to possess the "voice of Stentor" to denounce them—saying that the hermetic fire is a fire that does not burn, it is a *magic* fire, an *interior* fire, *subtle* and occult. "The Opus is accomplished neither by (vulgar) Fire nor by the hands, but only by means of the inner heat,"[3] as with a "rising fever," as the *Turba philosophorum* reveals to those who understand.

---

[1] *Filum Ariadnae*, 75.

[2] Crassellame, *Ode alchemica*, 3.1.1–2.

[3] Pernety, *Dictionnaire*, 397; *Fables*, 1:125.

On the other hand, the hermetic Philosophers recognize various fires, which are to be brought together in the work so that one may help the other. The main difference lies between "natural Fire" and "Fire against nature." Unnatural Fire is the Fire of the hermetic Art referring to the aspect of the "one thing" as the basis on which it is "Nature that dominates itself," "that kills itself" and thus is capable of reacting against the fact of being in order to infuse in it a higher discipline that sustains the fallen and erring natures, "rectifying" them."[4] After which, the two fires—that of the Art, directed by the operator's will, and that of Nature, which is the vital fire, that is to say, the psychophysical fire, by which perhaps it can refer again to the heat of the heart and the blood (in ☿)—are united and, as has been said, the one increases, fortifies, and develops the action in the inner depths of the other. Besides the fire called intermediate, unnatural, and composite, a third is mentioned, the "Fire that kills," which recalls the primordial "fixations," that is to say, the absolute individualization of the force.

But the first of these fires, if it is not fire of wood, neither is it a simple state of feeling but an "enthusiasm" of the spirit intensely energized, which is concentrated and reunited in itself, as one that embraces, shelters, nourishes, cooks, and "loves." And all of a sudden a special and subtle warmth permeates the whole body.

In the Orient they speak precisely of such an inner heat on which meditation is concentrated, a heat that is not just physical or psychic, which is evoked by special practices (for example, that of the breath) that produce special effects and favor the meditation and the awakening of the power contained in the formulas and symbols of initiation.[5]

All of this is proposed as a guide for the interpretation of expressions in the texts that are routinely encountered in great abundance. We shall limit ourselves to quoting Pernety, for whom "the philosophical Fire is that with which the philosophers wash the materia, that is, purify the Mercury"; and the "unnatural Fire," or "intermediate," is the "result of the union of the natural Fire and the Fire of the philosophers which is against nature." This unnatural Fire is the cause of the putrefaction and death of the composition and of the perfect and true philosophical solution"—and to this Fire "against nature" remains the task of "reanimating the

---

[4] The two symbols have another meaning. The natural Fire is that which has been specialized and personalized. The Fire against nature, on the other hand, is the not yet individualized power of creation and, as such, antithetical to the first: for which we sometimes refer to the Mercury in the free state as the "poisonous" Mercury. Cf. d'Espagnet, (*Arcanum hermeticae, BCC* 2, §54): "The Fire against nature is contained in the stinking menstruum, which transforms our stone into a certain poisonous Dragon, powerful and voracious."

[5] Cf. A. David-Neel, *Magic and Mystery in Tibet* (1932; reprint, 1971), passim; cf. "Psychische Schulung in Tibet," in *Die Christliche Welt*, nos. 1, 2, 3, (1928); *Bacot, Vie de Milarepa*, 157, 196.

hidden Fire in the other, liberating it from the prison in which it has been locked."[6]

The *De pharmaco catholico* also concerns itself with the three "hermetic" or "magical" fires, without which the "solution" cannot take place, pointing out by symbols the functioning of each; the text calls one of them "sympathetic" (in sympathy with the other profound and primordial Fire of the telluric entity), and says that it is increased by the careful kindling of the igneity of the metals, but as soon as the ignition occurs one must be sure to corporealize the Soul in order to keep it from dissolving in Air, by the action of such Fire (which returns the various powers to the undifferentiated point).[7]

And Artephius speaks of the three Fires and calls the first "Fire of the Lamp"— that is, light-Fire, *illuminated* Fire—"continuous, humid, airy, proportioned"; the second is the "Fire of the ashes," that is, a fire that is sheltered in the *interior*, analogous to the so-called natural Fire, on which the athanor is placed; finally there is the Fire against nature, "Our Water," which is related to the Fountain, and destroys, dissolves, calcinates.[8] But often these three Fires are used in the texts as symbols to mean the three phases of the Work.

The operators next call special attention to the Regimen of the Fire that "must maintain itself constantly at the same temperature and never go out." Nature itself will indicate to the enlightened mind the intensity of the occult Fire.[9] The prescriptions, as a rule, are of this type: "Ye must not force the Fire at the beginning of the Work on the Mercury, or it will be volatilized. But once having achieved the fixation, then the Mercury resists the Fire [that is, the "ego" active element can be made to intervene, without running the risk of the "Mercury" consciousness disappearing, and returning to the conditionalities of the body], and resists it all the more for having been in combination with Sulfur."[10] With a slow and patient reheating, with continous, gentle heat, it must be worked until one

[6] Pernety, *Dictionnaire*, 49, 163, 165, 402-3. Cf. Geber, *Summa*, 530-31; d'Espagnet, (*Arcanum hermeticae*, §80): "The Fire innate in our Stone is the Archeus of Nature, the 'Son and Vicar of the Sun' moves, digests [= ripens] and completes everything, if it is left free." Cf. G. Lenselt, *Les apparences de verité et vraye pratique de l'Alchimie* (ms. 3012, Bibl. Arsén., in de Givry, 413): "The Fire of the Sages is the only instrument that can work this sublimation: *no philosopher has ever overtly revealed this secret Fire;* who does not understand must stop here and ask God to illuminate him."

[7] *De pharmaco catholico*, 3, §§1, 2, 4.

[8] *Livre d'Artephius, BPC*, 2:148-49, 150-51. Each of the following attributes of Fire, given by Bernard of Treviso (*Philosophie des métaux*), for him who understands, contains a direction: "Make a vaporous Fire, digesting, continuous, not violent, subtle, *enveloping*, airy, closed, non-combustible, altering." Artephius has said of "our" Fire: "It destroys, dissolves, congeals, calcinates, is altering, penetrating, subtle, airy, non-violent . . . *encircling, containing*, and unique."

[9] *Livre de El Habir, CMA*, 3:93, 109, 110.

[10] Ibid., 79.

obtains the "occult World Spirit" [Archeus] locked inside the symbolic Stone.[11]

We shall abstain from further references because they would only lead us into more complicated mazes of the secret alchemical language. Who now possesses his own trusty thread of Ariadne, can venture farther by himself.[12] The general prescription is always to avoid using violent fires at the beginning, because the purpose is to awaken not the exterior and impure fire (the Red that appears prematurely), but the deep fire, which is at the same time Gold and Sun, enclosed within the body "and is not awakened before the [sense of] body has been dissolved." For this purpose one must first have reached the Water and the rebirth in the Water; whereafter the Water is extracted and flees from the violent Fires, which necessarily are stamped by the impure and terrestrial element of the person. The calm fire, subtle and illuminated, that "cooks"[13] little by little, is that which must be used until the mortification and the revelation of the Light, unless one may have chosen those particular methods of the aforementioned wet path that so frequently have the drawback of raising the residual and combustible parts along with the subtle principles.

---

[11] *Chymica vannus*, 259.

[12] We refer especially to Philalethes, *Epist. Ripley*, §§56, 57, 54; *Filum Ariadnae*, 82-83, 84, 89, 105; *Turba philosophorum*, passim

[13] The symbolism of "cooking" refers precisely to the specific action of fire, which little by little "ripens" the crude and brute substances. Whereupon the *Turba* says: "Understand ye by it everything according to Nature and Order. And believe ye me without seeking further. I command ye only to cook; cook at the beginning, cook in the middle and cook to the end, without doing any other thing than cook, and so Nature will be borne to the completion."

Thirty-Seven

Che white work: Rebirth

Whiteness—light, spring, resurrection, life, flow-ering, birth, etc.—hermetically expresses the state of active ecstasy that uplifts the human condition. It regenerates, restores the memory, reintegrates the personality with the noncorporeal state. "What more can I say, my son?" reads the *Corpus Hermeticum*, "Only this: a simple vision [ἄπλαστον] has taken place in me . . . I have come out of myself and have clothed myself in a body that does not die. I am no longer the same, I have been intellectually born . . . I no longer have a color, nor am I tangible or measurable. All of that is now alien to me . . . and I no longer see with physical eyes."[1] This is the foundation that we must bear in mind when we encounter the expressions of the enciphered language referring to the experience of Mercury or divine Water and, in particular, the *albedo*.

"The life-giving Magic Light" drawn from the center of the "Elemental Cross" (seat of the heart, see page 82), the "clearest water" or Mercury, is—according to Della Riviera—"the Spirit of the World Soul" [Archeus] and in this "are all things seminally contained." The author then explains that in this "Heaven" there is no "reunion of soul and body"; rather "the body is included in the nature of the soul and is almost the soul itself, extensive, visible . . . light without matter or dimensions." And he repeats,

---

[1] *Corpus Hermeticum*, 13.3. Cf. also 13–14, where it is said that the rebirth is "no longer seen as of bodies or three dimensions." Cf. Plotinus, *Enneads*, 5.3.7; 6.9.9.

"This celestial Mercury is spirit being perfect lucidity . . . nature in itself brilliant and transparent, almost diaphanous, and illuminated . . . not subject to any alien mixture or any passion; *an act of pure intelligence,* having an invisible and incorporeal illumination that is the source of this visible light."[2]

So the conferring of such a principle means transmutation (the first of the alchemical transmutations) and resurrection. "When the White appears in the materia of the Great Work, Life has conquered Death, their King has been resuscitated, Earth and Water have been converted into Air, it is the Regime of the Moon and the Son has been born." Then the Materia has acquired such a degree of fixation that the Fire can no longer destroy it (it is "the stability of the inititiate," no longer conquerable by death"). "When the artist sees the perfect whiteness, the [hermetic] Philosophers say that the moment of tearing up the books has arrived because at that point they are no longer of any use."[3]

An Arab text asks, "What do we call combustion, transformation, disappearance of darkness and production of the incombustible compound? All these terms apply to the compound at the moment of its turning white."[4]

Artephius speaks of "that which is clear, pure, spiritual and lifted up by the Air," farther on he speaks of "turning into Air,"[5] and then of being made alive with Life and made completely spiritual and uncorruptible, as the feeling that marks the "sublimation, conjunction and elevation, in which the whole compound is made white."[6] "Pure, subtle, brilliant, clear as the dew, diaphanous as unflawed crystal," these are, for Basil Valentine, equivalent to the qualities of "our Living Silver," extracted from the best Metal by Spagyric Art, that is, by separation. The Syrian texts refer to it as "matter that turns copper white, white cloud, Water of clarified Sulfur, transparency [$\delta\iota o\psi\iota\varsigma$], mystery unveiled."[7]

---

[2] Della Riviera, *Mondo magico,* 20, 47–48.

[3] Pernety, *Dictionnaire,* 58.

[4] *Livre de Cratès, CMA,* 3:69.

[5] Cf. Agrippa (*De occulta philosophia,* 2:26): "Air is the body of the life of our sensitive spirit and does not have the nature of any perceivable object beyond that of a spiritual and elevated virtue. Nevertheless it happens that the sensitive Soul rejuvenates the Air that surrounds it and that it feels the quality of the objects that act on it in an Air enlivened and joined to the spirit, that is, in the *living Air.*

[6] *Livre d'Artéphius, BPC,* 2:139.

[7] In *CMA,* 2:82. White Gold, White Sulfur, White Stone, etc., are other symbols for the ego principle in this state. Still another symbol is Magnesium by way of an ancient etymology that would derive this word from "mixing," $\mu\iota\gamma\nu\acute{\upsilon}\epsilon\iota\nu$, the Natures united by *combinatio* (see *CAG,* 2:202). White Sulfur, for Bernard of Treviso (*Philosophie des métaux, BPC,* 2:432), is "the simple soul of the Stone, upright and noble, removed from every corporeal density." Then he goes on to give instructions for converting this Sulfur, freed from all excess humidity, into an "impalpable and most subtle powder." This last expression may perhaps suggest a real inner experience, associated with the sense of "loss of weight," of lightness and airiness in contrast to the ordinary state of corporeal consciousness.

"By means of the Divine Water," Ostanes teaches, "blind eyes see, deaf ears hear and the thick tongue speaks with clear words." And he continues, "This Divine Water revives the dead and kills the living, for it makes natures leave their natures and because it revives the dead. It is the Water of Life: who has drunk thereof cannot die. When it has been extracted, perfected and mixed completely [with the principle that has been obtained], it impedes the action of the Fire on the substances with which it has been mixed, and the Fire can no longer disintegrate [in the lethal and negative sense] similar mixtures."[8]

Arnold of Villanova: "Our Water mortifies, illuminates, prunes and purifies. In one principle it makes the dark colors appear during the mortification of the body, but then come other colors, numerous and various, and finally the whitening."[9] And Raymond Lully: "This water is called *Water of Wisdom* . . . in it resides the spirit of the Quintessence that makes everything where otherwise nothing could be made."[10]

---

[8] *Livre du mercure occidental*, text in *CMA*, 3:213.

[9] *Semita semitae*, 12. Cf. *Turba*, §§16, 17; Philalethes, *Introitus apertus*, §11.

[10] R. Lully, *Vade mecum*. Cf. Boehme, *Aurora* 24, §38.

Thirty-Eight

the coniunctio
in white

O nce its "location" and meaning have been established, we must return to the importance of conferring an active character on the experience. It is necessary to recover the magical heroic sense hidden in the symbolism, according to which the Divine Water is represented by a Virgin, who is the Mother with respect to that which is reborn[1] out of her by "immaculate conception" (autogenesis, spiritual endogenesis), and simultaneously the Wife of this her own son who, serving as the male, possesses and impregnates her.

According to another allegory in the literature, while the mother engenders the son, the son engenders the mother, that is, his act accompanies, creatively and exactly, the entire process—provided this is always in accordance with "the rules of the Art." This generation of the Mother *purifies* her (what purifies is also purified), and at the same time it transforms the "Whore of Babylon"[2] into a virgin.

Here we have the "fixating" action that the reborn Gold, almost by its sheer

---

[1] Hence the alchemical symbolism of the "Virgin's Milk" by which the "Hermetic Child" is fed.

[2] Pernety, *Dictionnaire*, 408: "The Whore of the Philosophers is their Moon . . . or Babylonian Dragon: The Art purifies her of all filth, turning it into virginity. When in this state, the Philosophers call her the Virgin." In Hellenism, those allegories correspond to the myth of the "Perfect Man" who penetrates the Impure Womb and alleviates the pains of its darkness; when the mysteries are known, he drinks from the cup of Living Water that liberates him from the "garments of servitude" (in Hippolytus, *Philosophumena*, 5.10).

presence, exercises over the evoked power. If it has not been dissipated, the power is relieved of its desire nature and its "viscosity," by which it had been attracted and enslaved by everything (symbol of the whore). It is then reduced to "aqua *permanens*" (Eternal Water). This is the result of the "philosophical incest." "The True Mercury," so says one text, "does not work alone, but must be fixed by Arsenic," that is by the Masculine.[3] On his part Ostanes says that Mercury "used in the trial of souls," "transformed into ethereal spirit [liberated or extracted] is launched into the upper hemisphere; descends and reascends avoiding the action of the Fire [equivalent to the Masculine or Arsenic] until upon its fugitive movement being stopped, it reaches the *state of wisdom*. First, it is difficult to retain it and it is mortal";[4] but in the Greek enigma of the "four syllables and nine letters," knowledge of which confers *wisdom*, the key is, ἀρσενικόν, Arsenic, equivalent to the fire avoided by the "Virgin," the "fleeing demon," which must be restrained.

Here the hermetic exegesis of classical mythology also intervenes: recall the labor of Hercules in which he conquers Achelous, son of Earth and Ocean, who has assumed the form of a river. Della Riviera explains that in allegory this is the resistance necessary to oppose the waters attempting to sweep away the Earth (that is, individualization, speaking generally) via the wet element still hidden in the substance, which causes the latter to try to dissolve itself. "But the hero battling pyronomically [that is, opposing the Fire state of the Spirit], finally overcomes the powerful flow of the stream, keeping it to the destined Earth [which here expresses the supernatural form of individualization]."[5]

In the same way, on the Porta Magica of Rome we read *Aqua torrentum convertes in petram* (You will convert the water of the torrents into stone—Trans.). Surely not standing alone is another inscription that announces that Our Son who was dead, lives, and the king has returned from the Fire (after having conquered the water) and enjoys the occult mating: *Filius noster mortuus vivit rex ab igne redit et coniugo gaudet occulto.*[6] And again in Della Riviera: "Our Firmament is congealed Water in the likeness of the crystal which the Heroes are accustomed to call Dry Water or skinny water." Finally, the same concept of active congelation is also ingeniously related to the two "magical Angels"—now interpreted as the primordial forms in which the cosmic waters have been fixed—according to the formula: ANtico GELO [an Italian pun: literally "ancient ice," and thence *angelo* or "angel"].[7]

---

[3] *CMA*, 2:84.

[4] *CAG*, 2:276.

[5] Della Riviera, *Mondo magico*, 105.

[6] P. Bornia, *La Porta Magica* 32-33.

[7] *Mondo magico*, 80, 99-100.

The expression, already used in the Greek texts for the hermetic worker, "Lord of the Spirit," φύλαξ πνευμάτον, is found again in Basil Valentine, for whom man was "made Lord of this spirit [the mineral, required in the Work] to set it apart as something new, that is, a new world, having the power of fire."[8] The meanings as well as the expressions converge once again in the entire tradition. This is known as the hermetic "Coniunctio in White," Incest, and Dominion over Life.

---

[8] B. Valentine, *Aurelia, BCC,* 2:207. From the idea of transparency, associated with that of hardness (equivalent to congelation), proceeds the alchemical symbolism of Glass and Vitriol. Because of this Lully says, "A philosopher is one who knows how to make glass." According to Braccesco (*Espositione,* fol. 10a) the metals dissolved in the prima materia are vitriol, "which I call Dry Water" and which in the formula of Basil Valentine is linked to the precept of "descending to rectify."

. . . .
Thirty-Nine
. . . .

Che
ETERNAL VigiL

To make it through this experience means to overcome sleep not just in the symbolic sense, but in fact. The nocturnal state of sleep can be considered that darkness that has to be thinned out of the Materia so that the inner Light can begin to shine, Apuleius's "Sun shining in the middle of the night." So it is that every night we naturally attain the "separation" that the philosophers are seeking. As we have said before, we must actively work to witness it, as if we ourselves were the cause of its coming about, instead of falling into reduced and weakened states of consciousness.

Now perhaps we can understand these words of the *Corpus Hermeticum:* "The sleeping of the body became the lucidity *νῆψις* of the soul; when my eyes were closed they saw the Truth"; and also: "You can leave yourself without sleeping, just as they who, although sleeping and dreaming, are not asleep."[1] This explicit reference is of capital importance. It is an esoteric traditional teaching that there is a similarity between the mystery initiation—as partial catharsis with respect to death—and sleep that temporarily liberates the soul from the body by means of a separation that does indeed result in death if carried beyond a certain point.[2] The

---

[1] *Corpus Hermeticum*, 1.30; 13.4. Cf. Eliphas Levi (*Dogma and Ritual*, 158): "To sleep awake is to see the Astral Light."

[2] Cf. Proclus, *Commentary on the Cratylus*, 82, 133; V. Macchioro, *Heraclitus*, 128-29.

hermetic "diaphanum" is the Light that appears in the night for those who with closed eyes attain, while still in life, the state of death.[3] Once again, this Light is the ethereal and intelligible light of Mercury, which according to correspondences already mentioned, begins to shine in the symbolic "heart."

We have previously emphasized the white character attributed by a Hindu text to the garment of the "Spirit consisting of knowledge" when, "once the consciousness has appropriated the vital spirits, it resides during the course of sleep in the ethereal space of the heart."[4] And the correspondence is too precise to leave any doubt about the recognition, also in this case, of one of the "constants" of the symbology and primordial initiatic science. We might also include the Pauline reference to the heart that watches while the ego sleeps and, especially, the following quotation from the Qabalah: "When a person goes to his bed, his consciousness abandons him and goes up. But if every soul leaves the sleeper, not all rise to behold the countenance of the King . . . [the Soul] passes through numerous regions jumping from place to place. In its journey, it places itself in contact with impure powers that constantly surround the sacred regions. If the soul is contaminated by impurities, it mixes with them and remains with them during the entire night. Other souls ascend to the higher regions, and even beyond them to contemplate the glory of the King and visit his palaces. . . . A man whose soul reaches this supreme region every night can be assured that he will participate in the future life," which, mind you, is not as some decrepit survival, but as immortality in the highest sense.[5] Nothing less is the promise of initiation.

To arrive at the Light after the alchemical "black" means to possess the capacity to complete this "voyage" consciously, entering thus into the supernatural vigil. "That which is night for creatures, is the time of awakening for the man who has dominion over himself, and the awakening of all beings is night for the Sage of penetrating mind"; it is in these Oriental terms[6] that it is possible to express the conquest implicit in the realization of the white Work. We might also recall the battle of Jacob, who, once he was alone, engaged victoriously in battle against the *Angel*, or "Man," for the whole *night*, overcoming and resisting him until the *dawn*, whereupon he came to see the face of God without dying.[7] The hermetic

---

[3] Heraclitus (frag. 26 Diels) says: "Man lights his own Light when he extinguishes himself each night. And though living, he visits death when his eyes close in slumber."

[4] *Brihadaranyaka-Upanishad*, 2.1.15-17. We might also recall the "radiant white" color acquired by the robe of Christ at the moment of his transfiguration. (Luke 9:29).

[5] *Zohar*, 1.83b.

[6] *Bhagavad-Gita*, 2.69. Recall also that "Buddha" is not a name but a title—it means "The Awakened One"—and refers to the supersensible experience that the enlightened have during the four watches of the night. Cf. Evola, *The Doctrine of the Awakening*.

[7] Gen. 32:24-30.

content of this myth is evident, even aside from the fact that the "Angel" is, not without reason, one of the secret names chosen by the hermetic masters to signify "the volatile matter of their Stone."[8]

It has been said, besides, that alchemy repeats the theme of revelations concerning the Great Work obtained from the perspective of visions during dreams, the magical sleep, and analogous states; that is to say that they are allusions to a partial illumination dramatized by fantasy and propitiated by a certain support of the waking consciousness when, in a natural way, the "separation" is attained once the eyes of the body have been closed.

---

[8] Pernety, *Dictionnaire*, 33.

che booy of light
ano prooucciop
of silver

We have spoken of the active ecstasy in which liberation and transfiguration are exactly balanced by an equal degree of affirmation, in which any giving over to rapture or "combustion" is arrested and frozen. So we can speak of a "fixation" which is like an experience without form. From this, however, there may proceed another kind of experience, which is first set in motion by a descent that completely defines and confirms what is achieved.

The sensation of the body is introduced into the new state, experiencing corporeality as a function of the state of "light," "day," "life," etc.—and, vice versa, that experience becomes a function of the new corporeality. The result, in a special sense, is what is called the "White Stone": the first embodiment or projection of the spirit, the resurrection, by which the remaining dark dregs become white and a detached new form arises, abandoning the "sepulchre"; whereupon the consciousness of the body is transported into the full expression of those energies by which the body lives. The hermetic masters, referring to the ancient myth, call this new "body" *their Diana* and say: "Blessed are the Acteons who succeed in seeing their Diana naked,"[1] that is, seeing her completely, beyond the terrestriality she had been hiding behind; and thereby they also say that their stone "espouses a celestial nymph, after she has been stripped of her terrestrial form, to become with her a single thing."[2] This is the first hermetic transmutation: from the Lead or Copper to Silver.

Let us quote in this regard a few words that are characteristic of Gichtel: "In the regeneration we do not receive a new Soul, but do receive a new Body. . . . This Body derives from the Word of God or the heavenly Sophia [symbols equivalent to the heavenly Waters], which appears rising from the holy and inner Fire of Love . . . it is spiritual [this body], more *subtle* than air, similar to the rays of the Sun that penetrate all *corpora*, and as different from the old body as the brilliant Sun from the dark earth;[3] and though it remain in the old body, is inconceivable and incomprehensible to it, though at times it is felt."[4] And Artephius says, "Our Bodies are raised up in a white color, over the dissolving Waters, and this *whiteness is Life*"; with it "the Soul enters the Body, and this Soul is more subtle than Fire, being the true Quintessence and the Life that asks only to be born and to be stripped of the gross, earthly dregs."[5]

From what the literature says, concentrating on the stone we must *embody the spirit and spiritualize the body in one and the same act*. Silver, the hermetic "White Rose," first efflorescence of the seed sown in our earth,[6] corresponds then to the "astral and radiant body"—$αὐγοειδὲς$ ἢ $ἀστροειδὲς$—of Philoponus, to the Homeric aerosome, and, in a certain measure, to the Pauline, but above all Gnostic, "resurrection body"—$σῶμα$ $πνεῦματικον$. The most "noble" quality of Silver is found in Pelagius's teaching, according to which the subtilization produced by the Divine Water confers iosis, the active virtue, on the bodies, the general idea being that bodies in the Mercury pass from potential to actual; all this leads us back again to

---

[1] Cf. Philalethes (*Epist. di Ripley*, §51): "In this work our Diana is our Body, when it is mixed with Water." He adds that the Diana has a forest, because "in white the body produces vegetation"(a symbolism we have aleady explained, p. 84). The hermetic Acteon, as contrasted to the classical myth, does not suffer punishment for having seen Diana naked. Diana, as raiser of Apollo, means that this propitious state, in its turn, favors the supreme state that will follow the solar stage.

[2] *Triomphe Hermétique, BPC*, 3:276. We could draw one parallel, among others, in the possibly esoteric interpretation of this passage from the Song of Songs (2:13-14): "Arise, my dove, my friend, *my wife*. Hasten to come to the crevices of the *rock*, to the depth of the *Stone*."

[3] Cf. Della Riviera (*Mondo magico*, 95): "The very pure and simple magical land, that compared to the other [impure and unclean], is like the radiant and true solar body compared to opaque shadow."

[4] Gichtel, *Theosophia practica*, 3, §§13, 5.

[5] *Livre d'Artephius, BPC*, 2:137.

[6] Bernard of Treviso, *La parole délaissée*, (*BPC*, 2:434): in the subtilization "the white Rose, celestial, sweet, so beloved of the 'Philosophers', is completed."

the aristotelian and neoplatonic conception according to which every material thing, as such, is nothing more than something sketched out, a projected design that tends to be, but is not, because there can be no "being" in the world of becoming.

The same applies to human embodiment, which in its materialization almost expresses the stoppage and fading of an intellectual power whose complete attainment is the "body" of the regenerated ones (first with the white, then with the red), and which is designated also by the term—σῶμα τέλειον—the perfect body. This is why the hermetic authors insist that the transmutation is not an alteration but quite the reverse—a perfection, integration, realization, and consummation of something that is imperfect, a multiplication and vivification of the power of that which was "dead."

The phase of simple fixation of the Waters and that of the extraction of the Diana or Moon can, in practice, be confused with one another. This is especially so in the dry path, since on this path, from the beginning, we are dealing with something at once corporeal and noncorporeal, active and passive, that is, of one nature or the other. In any case, the formula—to release the corporeal and to embody the noncorporeal—as we have said, is a recurrent and central theme of the whole tradition. The hermetic masters recognize the difficulty of actively maintaining themselves in a purely noncorporeal state; which is why they say, unanimously, that the complete fixation is reached by simultaneously making the spirit body and the body spirit.[7] They admit the necessity of the body as support for the fixation and as antidote against the danger of escape and dissolution.[8] Even if the sudden repeated "precipitation" had not the power to transmute the materia into pure silver, a cycle of successive sublimations (separations) and precipitations (return to the body) all the way to completion would be desirable, in order not to lose contact with that which—although only in the Earth state—possesses in itself, nevertheless, the condition for individualization and the seed for the Red Work and the "Diadem of the King."[9] As a general precept, there always remains: *solve et coagula*.

And Potier explains: "If these two words are too brief and unphilosophical

---

[7] Cf. *Livre d'Artephius* (*BPC*, 2:168): "The solution of the body and the coagulation of the spirit take place in one and the same operation." Cf. also Pernety, *Dictionnaire*, 532.

[8] *Livre d'Artephius*, *BPC*, 2:122. Cf. also from the Syrian texts (*CMA*, 2:84): "The Water requires perfect bodies, the reason being that after having dissolved them it congeals, fixes and joins with them, in a white earth"; Flamel (*Désir désiré*, 318): "The Mercury is fixed by means of that in which it is contained," that is, the body; and the *Turba* (§40): "The spirit is not congealed except through the dissolution of the body and the body is not dissolved but through the congelation of the spirit."

[9] Cf. Zacharias (*Philosophie naturelle des métaux* 532, 534): "It is necessary to be attentive and vigilant so as not to miss the right time for the birth of Our Mercurial Water, to unite it with our own body."

The Body of Light and Production of Silver · · · · · · · · · · · · · · · 157

for you, I will speak more broadly and comprehensively. *Solve* is to convert the body of our magnet into pure spirit. *Coagula* is to make this spirit corporeal again, according to the precept of the philosopher, who says: "Convert the Body into Spirit and the Spirit into Body. Who understands these things will possess everything and who does not understand them will have nothing."[10] To the *solve* corresponds the symbol of the ascent; to the *coagula* corresponds that of the descent. According to the hermetic literature, the "descent" refers to the Water of Life that restores life to the "dead," and takes them out of their graves. It is the first liberation of the titanic vulture that cried out from the top of the symbolic mountain that he was "the whiteness of the black."

If we were to provide quotations referring to this phase of the Work we would never come to the end of them. All references speak of it; although they seem to say different things, they all say the same thing with diverse and complicated symbols. The expressions appropriate to the White Work, however, are often woven into those peculiar to the Red Work, because the two proceedings run analogously. We shall limit ourselves to two or three examples and refer the reader to the texts in which, if he has acquired intelligence, he will gradually be able to orient himself with the help of what we have said up to this point.

In one of his customary graphic analogies, Zosimos speaks of the Copper Man, "Chief of the sacrificial priests and himself an object of sacrifice [at the same time]—he who vomits his own flesh and to whom has been given the power over these waters," and who upon the altar says: "I have completed the task of descending the fifteen steps into the darkness as well as the task of returning thence to rise into the light. The Sacrificial Priest renews me by casting out the denseness of my body. And so ordained as a priest by means of the compelling power [of the Art], I am become a spirit . . . I am the one that is [ὤν] the priest of the Temple."[11] And the Copper Man, in a vision, is transformed into the Silver Man in the splendid form of the god Agathodaimon.[12] In technical terms, it is always said in the Greek alchemical texts that from

---

[10] Potier, *Philosophia pura* (Frankfurt, 1619), 64, quoted in *Ignis* (1925).

[11] In *CAG*, 3:118-19.

[12] Whose name means "good daimon." The classical daimon corresponds to the "double," that is to the lunar and subtle form, which then is actualized as the first transformation of the consciousness of the corporeality and is converted into immortal form. Later on we shall speak of the "cloud" or "smoke." Again, this is the "double" or ☿; the "soul-daimon" of which Empedocles speaks and which in Homer is designated by *thymus*, the same word, exactly, as Latin *fumus*. (Cf. Gomperz, *Geschichte der Griech. Philosophie*, chap. 4, §7.)

the stone rises a spirit like a cloud that rises up—νεφέλη διαβαίνει[13]—and the fixation of this spirit in our Copper produces Silver. It comes down to a matter of projection—ἐπιβαλλει—on the bodies of the sublimated, (that is, liberated spirits, which makes them unite with the inner nature, or Soul—ψυχή—in spiritualized bodies—σῶμα πνευματικόν—to the point of taking over the Matter and dominating it, while they are made corporeal and fixed—πῆξις—ready to produce Silver and Gold. [14]

An Arab text says more clearly that what is to be fixed in the body, until the "Body and Spirit share a single nature," is the "vital element," and that this is the symbolic "tincture" and the "path followed by the prophets, by the saints and by all philosophers."[15] Flamel teaches that, on descending, the Natures "are transmuted and transformed into Angels, that is, they become spiritual and very subtle";[16] and the De pharmaco catholico describes the transformation that takes place in the organic structure of the body as follows: "Freed of all pollutions and earthly encumbrances, reduced and reconverted into clarified Salt and illuminated soul, this liquid, [because it has been dissolved in water], drinkable Gold will be dissolved in the body or human stomach, and diffused little by little—or invade the body rapidly—until it occupies every member and the entire blood system, in order to exercise [as befits a universal pharmaceutical] a general effectiveness all the way up to the ultimate miracle."[17]

Nor do we wish to omit reference to the hermetic interpretation of the same myth in the Gospels serving as operations of the Royal Art. After the old man has been put up on the cross, he is then placed in the sepulchre (nigredo). Awakened to new life after having been hidden in the depths of the Earth, in Hell, he first takes celestial form and then human (ascent and descent) with the purpose that in the Pentecost "the Holy Ghost comes down to impregnate the entire Body and free it from death";[18] whence the relationship with the "birth, from dead flesh, of another celestial and living Body

---

[13] Cf. Livre de la miséricorde, (CMA, 3:167): "The action of the soul on the body transforms it and gives it a non-material nature like its own. . . . The innermost nature of the substances is that which is contained in the inner part of the body and this is united to the intimate nature of the soul, though it must be returned after the latter has been separated from the intimate nature of the body."

[14] CAG, 2:107, 112, 114, 122-23, 129, 130, 146, 151, 172-73, 195.

[15] Livre de la miséricorde, CMA, 3:183-84

[16] Flamel, Figures hiéroglyphiques, §6 (BPC, 2:251). Cf. Bernard of Treviso Parole délaissé, BPC, 2:345.

[17] De pharmaco catholico, 12, §5.

[18] Boehme, De signatura, 7, §53.

that knows and comprehends the Light."[19] An analogous exegesis can also be applied to the Old Testament: It is said, for instance, that Moses ascending Mount Sinai after seven days (possible allusion to the purification of the *seven*: see pages 60-61; regarding the symbolism of the "ascension" and the "mount," see note 10 on page 128), enters the cloud animated by a consuming Fire. Upon descending from it he has a form and "face" that irradiate light.[20] Actually, the symbols agree with those of alchemy: for "cloud," as we know, in the enciphered language, is a frequent name for the product of separation and the texts often say that a Fire is hidden in it; this Fire, apart from the power also designated as "venom," can also signify the potentiality of the following "red" stage. The radiant form is the "body of life" or Diana, ☿, regenerated and liberated. The hermetic exegesis can also be applied to the Flood, which expresses the "dissolution" phase, while the successive retreat from the Waters corresponds to the desiccation that gives way to the fixation of the volatile, the *coagula*. After which, the *black* raven no longer returns. A white dove instead brings an olive branch, the *semper virens* that symbolizes the renewed and everlasting life of the regenerated[21] as well as the "peace" to follow. As sigil of the alliance between "Heaven" and "Earth" the seven colors of the rainbow that appears in the "cloud" are manifested.[22]

We may also refer to the ascent of Elijah on Mount Horeb, also called the "Mount of the Lord," which, however, etymologically has a possible relation to desolation, *desert*, raven, and solitude,[23] that is, with the inner states that are manifested in the work of mortification and purification. And it is on Horeb that the manifestation of the *Angel* of the Lord takes place, in a Flame of Fire, and the revelation of the "I am that I am."[24] Also, the symbol of

---

[19] *Aurora*, 20, §66. Pernety (*Dictionnaire*, 349) thus sums up the hermetic interpretation of the Gospels: "Their elixir is originally a part of the universal spirit of the world, corporealized in a virgin Earth. From this it must be extracted by passing through all the required operations before it reaches its goal of glory and immutable perfection. In the first *preparation* he is tormented to the point of bleeding; in the *putrefaction* he dies; when the white color turns black, he steps out of the dark and the tomb and is gloriously revived, rises to Heaven, all quintessentialized; whence he comes to judge the "quick and the dead," the dead being everything in man that lacks purity, which succumbs to alteration, cannot withstand the fire and so will be destroyed in Gehenna."

[20] Exod. 34:28-30; cf. 24:12-18; Deut. 9:18-25; 10:10.

[21] Cf. the symbol equivalent to the dove that brought Zeus ambrosia. (*Odyssey*, 12.62).

[22] Gen. 7:4; 8:1-12.

[23] Cf. *Ignis*, no. 11-12 (1925), 379ff.

[24] This sentence—recalling the "I am that which is" in the alchemical text of Zosimos quoted earlier—could refer to the experience of the pure ego, which the preparatory purification (that very often in alchemy is associated with the symbolism of the period of "forty days") liberates from all heterogeneous elements. In his spiritual regeneration—according to Cagliostro (quoted in *Ignis* [1925], 148, 179)—the initiate says of himself: "I am that I am."

desert returns in the forty days of Jesus' retreat, and in the myth of a thirsty Dionysus, to whom Jupiter appears in the form of a ram (♈), the sign that evokes Sulfur or Fire; Fire which in Chaldean is expressed by the same word, *Ur*, by which the Old Testament refers to the companion of Moses in his retreat (also of forty days), who leads him across the *desert* to a fountain, in which he quenches his thirst.[25] The number forty reminds us also of the number of hours that Jesus lay in the "sepulchre," and that in the calendar of Catholic feast days, after *Carnival* follows *Ash* Wednesday and a period of mortification of forty days, culminating in Easter with the *resurrection*. Easter is immediately preceded by *Palm* Sunday, which reveals the well-known vegetable symbolism and is also associated with the symbols of Egg and Lamb, or Aries. We have then, again in Aries ♈, the allusion to the power of Fire and "transcendent virility" (*ios*, *virtus*, *vis*, *vīrya*, see chapter 24) and at the same time the astrological indication of the correct date for Easter, which falls on the spring equinox, under Aries. But at this moment a new association of symbols appears to us, now that in spring the Earth and the dead bark ("cortex") *open*, and grasses, vegetation, and flowers rise, that is to say, the emergences of the "powers" takes place. Many alchemists for their part— now Olympiodorus, now Rhases, Rudienus, the Cosmopolite, etc.—say that the beginning of the work (in the sense of the first positive result) is obtained when the Sun enters Aries; and Pernety[26] informs us of the correspondence between the immaculate Lamb, consecrated at Easter, and the "purified Matter of the philosophers."

This is one of those many cases of strange and exact concordance of traditional symbols resulting in a kind of illuminating short circuit in the sign of universality.

Returning to the practice, it must be noted that the "descent" and the new contact with the corporeal constitute the most propitious condition for the eventual return of those old resistances that we have discussed, owing to incomplete purification (see page 126ff.). We must be able, if that happens, to repeat the Herculean labor of the Erymanthean boar sent by Diana, which could only be tethered when, after the falling of the *white* snow, the animal was obliged to find refuge in a small fruit orchard.

We shall now quote Stephanius once more: "Do battle, Copper! Do battle, Mercury! Unite the male with the female. Here is the Copper that receives the red color and the *ios* of the golden tincture: it is the decomposition of Isis . . . Do battle, Copper! Do battle, Mercury! The Copper is destroyed and deprived of its body by

---

[25] In the zodiacal series, after Aries come Taurus and Gemini, whose correspondences to phases of the Art might be the Red Work and then the Androgyne, or Rebis.

[26] Pernety, *Dictionnaire*, 10.

Mercury and the Mercury remains fixed by virtue of its combination with the Copper."[27] This is the battle of the "two natures," of the "Equilibrium of the Water," which again requires a subtle and sublime art so that the one of the natures does not destroy, by some excess, the other; so that the corporeality and the human form of the ego do not tend to reestablish themselves as a new, if not even stronger prison; or that the spiritual is not transformed into a poison that corporealization can no longer support and use for its transfiguration.[28]

---

[27] Text quoted in Berthelot, *Introduction à l'étude de la chimie*, 292. The reader will separate the allusions to the subsequent phases. Here copper is the equivalent of the Body.

[28] We would point out to the reader who may be interested certain texts in which he can find the characteristic allusions to transmutation of the two natures to the white: d'Espagnet, *Arcanum hermeticum*, §68ff.; *Livre de El Habir*, CMA, 3:112; Zosimos, in *CAG*, 2:223; Geber, *Summa*, BCC, 1:557; *Livre d'Artephius*, BPC, 2:153; Boehme, *De signatura*, 5, §17; *Filum Ariadnae*, 100; *Turba philosophorum*, §§5, 6. We shall cite only Artephius further who, after saying that the Water or Mercury is "the Mother who must introduce and encapsulate in her womb her Son, i.e., Gold," and that "she must revive the body and restore Life to what was dead," adds, "In this operation the Body becomes Spirit and the Spirit is turned into Body. Thereupon are established friendship, peace, accord and union of the opposites, that is, between the Body and Spirit which interchange their natures . . . mixing and uniting down to their smallest parts. . . . Thereby is obtained a middle substance, a body and spirit mixture"; and it is clear that "this could not be possible, if the Spirit did not become a body with the Bodies, and if by the Spirit the Bodies had not been made volatile and if the whole was not fixed and permanent" (*BPC*, 2:131, 133, 134). We shall also recall a notable passage of Della Riviera (*Mondo magico*, 85, 86–87): "After the celestial union [of the Moon and the Sun, corresponding to the first fixation of the invoked force], the Moon is made equal to the Sun in perfection and dignity, such that having been linked so intimately to the Sun, she is raised from the lowest to the highest of positions: while the waters beneath the Firmament, that is to say, placed under it, retreat little by little to a single place and are reduced until finally the dry earth appears, which drier than ever, after the summer's extrinsic heat, and extremely athirst, draws back to itself again, by virtue of its power of attraction, particles of this water, like a celestial dew . . . which gently irrigating and fecundating the earth, excites and moves the vegetating virtues in her, of which the *green color* is manifestated evidence, that again appears on her. The *green color is the symbol of the vegetative soul and, at the same time, of the universal nature.* New natures are engendered "in a water that *substantially is nothing less than the pure Spirit* [of the Heaven and Earth], *brought from the potential to the actual, and made one thing, in the same way that two horns are one thing.* When all the celestial rain has burst from the sky and received by the Earth, the darkness of the Earth disappears and the *terra illuminata* returns all around." It is important to emphasize that this "terra illuminata" to which this passage refers is the radiant form or Diana, ☿, for which the explicit reference to Aristotle's vegetative soul, brought to actualization, has special importance.

Forty-One

BiRCh iNCO LiFE AND iMMORCALiCy

h aving arrived at the white, as we have said, the conditions for immortality have been met. "When the materia turns white, our king has conquered death." The "white stone" having been obtained, the preservation of consciousness stops depending on the ordinary body state and its continuity can maintain itself in states and modes of existence that no longer participate in the material world. At death, "the soul does not cease to live: it goes on to live with the purified body illuminated by the fire, in such a way that soul, spirit, and body illuminate one another with a celestial clarity, and are so embraced that they can never again be separated."[1] Then, for man, death becomes nothing more than the ultimate "clarification."

So the Diana whom the disciples of Hermes suddenly get to see completely naked is the equivalent, from this point of view, of the luminous form that, according to the Hindu tradition, is liberated amid the flames of the funeral pyre from the physical body and serves as a vehicle for the liberated to take celestial voyages that symbolize leaps to other conditions of existence, having no resem-

---

[1] B. Valentine, *Dodici chiavi*, 10.

blance to the "Earth."[2] This is equivalent, also, to everything that other traditions always designate in the most varied ways to indicate something like or analogous to the body, that replaces the fleeting flesh and expresses, metaphysically, the group of possibilities brought to the surface by the consciousness that has been victorious over death in the new modes of existence.

The closest agreement is found in alchemical Taoism. According to this doctrine, the condition for immortality is the actual construction of a subtle form to substitute for the gross body; this is obtained by a sublimation that returns said body to that "ethereal" state from which all things emanate, and by an extraction and concentration of the immortal and nonhuman elements making up the foundation of ordinary life.[3] In this case, as in occidental hermetism with its similar opposition to the mystical orientation, immortality relies on the concept of a "condensation" or "coagulation," and does not correspond to turning a light on or off, but to a return of the self to individualization.

It would not be amiss to emphasize the *positive* aspect that the idea of physical regeneration presents in such traditions. A contemporary Hindu alchemist has expressed it in very clear terms, and those who are beginning to understand will observe that the same teaching frequently lies behind the symbols of the ancient, Occidental hermetic literature. Narayāna-Swami[4] speaks of the power of life which, phase by phase, like a plant from a seed, has evolved the physical and psychic organization of man from the masculine germ deposited in the womb. This power lies at the base of every function and pattern of the organism, once its complete development has been reached. The goal of Hindu alchemy was to introduce consciousness into this vital force, causing it to become part of it; then to reawaken and retrace all the phases of the organization, reaching thereby an actual and creative rapport with the completed form of one's own body, which could then literally be called regenerated. "The living man," as opposed to the tradition of the "sleeping" and the "dead," esoterically would be precisely the one who has realized such direct contact with the innermost source of his corporeal life: with the force that makes his heart beat, the power that makes his lungs breathe and that by which the various physico-chemical transformations become what are considered to be "higher" functions.

When this happens the transmutation has been completed: it is no longer a question of physical transformation, but of the change from one function into

---

[2] *Brihadharanyaka-Upanishad*, 6.2.14–15. Note that in this same tradition at the same time it is affirmed (and Buddhism will be even clearer in this affirmation) that "there is no consciousness after death" (referring to ordinary consciousness) as in the image of a grain of salt that, cast into the water, dissolves and cannot be recovered (ibid., 2.4.12; 4.5.13). It is necessary always to bear in mind the basic ideas expressed in the introduction to this part of the present work.

[3] C. Puini, *Taoism* (Lanciano, 1922), 16–19ff.

[4] Narayana-Swami, *Transmutation of Man and Metals* in *Introduzione alla magia*, 3:176ff.

another function. The relation that the regenerated man maintains with his own body is no longer the same as that of its previous tenant and indicates a new existential condition. When the ego is simply joined or united to one's body, we can say with Boehme, that it is almost as if it were the body that generates the ego, that shapes it and gives it the clear sense of self, and by which the ego rules and falls according to the rule and fall of the organism—of a particular, unique and intransferable organism. But when the center of the body is situated in the life-force—which is not the body but that which produces, forms and sustains it—then things are competely changed. This life force is not exhausted by that which it has animated, but can be continued, from one body to other bodies, like a flame that jumps from one log to another; and whoever has come to be dominated by this force—which is altogether outside all ordinary consciousness—naturally will hardly be affected by the dissolution and the death of the body. He will not be touched by death, any more than the faculty of speech is lost when we fall silent or when a word has been interrupted, yet remains fully capable of being spoken sooner or later.

So much for the connection between re-(= new)birth and immortality. In Diana—White Stone, Silver, or Moon, etc.—"extracted" from the material body—Lead or Saturn—or in that which the material body has been transformed, one no longer has a "body," but rather the general power that can manifest a soul in a body in the fullest sense. René Guénon rightly says that "the glorious body" of Gnostic-Christian literature, to which corresponds the aforesaid Silver, "is not a body in the proper sense of this word but is its transformation (or transfiguration), that is, the transposition beyond the form and other conditions of individual (human) existence, or again, in other words, it is the attainment of the permanent and immutable possibility of which the body is no more than a transitory expression of manifested form."[5] Whence, also, the truly profound sense of the permanence and fixation attributed by the hermetic texts to the new body, and in which Body and Spirit have become one thing.

Finally, everything we have just explained can give us the meaning of this concordance—indeed even of the identity and simultaneity—of the two things to be done: the embodiment of the spirit and the spiritualization of the body, which as we already know, is an explicit teaching of alchemy. In fact, the spiritualization of the body is not—as the materialism of certain modern "occultist" views suppose—simply its becoming less physically dense, as though passing into a gaseous, atomic, or similar state. Quite the contrary, it is a matter of the body, while remaining as it is on the outside,[6] now existing solely as a function of the spirit and

---

[5] R. Guénon, L'Homme et son devenir selon le Védânta (Man and His Becoming, [Paris, 1927]), 150.

[6] Symbolically, this idea is expressed in the texts by expressions such as: "The tincture does not in any way increase the weight of a body, because that which tints it is a spirit which has no weight" (Livre de Cratès, CMA, 3:67).

no longer for itself, on the basis of a certain coincidental "cosmic" conjunction and on obscure processes falling below the threshold of the waking consciousness.

According to such an interpretation, the body is not "spiritualized" until the first moment that the spirit can live out the existence of the body as its own actualization, while the spirit at the same point "embodies" itself with the help of a "projection" and "coagulation," and it is this in-corporation as actualization that allows the body to become "nonphysical," that is, nonexistent, as a thing in itself.

The soul has already been dissolved, has reached that which possesses neither form nor conditions, that is, the pure state. Once it has done all this, it goes on to regenerate forms, conditions, determinations—in sum, those things from which it has been dissociated—so that by its own action, the "fixed" is no more than an active "fixation" of the "volatile." "This dissolution," says one text, "comes to reduce the body, which is terrestrial, to its First Matter [that is, to the state of pure, undifferentiated power or ether, of which it is the coagulation], so that the body and the spirit are made inseparably one . . . this is done in order to reduce the body to the same quality as the spirit, and then the body mixes with the spirit, inseparably [as the outer word mixes and is made one with the action of the voice that recovers it and says it again] without ever separating itself from it, just like water poured into water. To such an end the body, at first, is raised with the spirit and finally the spirit is fixed to the body."[7]

Obviously, the chemical terms "sublimate" and "elevate" must be understood metaphorically, as it is understood, for example, when one is spoken of as having been *elevated* to a certain charge or dignity;[8] in the case of the body it is exactly the assumption of a superior function, which is that of the superindividual spiritual principles to which symbolically correspond the most noble metals: first Silver, then Gold.[9]

Likewise, the word *androgyne* (or Rebis), used so frequently in the present special practice to designate the union of the two natures at different stages, should not give an impression of two separate and different substances or principles, as if they could be two things. The "materia" is no more than a stage, a phase of the Spirit's being; the Spirit, on increasing, incorporates nothing different from itself; on the contrary, in nothing other than in the practical inner realization of this nondiversity consists the true conjunction—says Rouillac in the *Abrégé du Grand'Oeuvre*: "it is called Rebis, because they are two things that *are not two*."

---

[7] *Filum Ariadnae*, chap. 51.

[8] Arnold of Villanova, *Semita semitae*, 12.

[9] "To change the natures"—says Pernety (*Dictionnaire*, 45)—is not to make the mixtures pass from one kingdom of nature to another, but on the contrary and precisely, it is to spiritualize the bodies and corporealize the spirits, that is, to fix the volatile and volatize the fixed. And, in synthesis, to achieve consciousness as a body and the body as consciousness through the pure action of the life-light."

And Pernety: "It is called Rebis because it makes the two one, indissolubly, although the two are nothing less than one and the same thing and Materia."[10] Artephius says even more explicitly of the reduction of Body and Spirit "to the same *simplicity* that will render them equal and similar," which is obtained precisely not by the addition of one thing to another, but by an action: "spiritualizing the one and corporealizing the other."[11]

The analogy to which we have already alluded here, can be expanded as follows: let us imagine ourselves before a manuscript written in an unknown language. The only thing that this writing means to me is that it is a group of signs that I have simply found and contemplated. Very similar is the ordinary state of the "fixed": such as I am, as far as a living individuality with given organs, faculties, possibilities, etc., for the most part I simply accept, I merely "am." "To be" is one thing, but to wish, comprehend, to be able to want something different, is something else altogether.

We can expand the analogy by saying that I know the language in which the inscription is written, and then I am no longer limited just to looking at it, but I can read and understand; the signs are then converted for me into a mere prop, a mere point of departure for an action of my spirit. In their physical sense it is as if they no longer existed: the inscription can be destroyed, but I will always be able to reproduce it beginning with my spirit and *finishing* with those signs instead of starting and ending in them, as was the case when they were nothing but incomprehensible hieroglyphics to me.

Carrying the analogy[12] to the corporeal being, one can understand how the corporeal in something can be transformed into that which is noncorporeal, without changing outwardly: because in fact, from the materialist point of view, no change has taken place in the signs. It is the same whether they have been encountered so or written automatically, or if they have been produced creatively as a free expression of a spiritual sense. So, a "spiritual body" would be completely indiscernible—externally— from any body, insofar as the supernormal possibilities that the former can manifest are left out and, in the scond place, if we disregard the fact that in this case "body" is no longer limited to an expression of the single condition of human existence.

---

[10] Ibid., 427.

[11] *Livre d'Artephius*, (*BPC* 2:164) adds: "This is impossible if it's not separated beforehand." Petrus Bonus (in *BCC*, 2:29ff.) speaks of an almost incredible subtlety (*subtilitas fere incredibilis*) and of a nature "as much spiritual as corporeal."

[12] In our *Yoga of Power* we have employed it to explain the tantric doctrine of the world as "word" and the "names of power," or *mantras*. We have also used it in our *Doctrine of the Awakening* to clarify similar analogies.

Birth into Life and Immortality · · · · · · · · · · · · · · · · · · **167**

Forty-Two

ChE REĐ WORK: RETURN ĈO EARĈh

We have taken somewhat longer with these observations because up to a certain point, what is true of the working of the White is also true of the Red. In fact, the distinction between these two phases (corresponding to the terms "small" and "great medicine") is simply one of *intensity;* they are two successive moments in the same process of "fixation." If the first labor is assigned to the Moon, certainly, as we have seen, the masculine Sun also plays a part. To arrive at the red all that needs to be done is to increase the Fire, which is now no longer united with the body by the Water, but directly, arriving by virtue of its nature at a depth the previous work had not touched: where the "limestone," the "almighty giant"[1] lies sleeping.

If we stop at the White Work we are reunited with Life, but Life that has a certain given form, subject to a kind of internal law that arises at once and which when followed, achieves its purpose but is not its own origin; much as one who having in his head a thought or feeling could represent or write about it freely, but could not claim he was himself its creator.

When we spoke of the quadripartition of the human being (page 46), we saw that

---

[1] Cf. *Triomphe Hermétique, BPC,* 3:296: "Just as there are three kingdoms in nature, so there are also three medicines in our Art, which are three different works in practice [corresponding to ⏚, ∇ and △] which are nothing more than three different *steps* that raise our elixir to its ultimate perfection."

it is not in its vital energies themselves that the order of the body lies but, more deeply, in its *minerality,* in its telluric, determined, unanimous essentiality, over which the laws of the physical world (Earth element) dominate, and not laws of biology or psychology. This aspect of the body is the first basis of its form and individuation. And behind that are hidden the primordial powers of all form and individualization. But when by increasing the Fire the clean, clear, life-bestowing water is reabsorbed, we come into contact with this region no longer via the ☿ energies, but through the individuating ♃ actions. In this way a new *solve* is obtained and a corresponding *coagula* imposed; and that is what constitutes the Red Work.

The ego is transformed by these actions, and *is* these actions—the "Fires of Saturn," the Gods of the "Golden Age"—to the point of reducing completely one's own individualization to that function of "nature which is dominated by itself" and corporeality to something that expresses nothing better than this same domination. It is to this stage that we attribute the purple, the sceptre, the crown, and all the other symbolic elements of royalty and empire. For only here is the regeneration complete. On the other hand, in this Work—in the *coagula* to which we refer—the supreme energy of the spirit is obliged to manifest: an idea clearly expressed in the formula of the Emerald Tablet that says the Telesma, "strong strength of all strength," is complete in its power only when it has been "converted into Earth."[2] And the Greek texts concur when they represent the third phase after the *nigredo* and the *albedo* as the true reanimation of the Fire—ἀναζωπύρωσις—and the resurrection of the dead.[3]

Characteristically, teachings of every tradition agree that *we must not stop with the "White" Work.* "The white elixir is not the ultimate perfection, because it still lacks the Fire[4] element as resurrection of the primordial Fire thirsting for the telluricity of the Body. "In the philosophic Saturn resides the authentic resurrection and the truly inseparable life," it is said elsewhere.[5] "The Earth found at the bottom of the cup [that is, the body, as that which remains after removing the subtle principles] is the Gold mine of the Philosophers, the Fire of Nature and the Fire of Heaven,"[6] whence we can

---

[2] Cf. *Filum Ariadnae,* 107: "The Work begins with the Earth element, which is reduced to Water; then the Water is reduced to Air, the Air to Fire and the Fire to Fixation, that is, in Earth, so that the work ends where it began. This is the philosophic conversion of the elements, from one to another."

[3] In *CAG,* 1:252

[4] Ibid., 145.

[5] *De pharmaco catholico,* 9, §2.

[6] D'Espagnet, *Arcanum hermeticae,* §§122, 123. An engraving of the *Margarita pretiosa* shows a coffin in which the king has been enclosed. Out of this comes a Child (first phase: the Regenerated) that the alchemist, nevertheless, must shut away again with the Father or King, which is an allegory of the necessity for the Regenerated to be enclosed with the still dormant and subterranean forces of the primordial individualization.

return to the different quotations already annotated (see p. 68ff.) about the richness of the scum, ashes, dregs, and other residues of earth, where in reality the "titan" hides, the "consummated act," the "Diadem of the King," the true Gold of the Philosphers, etc.

Here again, by the act of awakening and being awakened at the same time (the deep powers produce a transfiguration of the principle that has awakened them, in which, in the final analysis, they still participate), the mineral body, so to speak, returns the ego to the consciousness of its primordial and absolute act, of which the body expresses petrification, the neutralized state, sleep, and the mute state of dark slavery.[7] The Silver then is transmuted into Gold, not only as life and "light" ☿ (since spirit and body now form a single thing), but also as pure ego ☉.

The Greek literature speaks of a virility, or Arsenic, prepared with Egyptian niter (niter ⊕ again, indicates the specifically masculine qualification of the spiritual energy—while the "Egypt" in these doctrines is often the equivalent of a symbol for the body and of such a force ⊕ as is produced in the body) and they teach how to extract the divine water—θεῖα ὕδατα—from such substance, in which the spirits (then) take corporeal form: elevating themselves as divine or sulfurous mysteries—θεῖα μυστήρια—as celestial bodies—οὐράνια σώματα—and redescending "to the darker depths of the infernal, of Hades" (technically it is the inferior site ♈, of which we spoke on page 46, the organic correspondence of the "will" principle), and there they meet with the crude masses of "our Earth," that "Ethiopia," equivalent to the Lead and the Saturn of the later texts; they are the dead—νεκροῖς—who are reanimated—θνητὰ ἐμψυχοῦνται—and by alteration and transformation—ἀλλοίωσις καὶ μεταβολή—rectified, so that the black Earth produces precious stones, divine bodies—θεῖα σώματα.[8] Speaking comprehensively there is an "essential menstruum that washes the Earth and is raised to a quintessence in which the sulfurous thunderbolt in one instant penetrates the bodies and destroys the excrementa."[9]

---

[7] In symbols that must by now be rather transparent to the reader, Zosimos (CAG, 2:93, 95) says that the black Lead is fixed in the "Spheres of Fire." Its heaviness attracts a new soul, and "in that consists the Great Mystery," called the "Great Medicine" which induces new colors and new qualities in the subject.

[8] CAG, 2:292-94, 296ff. In the traditons of some primitive peoples, which we have to consider as degenerated and materialistic survivals of more ancient traditions, they speak of magic "stones" or "crystals" substituted by the spirits in place of the body organs, put in them during the magical sleep of initiation leading to rebirth. Cf. Hubert-Mauss, Mélanges d'histoire de la religion (Paris, 1929).

[9] J. M. Ragon, Initiation hermétique, 45.

Let us see what Eliphas Levi has to say: "The power that proceeds from the gold is comparable to *lightning* that, at first, is a dry terrestrial exhalation united with the humid vapor but then, when exalted, takes on a fiery quality, and acts on the humidity inherent to it, attracting it and agitating it in its own nature, until it precipitates dizzyingly to Earth, where a fixed nature *similar* to its own [corresponding to the "projection" of the primordial act that has determined the essentiality of the physical form] attracts it."[10] Synesius says that with the "descent" the airy substance begins to coagulate whereupon the Fire Devourer appears, from which proceeds the destruction of the humidity, that is, the root of the waters, the ultimate calcination and fixation.[11] The philosophic basilisk—says Crollius[12]—in the guise of a *thunderbolt* instantly penetrates and destroys the "imperfect metals." Now we have repeatedly referred to the correspondence of such a bolt with that by which the "titans" were struck. We need only add that the "imperfection of the metals" means specifically debility and insufficiency (the "incurable disease of privation") with regard to the total action: that of identifying oneself with the original power in order to be reintegrated supernaturally—but to avoid being "fulminated." Such is the perfection of the Opus Magnum or Great Work.

Just as there has been a "trial by Water" and a "trial by the Void," so in the new experience we can expect a "trial by Fire," more risky but to no different purpose. But in the first trial the separation of the vital principle from the denser body combination that kept it immobilized did not affect the combination itself, which went on existing and kept the seals of individuality. But now these seals have been broken and we pass beyond the absolutely undifferentiated point, beyond the point from which every individuating act successively has taken origin, but that as such can likewise serve as the central point of the "great dissolution" and, to tell the truth, not only with regard to the human condition or to some other particular state conditioned by this or any other "world," but in general. Every awakening demands an act of mastery (the repetition of a primordial act of control) so that the revived Fires do not act destructively.

According to some texts both operations, the white and the red, blend into one another to some extent.[13] In any case, only when the consciousness has been "subtilized" so that the ego learns a mode of being that is no longer supported by the corporeal and is able to perceive the forces directly and not

[10] E. Levi, *Dogma and Ritual*, 395.

[11] *Livre de Synesius*, BPC, 2:185.

[12] Crollius, *Basilica chymica* (Frankfurt, 1609), 94.

[13] Cf., for example, *Entretiens*, BPC, 2:92.

by the sensations or emotions of the body, only then can one hope to reach the depth of the Earth and there find no limits, but the beginning of the awakening of a higher wave in an absolute self-union, a resurrection without residue.[14] The separate phases are always: first, the *tincture*, that is, the infusion of ☉ or △ into ☿; then *penetration*, realized by means of ☿, which is introduced into the forms animated by it; and finally, *fixation*, in the full manifestation of the primordial forces contained in such forms.[15]

---

[14] See *Livre de El Habir* (*CMA*, 3:107): "The soul cannot tint the body, if one has not extracted the spirit hidden within it; then Body is left without Soul (the dross or scum), during which we possess a spiritual nature whose gross and terrestrial parts have been eliminated. When this has been made subtle and spiritual, it is in condition to receive the tincture that is introduced into the Body and tints it." Geber, *Summa* (*BCC*, 1:537): "The dissolution takes place with the help of the subtle, airy, caustic Waters free of all sediment. It has been fabricated by rendering more subtle the things that are not fusible or penetrable [*fusionem nec ingressionem habent*] that possess very useful fixed essences, which would be lost without this operation." Cf. Arnold of Villanova, *Thesaurus* (in *BCC*, 1:665): "*Nisi corpora fiunt incorporea nihil operamini*" [Unless the bodies are made incorporeal your work comes to naught].

[15] The three powers of the *xerion* or Projection Powder: βαφη, εἴσκρισις, κάτοχον, according to the Greek alchemists (*CAG*, 2:205). The alchemical idea expressed by the symbol of the "grain of incombustible Sulfur" has its correspondence in that other symbol of the "tiny bone," called luz, from which, according to Agrippa (*De occulta philosophia*, 1:20), "as plant grows from seed, the body is regrown in the resurrection and which has the virtue, moreover, of not having been destroyed by the fire."

Forty-Three

Che Alchemical Colors and Multiplication

In addition to the three fundamental colors—black, white, and red—others are also found within the literature. Essentially there are seven in all, which brings us back to the planetary correspondences mentioned before (chapter 14). But as for their place in the Work more than one interpretation is possible.

For Flamel, for example, the appearance of seven colors expresses the operation of the Spirit that adapts itself to the body by means of the soul;[1] the colors are equivalent to the seven colors of the rainbow appearing after the Flood as a sign of the alliance between "Earth" and "Heaven"—after the *black* raven did not return and the *white* dove flew back with the olive branch.[2] Thus the colors are so many phases of the physical regeneration that follow the rebirth in the Water. The opening of the seven doors or seven seals, the passage through the seven planets, the knowledge of the seven gods or seven angels, the ascension into the seven heavens and the various septenary figurations whose possible reference to the seven

---

[1] Flamel, *Désir désiré*, 314. Cf. Arnold of Villanova, *Semita semitae*, 12.

[2] Note that it is also the doves that bring the golden bough to Aeneas, so that he may descend to the underworld and return from it, a myth that even in antiquity referred to the initiatic mystery.

"centers of life" in the body—all these correspond to the hermetic colors, which express the successive "tyings" and "untyings" of the "knots" of the telluric being as it is worked by the Fire power.

Among other things, here we can discover the alchemical process of *multiplication* at work, which happens when, instead of a gradual total transformation, the conquest of one principle or spiritual state comes first. This principle or state is then "multiplied" by the transmutation of other natures into its own. As one flame ignites another flame, so one awakening awakens another. Such "multiplication" can be *quantitative*, when the resultant new elements do not change the nature of the function in which they are resolved (they do not lead, for example, from the White to the Red, but they infuse the white quality to successive orders of principles); or it can be *qualitative*, when said new elments are instead such that, to dominate them, the function that invests them must itself be transformed and pass through "exaltation" (*exaltatio*) into another higher function.[3] It is said, in any case, that "if we are satisfied to arrive at the perfect white or red without making any 'multiplications,' then we have settled for very little, because the multiplications build up a treasure and growth of power approaching the infinite,"[4] a saying that refers to the teaching that the Spirits, although they may have attained the strength of physical entities, multiply and reach their maximum intensity only when they combine with living bodies.[5]

Expressive symbols for multiplication, in the texts, are the allegories of personages (especially the King) who give their own "flesh" (their own nature) to other personages—frequently these are six or seven—which represent the principles that must undergo the transmutation; that is, each of the Six or Seven ask the One (a King on a throne, in the illustration of the *Margarita pretiosa*) for a kingdom or crown, that is, for the conquered and spiritually revived quality of royal Gold or the Sun.

Flamel, on the other hand,[6] associating multiplication with the symbol of the

---

[3] Presently we shall say something more about "multiplication" in its aspect as regarding the transmission of a quality or "tincture" (color), not to the principles still untransformed ("crude") in the same being, but to different beings, so that the same spiritual influence of the initiate is transmitted to them.

[4] *Filum Ariadnae*, 124.

[5] *Livre de la miséricorde*, CMA, 3:180. In this text it is specified that those energies that, combined with the Body, reach their maximum of intensity and resist the Fire "are *not the ones that can be reached through the ordinary senses*."

[6] Flamel, *Figures hiéroglyphiques*, see fig. 7 (BPC, 2:257). Other symbols of multiplication are: the pelican that feeds her own flesh to her children; the Phoenix (after all, *phoinix* means "red"), from whom come other birds as seen in an engraving of Libavius (in *Alchimia recognita, emendatam, et aucta* [Frankfurt, 1606]) which is accompanied by the legend: *Crescite et multiplicamini* [be fruitful and multiply].

key (= opening and closing) brings us back to a well-known meaning: to open, or *solve*, is what happens to each contact when energies are released into the free state; to close, to fix (*coagula*)—and even more expressly, to fell, to kill, to decapitate—is to reseal, awakening the "nature that dominates and contains Nature," and arresting the return of the dampening power of chaos that would try to sweep away and drown out whatever has brought on the turmoil of awakening.[7]

In the hierarchy of the Seven, every "closing" also establishes a quality by means of which one is attracted automatically to the next principle. For these interior experiences one could employ the image of a nucleus [or kernel] that lets the influence of a magnetic field in which it enters act upon it, allowing itself to be drawn into and identify with the nucleus, in turn, of the field—except that it detaches itself and becomes independent again once that identification is perfect. It then goes on to a higher force field in which the same phases are repeated: until it has traversed the entire hierarchy, fixating it and resealing all the powers—powers that, in turn, have allowed into their dissolutions universal and nonhuman forms of vision and power—in the full possession of the recomposed corporeality.

At this point we return to the cipher language of *dosing*—exact quantities in "mixtures" of active and passive, attraction and repulsion, abandon and mastery—the so-called science of balances, concerning which it has been taught: "If we could take a man, dismantle him in order to *balance* the natures in him and return him to a new existence, such a man would no longer be able to die"—moreover, "Once this equilibrium has been obtained, beings are exempt from change, no longer altered or modified."[8] It is the supreme stability of the Philosopher's Stone, responding to the command of the Arab alchemists: "Make ye immortal the bodies,"[9] which expresses the *other* nature's way of being: that of the no-longer-men.

Because of the equivalance of "dissolve" and "elevate," of "coagulate" and

---

[7] The work of extinguishing the resurgent gushing forth of the waters with every contact is hermetically related to Hercules' labor of killing the Hydra—whose name betrays its connection to that element—hacking off the immediately reborn heads that are the ever-renewing trunk of desire in the primordial energies; and also because *seven* are the heads sometimes attributed to the Hydra. Before this rebirth—says Della Riviera (*Mondo magico*, 103)—"stands the unconquered Hero, and to extinguish its origin [as water] by the fire of Nature, he conquers it; that is, he transmutes the body fluid into Earth, though still imperfect." An equivalent enterprise is the killing of Geryon, who assumes three forms, which it is necessary to conquer in order to be able to take away the "flock": forms that correspond in the hermetic interpretation to the three critical points—separation, trial by Water, and trial by Fire—which, moreover, are related to the three sites: head, breast, and trunk (see page 82ff.). These are also found in Hindu esotericism, which speaks of the three "knots" localized in the basal, cardial, and frontal centers (*mūlādhāra, anahata, ājñā*), where the force that tries to arrest the initiation process is particularly difficult to overcome (cf. Evola, *The Yoga of Power*, 173)

[8] *Livre des balances, CMA*, 3:148.

[9] *Livre de Cratès, CMA*, 3:52.

"descend," multiplication can also be called the "circulation" of the substance that, by the power of Fire, is obtained in the hermetically sealed vessel—seven times, according to some authors—which substance, when subtilized into vapor, is raised, condenses upon touching the upper part of the vessel or *athanor*, and is reprecipitated in the form of a sublimate that transmutes a part of the remains below as *caput mortuum*. When because of the greater heat the substance reascends, it transports this part with it, in order then to be condensed and redescend with an even more energetic "tinting power," which in turn acts on a further part of the substance, and so on successively. We have spoken of this merely chemical symbolism before.

Returning to the symbolism of the passage through the planets, Basil Valentine shows us the whole process in the following apocalyptic form: "Then the old world will fade away and a new world will take its place, and every planet will spiritually consume the other, in such a way that the strongest, having fed on the others [see below: the reduction of the subsolar planets through the agency of those of the higher symmetrics], will be the only ones that remain, and two and three [the two expresses the generic principle of opposition, while the three is the number of planets in each group: ♄, ♃, ♂ and ♀, ☿, ☽] will be conquered by the One alone [the final simplicity, corresponding to the state beyond the Seven]."[10] We can also quote the following passage of Boehme, concerning the moment when "Mercurius judged in the Sulfur Saturni is transmuted according to the lust for liberty": "The cadaver is raised up in a new body with a beautiful white color. . . . The Materia delays resolving and when it has been made desirous again [reference to the impulse that leads to further contact] the Sun rises from it . . . in the Center of Saturn, with Jupiter, Venus and the seven forms. And it is a new Creation, solar, white and red, majestic, luminous, and fiery.[11]

Petrus Bonus has this to say: "The ancient alchemists, thanks to the recognitions of their art, were well informed about the end of the world and the resurrection of the dead: because the Soul unites again, for eternity, with its original Body. The Body becomes completely glorified and incorruptible, so incredibly subtle that it can penetrate all densities. . . . The ancient philosophers saw the Universal Judgment within the operations of their art, that is to say, in the germination and birth of the Stone, because in it occurs the union of the Soul to glorify with its original body, in an 'eternal glory.'"[12] According to Michael Maier the last phase is a sempiternal fire, the *rubedo*, whose emblem is the circle in which the perfect triangle of the Body, Soul, and Spirit can be found.[13]

---

[10] B. Valentine, *Dodici chiavi*, 59 (ninth key).

[11] Boehme, *De signatura*, 12, §23.

[12] P. Bonus, *Margarita pretiosa*, BCC, 2:29

[13] M. Maier, *Scrutinium chymicum* (Frankfurt, 1687), 63

Forty-Four

. . . .

Che planecary
hierarchy

At the beginning of the previous chapter we mentioned that there are different interpretations of the seven. These differences also have to do with part of the disagreement over the order of the planets as given in various texts. This inconsistency, when not a question of distortions, proceeds either from the designation of different terms and symbols for the same things, or from an actual difference of the methods followed. When we speak of the seven "centers of life" we must also bear in mind that present in each are the forces of the others alongside its own, which is the dominant one.[1] Thus, by way of a given method or of a temperament more akin to one of the secondary energies than to the dominant one, there can be produced in a given center the awakening of a principle that normally should correspond to another center; so that one planet in the symbolism may take the place of another. So, for example, that same tiny *luz* to which we have alluded (see page 172, note 15), from which "the body sprouts or recreates itself in resurrection" according to the qabalistic tradition Agrippa refers to (and in full accord with the analogous Hindu teaching), is situated in the mystic region of the sacrum—but in certain Teraphim figures is found between the two eyes and also in the heart. So one and the same force, or state, is manifested in different centers.

Della Riviera gives the following order: Saturn, Jupiter, Mars, Earth, Venus,

---

[1] See Boehme (*Aurora*, 10, §40): "The seven are not separate, but they are as you see the stars in heaven, standing apart from one another and yet all together, one in the other, like a single spirit."

Moon, and Sun.[2] The interpretation is double and depends on whether it is a question of the dry path, that is, of a *continuous* line of purification and transformation up to the light form (Moon) and then to the Sun—or a question of phases *succeeding* to a preliminary realization of the Sun, in the sense of the grades of resurrection that the Sun itself works through when it goes to work on Saturn, the Body (or Earth). In this instance Saturn generates, as the myth says, the different gods (corresponding to the planets) and rises finally to the absolute perfection of the Sun or Gold, wherein, by "the removal of all their infirmities, impurities and heterogeneous ingredients," the "magic metals"[3] are transformed.

Pernety provides this order: Lead (Saturn, black), Tin (Jupiter, gray), Silver (Moon, white), Copper (Venus, reddish-yellow), Iron (Mars, rust), Purple, and Gold (Sun, red).[4] Here it is clear that the planets and the metals correspond to the phases of the diminishing of the darkness (from black to gray to silver) and of progressive ignification (orange, rust, red).

In Philalethes, the Lordship of Mercury takes first place as the "Labor of Hercules," of "separation" whereby the Gold "is stripped of its gilded garments," "the breaking of the Lion by such a struggle that he is reduced to the greatest debility." The rulership of Saturn follows, the black color, and here "the Lion is dead." Jupiter comes next, the God that dethroned Saturn, who now approaches but the first traces of the *albedo*. The immaculate white is the domain of the Moon. Venus follows—going from the white to the green—expressing the first symbolic plant growth from the Earth-body's cohesion, which rises up as ☿, freed of the impure *heat* of the dead Lion. The green then becomes sky blue, turning livid and changing to reddish brown, then pale purple, colors that indicate the iosis or combustion that begins to be produced within the heart of ☿. But now Mars intervenes, virile and ironlike, to produce the desiccation: "Here the Matter is enclosed and sealed in the bowels of her son and purified until having cast out of the composition all impurity and having replaced it with eternal purity": it is the color orange (which in Pernety corresponds to rust). Finally the Lordship of the Sun is reached, in which "from thy Materia a light hardly to be imagined will irradiate," which after three days becomes the most intense red.[5]

---

[2] *Mondo magico*, 207.

[3] Ibid., 208, This passage is rather important because it says that the Gold is "the Soul and Life of the thing itself," which when it has been "magically regulated and prepared" is transformed into this Gold.

[4] Pernety, *Fables*, 1:73.

[5] Philalethes, *Introitus apertus*, §§24–30. Another symbol used for the different symbolical colors is the peacock's tail. In Boehme (*De signatura*, 7, §§74–76), the order is the following: Saturn, Moon, Jupiter, Mars, Venus, Mercury, Sun. The process is described as follows: "When the corporealization of the Child has begun, Saturn carries it off and drops it into the darkness . . . the Moon's taking possession of it follows, mixing the celestial properties with the earthly, and thereby manifesting the vegetative life [i.e., ☿]. But there still remains a danger to be overcome [see p. 130–131]. After the Moon, Jupiter

In the ancient Hellenistic tradition transmitted by Stephanos,[6] the order varies again. The sidereal regions, associated with the gods and sacred metals, have the following order: Saturn (Lead, ♄), Jupiter (Bronze, ♃), Mars (Iron, ♂), Sun (Gold, ☉), Venus (Copper, ♀), Mercury (☿), Moon (Silver, ☾). This disposition can be turned around, however, according to a symmetry that has the Sun in the center with Saturn, Mars, and Jupiter above it as a triad of masculine divinities, with Venus, Mercury, and Moon below it in a triad of feminine deities (Mercury being the "Lady of the Philophers"), as in the diagram reproduced below. The spiritual itinerary, so to speak, then proceeds in a spiral: starting from a higher masculine god, it descends to join the symmetrical feminine divinity, then rises again and arrives finally at the center occupied by the Sun. The rising and falling movement that unites the symmetrical pairs corresponds, thus, to the successive sublimations and precipitations also circulating within the enclosed *athanor:* a descent to the "Infernal," where each "Arsenic" encounters a Water with which by dissolution, recomposition, and resurrection, prepares it to be converted into a metal each time closer to the Gold.

It is a peculiar "coincidence" that this same disposition of the planets is found in Gichtel, the same spiral journey beginning with Saturn ♄ and ending in the Sun ☉; an itinerary we have already interpreted (see pages 57-58) in its other possible sense as an involutional process. We know, however, that Gichtel connects each planet or god to a specific region of the body and we have remarked how these regions correspond, if we refer them to points on the spinal column, to approximately the places that Hindu esotericism assigns to the seven "centers of life."

The spiral also allows us to express in synthesis the whole process of the Art if we consider it to have a double course: centripetal from ♄ to ☉, and centrifugal from ☉ to ♄. In the first case, the upper triad expresses the elements of the vulgar state that are covered in "shadow," which encounter in their respective lower elements their liberating "dissolution." If we base ourselves on the teaching of Macrobius (*Commentarium in somnium Scipionis*), Saturn ♄ corresponds to the *intelligentia*—τὸ θεωρητικόν—and to the *ratiocinatio*—τὸ λογιστόν—which in

---

constructs a dwelling place for the life in the Mercury and starts the movement of the wheel that elevates it to but greater anguish, where Mars furnishes the Mercury with the fiery Soul. In *Mars* the more sublime life is enkindled, dividing into two essences: a body of love and a spirit of fire. The life of love [the sympathetic power of attraction and of the penetration of the 3] descends into the fiery interior effervescence and is manifested in all its beauty; but Mercury gobbles up this Venus. The Child then turns into a black raven, and Mars oppresses Mercury to its annihilation. Then the four elements are liberated from it and the Sun gathers up the Child and presents it in its virgin body to the pure Element. The light has shone in the quality of Mars, in this is born the true life of the Unique Element, against which no Choler and no Death can stand." These expressions can be interpreted in various ways: possibly also from the perspective of the episodes of the White work alone.

[6] Cf. Berthelot, *Introduction*, 84.

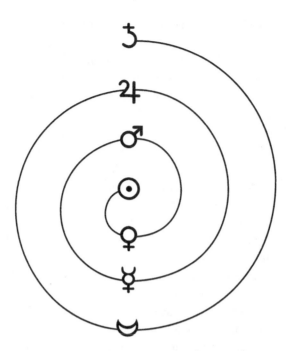

the first descending arc are dissolved in the Moon ☾. This is an allusion to the immersion of the reflective waking consciousness in certain vital energies, designated by the term τὸ φυσικὸν. The successive ascending arc rejoins Jupiter ♃, to which corresponds in the external consciousness the *vis agendi*—τὸ πρακτικόν—(we could also call it the "will," in its narrow modern sense); this is dissolved in Mercury ☿ as in the energy, frequently infraconscious, of the subtle intellect that runs invisibly through the woof of the common psychic processes—τὸ ἑρμηνευτικόν. It returns to rise up to Mars ♂, as *ardor animositatis*—τὸ θυμικόν—which finds its dissolvent in Venus ♀—τὸ ἐπιθυμητικόν; after which the descending arc enters the renascence or reminiscence of the *solar* ☉ consciousness, which begins to shine out through the dark masses of the body's prison.

Now follows the second movement, starting from the exact center ☉. The Sun, as *virtus, ios,* ferment, "stem," virile force of "rectification," etc., projects itself onto Venus and transforms her into Mars. With this power it agitates and fixates the Mercury and from it extracts the Jupiter. Finally it descends into the radical power of the Waters, understood as the outer limit of the vital force ☾ irradiating "Our Earth" and with that, it reascends, rejoins Saturn and recognizes it as the God of the "Golden Age." Thereby—and in accord with the gnostic precept—that which is above is extended to that which is below, and that which is below is carried above. Saturn, Jupiter, and Mars in this phase are "regenerations," noble metals no longer dead, out of which is produced an elixir of treble potency, capable of curing the "incurable disease of privation," that is, of the state of necessary materialism (see pages 77-78), of the three kingdoms, mineral, vegetable, and animal.

Here essentially are the deep entifications of man, and because of the not only symbolic and analogical but also magical correspondence of these entities with the kingdoms of nature in the true sense, this can also signify an introduction of consciousness into those nonphysical entities, of which these three kingdoms are the cosmic avenues of perception. "Mars" must be recognized, then, as that which is manifested tangibly in the form of the collective energies of animality; "Jupiter," as that which is reflected in the structures and growths determined by the nature of the forces of plants; while "Saturn," would be the "gods" that produce the world of metals, salts, and crystals within the mineral Earth:[7] together these planets constitute the triad of the great Uranian Gods.

The other three planets or principles, below the Sun or heart, act as dissolvents of the three vulgar suprasolar forms and represent macrocosmically that which corresponds to the human subconscious. They are the "nether" powers where the principle of chaos dwells. The "dissolution" that the initiate confronts as he descends into these *interiora terrae* is equivalent to that dissolution which, at the moment of natural death, returns the individual principles of the human being to the original impersonal macrocosmic roots whence they derived and on which they were fed. This region can properly be called the realm of Hades, that is, *where the dead go*, and when the portal is opened—not by a stream flowing down from the upper to the lower, but, on the contrary, by a nether force moving toward the higher spheres, the faculties of the awakened higher consciousness—then occurs the phenomenology of mediums, diabolical possession, confused and instinctual clairvoyance, visionary and nebulous mysticism with its angels, demons, and divers apparitions. This hybrid result of noncorporeal experiences mixed with repercussions of organic states and subjective residues, takes the form of uncontrolled and schizophrenic imagination.

This danger is greater in the methods of the wet path because these try to seek the objective precisely through the ascending path that the power of the liberated dissolving waters open. We have to insist here on what we have already said about anything deriving from the presence of unreduced elements, whether their presence is due to an inadequate preparation of the material or to insufficient energy of the awakened forces, which in the wet path are necessary to neutralize completely ("decapitate") every faculty of the external human consciousness.

---

[7] In this context, we might recall the images of the poet A. Honofrius in his *Terrestrità del sole* (Florence, 1926): "Beings all made of power come to us from above—Celestials, thinking diamond and iron, within their craggy graves. . . . Lightning-flashing powers, out of you comes the perfect form of the crystals." "In the head and shoulders is the power—that in mighty angels thinks earth—as in the breast, blood, and rhythm are the Sun."

However, when the current descends from the upper spheres, bringing with it a "quintessence"—obtained by means of asceticism and purification—of the faculties of the higher level of awakening, which have become independent of all infrasensible and affective influence, then such a "quintessence" acts as one of those chemical reagents a single drop of which is enough to clarify and make transparent certain very muddy solutions. The light is extended through the netherworld and its dark and vague forms change into definite and divine forms of the higher world: the one and the other being ultimately—as the septenary declares—the same reality that presents itself in two different states or experiences.[8]

Let us add a few words about the correspondences between the metals, gods, and centers of power in man from the practical point of view. In the same way that the energies of a "god" are expressed in the processes that form those metals in the bosom of the earth that traditionally were consecrated to it; and, moreover, as they are manifested also in the kinds of life energies which in man are expressed by designated organs and centers—so between certain forces locked in the body and certain metals there exist analogical relations of a "magical" (sympathetic) type, which serve as a basis for three distinct practical possibilities.

First, the introduction into the organism of certain metallic substances in given doses and forms, when the consciousness has been "refined" enough to be able to accompany and surprise what happens behind the scenes of the densest corporeality, can serve to introduce the same consciousness into the corresponding "centers" that have been especially energized by those substances. Moreover, if the imagination has a certain independence of the corporeal senses, it is possible for the resultant experience to be dramatized in the form of visions of figures and divinities, often utilizing the images that the operator keeps latent in his subconscious as vestiges of his faith or tradition.[9] As can be seen, this brings us again, in a certain

---

[8] In this regard it is very interesting to read in the *Bardo Thödol* (Tibetan Book of the Dead) about the *post mortem* experiences (which in initiation, in a special state of consciousness, are produced while still in life). It is taught that the dark and infernal gods are all one with the luminous ones: they are the same gods, but realized by an understanding incapable of identifying with the first, incapable of recognizing them as part of its own transcendent being, and dominated by irrational impulses.

[9] A Christian or a Brahman will have visions conforming to his beliefs, as different vestments for the same experience. The teaching about the correspondence of "all the members and parts of the human body" with "sacred forms" is explicit in the Qabalah (cf. *Zohar*, 1.272b). In Hindu esotericism there is a practice known as *nyāsa*, in which the divinities that correspond to the different parts of the body are ritually imposed on them. (cf. Evola, *The Yoga of Power*, 105-7.) Agrippa (*De occulta philosophia*, 3:13) writes: "If a man capable of receiving the divine influence maintains one clean and purified member or organ of the body, this becomes a receptacle for that member or organ corresponding to the god [that is, of the primordial Man contained in the sepulchre of the body] which is hidden in him as behind a veil." In the medieval texts we often encounter human figures, in which the astrological signs of the metals and planets placed in each part of the body serve to indicate the respective correspondences. In order to cover all the variants of such correspodences, we would have to penetrate far into the terrain of astrology, which would exceed the limits of the present book.

way and at least from a more precise direction of efficacy, to the technique of the "sacred beverages" and the "corrosive waters" in general (see pages 135–137).

Vice versa, once the consciousnesses sleeping in designated centers or organs of the human body have been extracted, it is possible thereby to be introduced into the "mysteries" of the forces acting occultly in the corresponding metal natures. Or in more mythological terms, it is propitious to contact the gods under whose influences these metals are formed. *This is one of the fundamental premises for the operations of alchemy, strictly speaking; that is to say, the actual transmutation of real metals by means of the hermetic power* (see page 202).

Finally, by certain rites known to ceremonial magic and theurgy, or by other techniques not excluding cases that seem to be in the category of spontaneous phenomena or "revelations," it is possible to arrive at the beginning of an experience that takes on the form of a god and whereby one can be introduced into the "mysteries," either of the body or of designated metals. This can go so far as to provide the illusion of a transmission of wisdom on the part of a being considered to be real and existing in it. This is, in any case, the foundation of ancient traditions within memory, according to which certain divinities taught men the sciences and arts, but kept the secrets of them to themselves (an echo of this is preserved in Christianity in the form of the "protector" saints of certain human activities). In the traditional world it is this aspect of that organic and unitarian conception of the universe by virtue of which every art and craft also had grades of initiation that conferred a sacred mystery upon it.

In this way physiology was, in ancient times, also a mystic theology; and theology was at the same time a "physics," an introduction to the actual interior knowledge of nature. And it was also a "medicine,"[10] as much in the practical matter-of-course sense as in the transcendental sense; and this double sense, inconceivable to the modern mentality, reveals the *synthetic* point of view of *sacred science*, which can be reached only through the spirit.

---

[10] In ancient Greece, for example, medicine was considered a sacred and secret science. And now we have said enough to make the reason for this secret understood. Galen (*De usu part.*, 7.14) compares medicine to the mysteries of Eleusis and Samothrace. Asclepius, "inventor" of medicine, gives his name to one of the books of the *Corpus Hermeticum*, and the Asclepiads who followed his tradition made up a kind of sacerdotal caste. In the *Vita* with which the works of Hippocrates begin, it is said that he taught his arts only to consecrated men and under the seal of silence. All this leads us to suspect a medicine different from that vaunted today and presented as science. And it would be interesting to show how often modern pharmacological medicine can be related factually to correspondences between certain substances and certain organs or functions that were spelled out in the initiatic teaching.

Forty-Five

KNOWLEDGE OF
THE RED AND THE
TRIUNITY

Let us move on now to some references to the final stage
of the work: transmutation.

In the *Corpus Hermeticum* a "Robe of Fire" is mentioned, which the intellectual being ☉ dons when it has been liberated from the body and which could never be endured here below. For a single spark of this fire would suffice to destroy the Earth (were it not for the guardianship of Water), yet it is said that it is just the absence of this Fire that prevents the soul from completing the divine tasks.[1] The Art—as we have seen—is directed, on the other hand, precisely toward making the organism strong enough to support this fiery element, whence the alchemical adage: "Mastery has been achieved when the Matter has reached perfect union with its mortal poison."

More specifically we can say that the true cause of all corruption is often the abnormal manifestation of a power higher than what the rigid circuits of the body can handle. Therefore, once the body's organization has arrived at its fulfillment it is disintegrated, consuming itself little by little, which is what *death* means for whomever has

---

[1] *Corpus Hermeticum*, 10.17–18.

not assimilated the inner nature of this flame and has not transferred his form[2] into it.

The *Corpus Hermeticum* teaches that for any body to become permanent it must be transformed—but, unlike mortal bodies, the transformation of *immortals* is not accompanied by dissolution:[3] precisely because the soul has been united with the "dissolvent" and with it has designed and established the nature of the new individualization,[4] in whatever form of existence it may manifest or maintain. For which it has been said that the adept of yoga will not suffer any destruction, not even in the final dissolution—*maha-pralaya*—as laid down in the traditional doctrine of the cycles.

If the τέλος, the final goal, is the sense that colors this development in its entirety, there is nothing better than the nature and dignity of the Red Work to help us penetrate the spirit of the hermetic Work.

This is especially so when we come to the problem of immortality. The hermetic Work carried to the Red stage is related to the supreme "supercosmic" conception of immortality. This conception is not easy to understand for a civilization that has long lost it; God understood theistically as a "being" and our identification with that being serve as limits beyond which it is absurd to imagine

---

[2] The hermetic symbols for birth out of fire and ability to prevail within it without changing are the Phoenix and the Salamander. Cf. Pernety (*Dictionnaire*, 434, 446), where for the term "residence" this explanation is given: "Mastery of the Redness, that with the Mercury, comprises a whole capable of remaining eternally within the Fire and of resisting its violent attacks." For the state of union with the "poison," cf. also Flamel, (*Désir désiré*, 315): "The Fire is born out of and feeds itself on the Fire and is the son of the Fire, which is why it returns to the Fire and does not fear the Fire.

[3] *Corpus Hermeticum*, 16.9: cf. with the passage of the *Virgin of the World* (213): "Between an immortal body and a mortal body there is but one difference . . . one is active, and the other passive . . . one is free and governs . . . the other enslaved and subject to impulse."

[4] Cf. the Upanishadic "to triumph over the *second* death," because "death has no further hold on him, death has become part of his being and he has been transformed into one of these divinities" (*Brihadaranyaka-Upanishad*, 1.2. B). For the same idea, extended to every partial form of negativity, cf. *Metaphysic of Sorrow and Sickness*, in *Introduzione alla magia*, 2:182ff.; and *Vie de Milarepa*, (277): "The world and liberation are visible in plain light. My hands are tied to their deed by the seal of the Great Seal . . . my daring knows no obstacle. Disease, evil spirits, sins and miseries adorn the ascetic that I am—in me they are arteries, seeds and fluids." "Seal" and "daring" here are related to the spiritual characteristics of the Red Work. Cf. also Boehme (*Aurora*, 10, §50): "If every fountain still has its sap when you separate from this world [that is, at the transference into the incorporeal of the different roots of vital force], then the fire that blazes in the Final Judgment does not damage us: it will have no power over the spirits that serve the organs of your lifeblood, and after this terrible tempest you will be, in your resurrection, an angel and one who has triumphed." We may also recall the most ancient teachings of the Qabalah (*Book of the Hekhaloth*) that speak of the passage through the seven celestial palaces, in each one of which we meet the adverse powers against which we must defend ourselves by means of a magical seal created by a secret name; with this the initiate seals himself as well. It is said that little by little the difficulties increase and "a fire that proceeds from his body threatens to devour him." It is the same transformation "of the flesh in the burning torches" that Enoch is subjected to; but he who is not as worthy as that prophet runs the danger of being destroyed by the flambeaux. According to one fragment of this literature, one must be capable of remaining standing upright "without hands or feet." Cf. G. Scholem, *Mystique Juive*, 63-65.

or to want anything else. But in the initiatic teaching the supreme *state lies beyond being and nonbeing.* According to the cosmic myth of the cycles, in this nondifferentiation, which is identical to the absolute transcendence, even this personal God Himself and all his Heavens are reabsorbed in the moment of the "Great Dissolution."[5] The ultimate perfection of the Work, which has been attained when the Earth has been entirely dissolved and united with the "Poison," means to have succeeded in reaching this outermost limit. At that point no further "reabsorption" is possible. The royal initiate, garbed in Red, is a survivor who remains, even (as in the myth of the cycles) when worlds, men, and Gods go under.

There is a measure of legitimacy in connecting the White Work and the Red Work, respectively, to initiation into the Lesser and Greater classical Mysteries. The promise of both was immortality, which is, let us reiterate, something positive and very different from the vague "spiritualist" conception of simple survival. But the first immortality was only such in terms of "life," even Cosmic Life, and therefore, ultimately, a conditional immortality linked to manifestation. The second, that of the Greater Mysteries, was a "supercosmic" immortality in the sense just indicated, and it was in the Greater Mysteries that use of the royal symbolism predominated.

Another point: It is interesting to note that in hermetism the White Work is always subordinate to the Red Work, and as a consequence the Light is subordinated to the Fire. This is no mere variation of symbols, but an eloquent *signature* for the experienced eye, because the hierarchical associations of such symbols within other traditions are the opposite, and not by accident. It can be observed that where White and Light take primacy they denote a spirituality that may eventually also have an initiatory character, but which falls predominantly within the boundary of contemplation, "knowledge," and wisdom, and so is nearer the sacerdotal tradition than the royal.[6] But when the Red and Fire take primacy, they are indications of the Royal Mystery and the magical tradition in the higher sense. In hermetism the latter primacy is clear.

Let us now pass on to the human analogy. The Orient knew long ago the ideal of the one for whom there no longer exists either this shore nor the other, nor both together—who, without fear of any kind, has forsaken his human chains, has broken his chains to the divine and has been delivered from all chains: the *Hero*, whose path is known neither to Gods nor to men.[7] But behind the hermetic symbolism of the Androgyne and "Lord of the Two Natures" we

---

[5] Cf. Guénon, *Man and His Becoming;* Evola, *The Doctrine of the Awakening.* The approximate equivalent of the "Grand Dissolution" in the ancient Western traditions is the "cosmic burning"— ἐκπύροσις—returning here to the idea of Fire, the element that is Death and Life in the Red Work.

[6] Likewise, in Catholicism the supreme chief of the hierarchy is dressed in white, while the red is worn by the "Princes of the Church," who are subordinate to him.

[7] Expressions of the *Dhammapada*, §§383, 417, 420.

can discern a very similar conception of the adept. As we have seen before, the "race of hermetic Philosophers," says Zosimos, is autonomous, above destiny, without king (because it itself is royal). According to the *Corpus Hermeticum*, the double nature, far from being an imperfection, is considered the expression of a power that is beyond mortal and immortal. It is said time and again in the texts, that the Son engendered by the Royal Art is nobler, greater, and more powerful than his cosmic progenitors, Heaven and Earth. He is called *magnipotens;* he holds in his hands the sceptres of the spiritual kingdom and the temporal kingdom, and has wrested the glory of the world and has made of himself his own subject;[8] he has been crowned eternal King, says the *Chymica vannus*.[9] He is "the one who Lives," because in the act of receiving the "tincture" of the Fire—death, evil, and darkness flee from him: his light is living and resplendent.[10] Iero of Peace whom the world awaits, known as the *seven-times-purged* by Fire, there is none like him and he is the conqueror of all red Gold;[11] his might is sovereign over all his brothers;[12] he has been called all things, everything in everything, the very "Prima Materia" itself;[13] and accordingly, say "Hermes" and Chymes the ξήριον (Powder of Projection) possesses the "great Pan," the Mystery "sought for eons and now found at last."

At the center of the planets, with the emblem of the universal empire ☉ in his hand, one text puts these words into his mouth: "Radiating great brilliance, I have conquered all my enemies, and from one I am become many, and from many, one, descended from an illustrious lineage . . . I am one and many are in me [*unum ego sum, et multi in me*]"[14]—whence it is clear that the initiatic "we" (which can be associated with the *pluralis majestatis*, the royal or pontifical plural) expresses a state of consciousness that is no longer that of a particular being, but that which reigns over the possibility of multiple individual manifestations.

In particular, the assimilation to the "body" state corresponding to the Aristotelian "pure forms" or to the "angels" of Catholic theology is the same as expressed in hermetism, since in this "the enlightened man will not be less than the celestial spirits, will be in all and for all like them "in one impassible and incorruptible Body."[15] "A new glorified soul will be united to the

---

[8] *De pharmaco catholico*, 3, §§13, 17.

[9] *Chymica vannus*, 278.

[10] *Sette capitoli d'Ermete*, §3.

[11] B. Valentine, *Aurelia, BCC*, 2:214.

[12] *Triomphe Hermétique, BPC*, 3:255.

[13] B. Valentine, *Dodici chiavi*, 21. This is not understood naturally in a pantheistic sense, but in the sense of release from the "fixation" and the possession of the unlimited possibility of manifestation.

[14] B. Valentine, *Aurelia*, 215.

[15] B. Valentine, *Dodici chiavi*, 46 (key 7).

immortal and incorruptible body: thus will be made a new heaven."[16]

And in one of the Gnostic-Mystery traditions there is a similar symbolism in "the tunic of Tyrrhenian purple," "scintillating and flaming, incapable of change or alteration[17] and over which neither heaven itself nor the zodiac have power; whose radiant splendor and bright lustre convey to one a supercelestial aura[18] which, on being made known, amazes, terrifies, and makes one tremble all at the same time."[19]

Finally, now that we have given the sense of the ultimate union of the natures, or triunity, we will cite an ancient text characteristic of Comarius. The first thing mentioned is the "shadow," because of which the "Body, Spirit and Soul are debilitated" (cf. the πένια as a state of "privation"); the "dark spirit, made of vanity and flabbiness," an obstacle to the attainment of the Whiteness, and an image of the phantom created by the body; and finally, the character of that which is divine or sulfurous, consisting in the power by means of which "the Spirit acquires a Body and mortal beings acquire an [immortal] Soul, being dominated and dominating at the moment of receiving the spirit [or Mercury] which emerges from the substances [when it is liberated from these conditions]." After which, the text continues:

> When the dark and fetid spirit has been rejected, to the point where neither its smell nor dark color can any longer be perceived, then the Body becomes luminous, the Soul rejoices, and with it the Spirit. The darkness having fled from the Body, the Soul calls out to this now luminous Body and says to it: "Awake from the depths of Hades and rise from the darkness! Awake and break away from the darkness! Truly thou hast assumed the spiritual and divine state. The voice of resurrection has spoken; the Pharmakon of Life has penetrated thee." Moreover, the Spirit [in the text the symbol of Cinnabar, the red sulfur of mercury, appears here] rejoices in turn in the Body [♄, Lead], just as in the Soul [☾, Silver] in the body [☉, Gold] in which it resides.[20] This runs with joyous

---

[16] Philalethes, *Experimenta de preparatione mercurii*, §17.

[17] It should not be forgotten that initiatic immutability does not refer to any one manifested form, but to the immutable function that comprises the possibility of manifesting various forms, without being in any way altered by such appearances.

[18] In the *Corpus Hermeticum* (4.5) it is said that the hermetic initiates "embrace with the intellect what exists on earth, in heaven and *beyond heaven*," whereupon we are again facing that unity and uniqueness beyond the corporeal and the noncorporeal. The twelve signs of the zodiac correspond to twelve dominant archetypes of the forces of life: to be emancipated from them, means to be superior to the same power that has acted in the White Work.

[19] Flamel, *Figures hiéroglyphiques*, 259.

[20] It is interesting to look at the metallurgical symbols of the signs accompanying the text. Cinnabar,

precipitation to embrace it—does embrace it and then the darkness ceases to dominate it, because it has reached the Light [♈, the sign of the Sulfur in a nascent state, that is, before its passage to the amalgams]. The Body does not [any longer] support its separating from the Spirit [as happens in death], and takes pleasure in the permanence [☉, the Gold] of the Soul,[21] which, after having seen the Body hidden by the darkness, is now full of light [♈, Sulfur in its nascent state]. And the soul is united to it, after which it has become divine with respect to it, and has taken residence in it. Once the Divine Light has been assumed, once the darkness has fled from it, the three are united in tenderness [perhaps in the sense of "tenuousness" as the first dissolving of the dense—in the text, the Mercury sign as the Greek letter μ (mu) interpreted by Berthelot as an amalgam of Mercury]: Body [☉, Gold], Soul [☿, Mercury][22] and Spirit [Cinnabar]. They are transformed into one. And in such [unity] the Mystery is hidden. With their union, the mystery is completed. The dwelling place has been sealed, and a statue has been erected, full of light and divinity. Insofar as the Fire [♈, Sulfur in the nascent stage] has united and transmuted them, and they have departed from its bosom [sign of the ios of the Copper].[23]

In the interest of rendering everything clear in this text, the reader may put to the test what he has learned of that which has been revealed up to this point.

In general, the hermetic achievements have various levels of permanence. "To fix," in such a sense, can also have the special meaning of appropriating, in a stable way, the stages reached by the operations of the Art. Thus Geber distinguishes between a "medicine" of first, second, and third grade.[24] The first has merely a momentary action, as in the case of anything that can be attained by violent methods with a blow of the hand. The second produces an incomplete transformation, as in the case where spiritual states do not succeed in producing the corresponding body transformations. The last is the "total medicine," which acts integrally with a permanent transformation.

---

here, means Mercury united with Sulfur (☿) in the organic compound. Notice also that the Body in the vulgar Mercury function is combined with Lead, but in its Soul function with Gold.

[21] The body, immersed in light, is manifested as Gold and the individualized form of the Soul. Cf. page 76.

[22] Here we employ a symbolism according to which the Body, in the redness, takes on the masculine and Gold function by virtue of the personalizing powers of fires whose entry it brings about, while the Soul, as still distinct from such powers, is assimilated to the Mercury.

[23] Comarius, text in CAG, 2:296-97. The ios of Copper is the profound power that stands at the root of the common reddish "metal" (Copper) and that is liberated by the Work and transformed into the root of all resurrections.

[24] Geber, Summa, 1.4, proem, §2.

Forty-Six

PROPHETIC
KNOWLEDGE

Let us briefly discuss the supernatural possibilities deriving from the various levels of the Work.

In general, the *separation*, as it breaks the chains of the body, to all intents and purposes can liberate the faculties of the awareness of, and ability to deal with, the conditions that weigh upon the body itself: that is to say, the conditions of space, time, and causality. Thereupon the adept can pass on to stages and activities that in some measure are free of such conditionings, provided he succeeds in "fixating" or mastering the process of separation.

Thus Della Riviera, having identified as "Magic" the conquest of the Tree that stands at the center of Paradise, says that the first result is the illumination and exaltation of all the human faculties. Liberated from the petrification of the animal organs, the energies resulting from mental unity ⊙, "without obstacle of any kind, can freely perceive future things, as easily as present and past."[1]

Various hermetic authors such as the Cosmopolite and Philalethes discuss this prophetic ability; but it must not be seen as separate from a faculty of *realization*, as Agrippa says: "The soul having been purified, released from all mutation, glowing externally with freedom of movement . . . imitates the angels in its own nature and obtains what it desires, not in succession or time, but in a single instant.[2]

---

[1] Della Riviera, *Mondo magico*, 4, 5, 116, 118, 149.

[2] Agrippa, *De occulta philosophia*, 3.53.

This prophetic science—insofar as it is a *science*, and not a sporadic or spontaneous phenomenon—proceeds, as a rule, from a new experience of time and events
that is peculiar to the hermetically renewed consciousness. It is not explained by
fatalism (wherein the future is predetermined and therefore foreseeable), but by an
ego-state united with certain influences that determine the events of the external
world, in the same way that the ordinary person is united with the active powers
of his material body.

It is stated clearly in this passage from Plotinus:

> For a superior soul the stars are not only prognostics, but the soul is part
> of and evolves internally along with the All, in which it participates ... the
> knowledge that [the superior man] has of the future that we attribute to him
> does not at all resemble the knowledge of fortune-tellers, but is like that of
> active participants who have a certainty of what must be; and such is the case
> with genuine rulers. For them nothing is undetermined, nothing is uncertain.
> Their decision persists as it was in the first moment. Their judgment of things
> to come is just as firm as their vision of present things is exact. . . . The adept
> persists in wanting that which he must do and, in this persistence, he will do
> only what he wills, and nothing else but that which derives from the idea in
> himself. . . . When one rules alone, on whom does he depend? On whose
> desires? To such an agent action does not come from anything else, any more
> than Wisdom comes from others. He needs nothing else: neither argument,
> nor memory, since these things [compared to the superrational and absolute
> "awakening" that he possesses] are useless.[3]

In this sense prophetic knowledge, rather than being based on fate, is based on
its mastery. Moreover, the unanimous teaching of hermetism, especially hellenistic
hermetism, is that the power of fate does not extend beyond a certain limit and that
this limit does not stop an adept. Zosimos's declaration has been repeatedly quoted,
according to which the race of Philosophers is beyond destiny and "autonomous":
"The race of Philosophers acts without undergoing the action [ἐπαθῶς γὰρ
ἐργαζεται]";[4] after having "separated the sulfurous Soul from the elements," it has

---

[3] Plotinus, *Enneads*, 2.2.9; 4.12. The investigations made by Lévy-Bruhl in *Primitive Mentality* and The
Primitive Soul demonstrate how, interestingly, under the surface of many rites for the "knowledge" of
the future, there is actually a hidden magical operation for determining the future; thus, the exactitude
of the presumed prophecy and the efficacy of the operation or rite would be the same thing. That even
turns out to be the case, in certain aspects, with the ancient Roman augural science

[4] Text in *CAG*, 2:213. Agrippa (*De occulta philosophia*, 1.13) speaks of a double experience of the action
as command in the first causes, and as "necessity" in the domain of those "ministrants" from whose
circle, according to a hermetic text already quoted, the immortalized soul escapes.

been reintegrated into the principle of pure action and is no longer subject to conditions.

Thus Agrippa speaks of a magical power "acting without limits or external help," residing in the "permanent and nondecaying soul."[5] The relation of this power to the "separation" is confirmed by this passage from Braccesco: "The subtle and formal substance, submerged in quantity and matter, cannot exercise its potentialities, but the more spiritual and formal it is, and the more *separated* from matter and quantity, the more it can extend its powers to produce many effects. And since our medicine is composed of subtle spirits and is almost *separated* from all elemental matter it can, but without any obstacle, be extended to all curable infirmities." And here we can interpret "infirmity" in the more general sense of imperfection, limitation, and privation of being.[6]

But to speak in detail of the different powers it is necessary to consider, by reason of the various occult "entities" enclosed in corporeality, the profundities that the work of separation and recomposition, of *solve et coagula* can reach.

---

[5] Agrippa, *De occulta philosophia*, 3.44.

[6] Braccesco, *Espositione*, fol. 82a; cf. with Agrippa, 3.50.

Forty-Seven

Che FOUR STAGES OF POWER

The first "Materia" that we encounter with which the ordinary ego has the most immediate rapport is mental energies. Once they have been freed from the conditions of the body (and specifically from the brain), these energies acquire a "penetrating" and ubiquitous virtue: they can communicate directly with other minds, bridging the spatial separation between individuals. But this ability commonly referred to as "reading minds" is not the only faculty acquired. There is also the power to arouse, in other beings, specific thoughts, visions, and plans of action (mental commands).[1] The experience itself of a particular thought, moreover, can vary, and shows that our usual consciousness derives not so much from thought as from the repercussions of deeper energies. Such surges of energy at this point are picked up directly and isolated by the brain, which acts as a "transformer." It is in this state that the supernormal psychic abilities we have mentioned are manifested.

And the same can be said, analogously, for the deeper stratum of the human entity that is the seat of the emotions, passions, and sentiments. Nonhuman influences are at work behind the subjective forms of the stirrings of the soul and senses. The various feelings of the human emotional spectrum result from different primordial energies, of which the types of the animal world are often considered

---

[1] Agrippa, (De occulta philosophia, 3.43): "He will thus succeed in obtaining great power to immerse and insinuate himself into the spirit of other men, even at great distances, and convey to them some of his conceptions, will and desire."

their avenues of sensitivity. It seems then, that what appears in man in the form of a particular passion or emotion is the same that is manifested in Nature by a specific species of animal. The twelve animals of the zodiac refer to this; and the "marriages with sacred animals" mentioned in certain traditions must be understood as the union with energies acting through the world of human affectivity, as general, invisible, nonhuman causes of the forms of it.[2]

This is the point at which we also acquire the virtual faculty of "projecting" to other beings not only ideas and images, but emotions and affective states in general, even "charging" objects and places[3] with specific emotive states. This provides a supernatural authority over the animal kingdom as well, as recorded in the lives of many saints and ascetics.

And all this is an effect of the separation, purification, and stripping of everything that is manifested in the double aspect of thought and feeling in the common man. But now let us go on to the third "level": to the plane of the vital forces corresponding to the sign ☿ of the "lunar Mercury" (vegetative soul). After the "separation" has taken place (that which occurs in the "Whiteness" with the consequent transmutation of the Lead into bright Silver), there follows a control over a "form" or "subtle body" that can be detached from the physical body. Thereupon it becomes possible to project one's own "double" which, as a regenerated consciousness, has the power to transport itself instantaneously to any given point in space, resulting thereby in a corresponding apparition.

This "form," being sustained solely by the mind, can assume whatever shape the mind imagines and imposes. Hence not only bilocation, but also the ability, that the Orient attributes to the yogis, to appear simultaneously in several different forms apart from those which (up to this stage) the unity of a single physical body lying in abeyance maintains. If in many popular traditions or among primitive people there are witch doctors said to have the power to manifest themselves and act in the forms of animals, while remaining elsewhere and lying in their human body, there is reason to think there are other phenomena substantially like these. But in the greater part of these cases (if they are authentic), they are not the deliberate acts of the Higher Soul. Such phenomena are the result rather of a dark promiscuity on the part of the sorceror with one of the occult forces of animality, which erupting in him, dominates the "double" to whom is transmitted the figure of the type that corresponds in the visible animal kingdom ("werewolves," "leopard-men," etc.): dissociated projections

---

[2] When the connection is established passively so as to overwhelm the personality, we have what is called totemism; in that case the person is, in a certain way, the incarnation in human form of the spirit of a given species of animal.

[3] Here we can also point to objects and even to places (for example, certain traditional sanctuaries) that by consecration and imposition, have become, so to speak, storage batteries of "spiritual influence," either benefic or malefic. Cf. Magic of the Creation in Introduzione alla magia, 2:283ff.; and A. David-Neel, Magic and Mystery in Tibet, passim.

in which are dramatized the *totemic* rapports mentioned in footnote 2.

That which is dissociated, in any case, is that which in the subtle forces of man corresponds to the vegetable kingdom; and as affectivity in itself opens the way to extrasensory knowledge of the "sacred animals," so the "extraction" of this group of subtle forces opens the way to the extrasensory consciousness of the vegetable essences, a consciousness distinguished by a corresponding "power." The phenomena of desiccation or the abnormally rapid growth, well known in the Orient, of plants and herbs are also mentioned in the hermetico-alchemical texts.[4] As for the strictly human application of the "Medicine," the acquisition of the "White Stone" confers on the soul the capacity to act on disturbances or ailments of the body not merely in a functional way, but also organically.[5] An intuitive knowledge of those natural remedies can also be acquired which, according to the circumstances, can act on the sick body. This is the method followed, for instance, by Paracelsus, for whom the basis of true medicine [the knowledge of signatures] was essentially alchemy.

Finally, when dissociation, purification and reconstitution vest the same cohesive telluric structure in the body—apart from the possibility of transporting into the invisible everything that makes up visible man, (invisibility, death without leaving a body—"raising the whole body to heaven by Assumption," "the body raising itself, by its own power, to the region of Brahma," etc.)—and apart from the possibility of magically dissolving the body in one given place in order to recompose it and cause it to appear intact in another, and not just in its double (in that case there occurs in the human body what today we must admit under other conditions, that is, *mediumistic* conditions, which take place in the metaphysical and "psychic" phenomenon of the "apport")[6]—beyond all that, is the not inconsiderable power to act on substances and on the laws of external minerality, on the occult forces active in them, that henceforth the initiate has activated within his own magically enlivened organism.

---

[4] Cf., for example, Della Riviera, *Mondo magico*, 178-79.

[5] The true "medicine," say the alchemists, "is the stellar body," that is, the power of life, root of the organism, with which it is now joined directly in such a way that one has the power of concentrating it on a given organ and conquering the forces that are disturbing it. Cf. Della Riviera (*Mondo magico*, 169): "In the same way that the life of the branches lies in the roots of the tree, so sick bodies are magically healed by the help of the radical humor, the Spirit of Life and in sum even Nature itself, by no other agent than themselves."

[6] Cf. Agrippa, (*De occulta philosophia*, 3.43): "The Chaldean philosophers expound at length on the power of the mind . . . which can be so full of light that it pours out its beams through the particular intermediaries [☿ and ☿] even as far as the dense, dark, heavy and mortal body; bathing it also in abundant light, making it radiant as a star and, because of the abundance of the rays and their lightness of weight, it can be raised to the heights as a flake of ash is raised by the fire, and so transported at once with the spirit to faraway regions." One of the names given to the Philosopher's Stone is *Lapis invisibilitatis*, Stone of Invisibility (cf., for example, Sendivogius, *Novum lumen chemicum* in *Musaeum hermeticum*, 547).

Forty-Eight

METALLIC TRANSMUTATION

o this final stage we attribute the possibility of alchemical transmutation as it is commonly understood: the transmutation of metals.

If you have followed our explanations up to this point, we trust you will have no need for specific arguments to be convinced that alchemy cannot be reduced merely to chemistry in its infancy—unsystematic, superstitious, and overshadowed by modern chemistry. When alchemy is understood in the entire context of Western history, it surely has more than one aspect. In its essence, however, it remains a traditional science of a cosmological and initiatic character.

Given the *synthetic* nature of this type of science, alchemy must of course include a chemical side, particularly as a basis for symbolic transpositions. In the same way that the art of construction, or masonry, could be used to express aspects of a spiritual, ritualistic, and initiatory process (an echo of this has been preserved in Freemasonry), so the physical understanding of the elements and certain operations involving the metals can be said to have a similar function.[1]

Secondly, some hermetists were also practical chemists, and were able to make certain precursory discoveries as, for example, the different compounds of mercury, silver sulfide, various kinds of ether, quicklime, aqua regia, and various dyes

---

[1] Cf. *Introduzione alla magia* (third ed., [Rome, 1971], vol. 2) in which Pietro Negri has made an attempt at an interpretation that in an alchemical text on lead considers simultaneously, the two possible aspects: the chemical and the hermetico-symbolic.

("tinctures"). But this kind of knowledge took only a secondary and subordinate place in a system whose premises, methods, and spirit had absolutely nothing in common with the chemical domain or any other modern science.

So if in this special sector the objective of the production of metallic gold is sometimes pursued and sometimes even attained, it is a question neither of a sensational phenomenon nor a scientific discovery. It is a question, on the contrary, of the *production* of a *sign*, that is, of something that Catholicism might properly call a miracle, particularly as opposed to a simple phenomenon; or better yet, what Buddhism would call a "noble miracle"—*ariya*—in contrast to "vulgar" prodigies—*anariya*—which even though they may be supernormal phenomena, are not accompanied by any higher meaning.[2] The production of metallic gold was to alchemy a *proof of transfiguration given by a power* the testimony of having realized the Gold ⊙, *in oneself*.

But with the diffusion of alchemy through the West these understandings were separated from the others and lost their true spirit; the desire and greed for pure and simple gold, for monetary gold, became the main interest. And so that brand of alchemy was born that could be considered the infantile stage of scientific chemistry. But hermetic or traditional alchemy has nothing to do with the origin of modern chemistry, says René Guénon correctly;[3] and he adds:

> It was rather the deterioration of Alchemy, in the strictest sense of the word, which took place perhaps in the Middle Ages, with the incomprehension of certain persons who, incapable of perceiving the true meaning of the symbols, took everything literally and believing that in them there was nothing but a description of purely material operations, gave themselves over to more or less disorganized experimentation. Such persons, forever obsessed with the fabrication of gold, made, here and there, some fortuitous discoveries. And it is these that were the true precursors of modern chemistry. So we can say that hermetism and the Alchemical initiation are not related to modern chemistry by evolution or progress, but quite on the contrary, by *degeneration*. In this, as in other fields, modern science is built on the remains of ancient sciences, which have been gutted of their substance and abandoned by the ignorant and profane.

That modern science should have acquired the precise experimental knowledge and technical mastery of a quantity of natural phenomena and in less than a century changed the face of this earth to a degree unmatched by any ancient civilization; and that in particular, it has pragmatically solved the problem of the

---

[2] Cf. Evola, *Maschera e volto dello spiritualismo contemporaneo* and *The Doctrine of the Awakening*.

[3] R. Guénon, *La crise du monde moderne* (The crisis of the modern world), 106-7.

transformation of the base metals into gold by means of the disintegration of atomic nuclei,[4] may be quite interesting and may enormously impress the profane, but it says nothing to anyone who has any idea of what true consciousness and power are or the means of acquiring them.

Modern science enjoys general accomplishments within the reach of everyone. In the premodern world only sporadic, exceptional, enigmatic conquests were made, like flashes of lightning. But the achievements of modern science possess only a material value; and airplanes, penicillin, radio, and similar products up to the atomic bomb and other dibolical creations say nothing to anyone beyond their physical meaning. Altogether different, we reiterate, was the case for things that could be realized in the ancient world, because every phenomenon, conquest, or realization was a sign or a symbol. It testified to a spiritual level or sacred tradition, illustrating what was concurrently possible—as a culmination—for whoever had followed the path of overcoming the human condition, had risen to the supersensible and had made a tiny rip in the veil of transcendent meaning.

And precisely because to have considered these "signs" from their utilitarian point of view would have meant a profanation and a degradation, the hermetic masters harbored a natural repugnance to produce them, and the alchemists themselves repeated the gospel saying: "Do not cast pearls before swine"; finally, at a certain point, alchemy *retired,* without further ado, from the Western world of technology and scientism.

A few mysterious hermetic adepts continued to appear here and there, perhaps in order to confound and rock, by the miracle of gold made before their very eyes, the edifice of researchers of the "positive" mentality;[5] or perhaps in order to enlighten someone who was on the point of being overwhelmed by doubt and despair; or perhaps in order to change the course of some human existence by gifts of an irrational or capricious form. Nevertheless, the "making of gold" continued to remain a mystery for those who thought that it depended on a secret formula, or on this or that jealously guarded procedure, or on special substances, instead of understanding that they needed to direct the attenton and action elsewhere, that

---

[4] It is known, however, that until now this achievement has not been feasible in practice, because the expense of producing gold in the laboratory is higher than the value of the gold to be obtained. We could almost apply—ironically—the truth intuited by Bernard of Treviso at the end of a lifetime of struggles, labors, and vain attempts: "To make gold one must already possess it." But Bernard was talking about hermetic gold, presupposed for eventually producing physical gold.

[5] The noted chemist Van Helmont, and Helvetius, physician to William of Orange, were visited by strangers who produced gold, after which they entertained no further doubts about the "holy science of transmutations." The same was repeated by the physician Poisson who, although the operaton of producing gold was controlled by Boyle, contrary to Galileo's *"Eppur si muove,"* maintained his anti-alchemical ideas to the end. We could also cite other cases of positive testimony.

what was missing was the understanding, in the first place, of the mystery of inner transmutation.

Thus, in what can be regarded as the specific argument of this chapter, it can be said that hermetism may *also* contemplate the transmutation of metals, but not as a purely material operation. Among others, Artephius and Morienus say, and in the clearest terms, that "the work that the magister does is not a work done by the hands" and that it depends, on the contrary, on artifice: "*subtle* plans and procedures";[6] and everyone else repeats that the substances and elements of which they speak are not the same as those of the common man.

Yet even when chemistry had begun to take shape as a "science," there were still alchemists who went on talking exactly like their Arab, Syrian, and Alexandrian predecessors. An example given by Pernety shows us the difference between hermetic and vulgar chemistry. "The first," he says, "takes Principles as its material, and acts on them following the ways of nature itself; vulgar chemistry, on the other hand, takes the "mixtures" after they have reached their goal, and works on them with extrinsic decompositions, which destroy their natures, and its results are monstrous."[7]

By these words he wishes to convey to us that profane chemistry acts on that which the physical form has already taken, on the "corpses" of processes already used up, without considering these same processes in their supra- and presensible aspect. Hermetic chemistry, however, starts on the contrary, from the spiritual understanding of the Principles (that is, from the primordial powers of elemental qualification), and acts on the formation processes that precede ontologically that state in which the substances belong to the nature of this or that metal and obey the laws that chemistry and physics have discovered in the realm of simple phenomena.

Alchemy, then, is differentiated from profane chemistry by a "metaphysic," that is to say, by an order of consciousness beyond the senses, which ultimately presupposes the initiatic transmutation of human consciousness. Between this transmutation (the latter) and the transmutation of metals no longer in the symbolic sense, but now real, there are analogical correspondences. So certain teachings and principles that first of all have a cosmological and metaphysical sense, can be applied not only to one but to the other transmutation—to that of man and metals "because the furnace, the path to be followed and the Work are all one."

For the operations of physical alchemy "different spiritual and corporeal forces are necessary," says an Arab text.[8] "These forces must be converging and not

---

[6] *Livre d'Artephius, BPC*, 2:162; *Entretiens, BPC*, 2:92.

[7] Pernety, *Fables*, 1:16, 21.

[8] *Livre de la miséricorde, CMA*, 3:136.

moving apart . . . the spiritual and physical forces must be similar . . . so that they can mutually help each other." "It is necessary that the operator be immersed in the work [oportet operatorem interesse operi]." Petrus Bonus says that the work is completed "by the adjunction of the Occult Stone, which one acquires not by the senses, but only by intelligence, inspiration, or divine revelation, or by the teaching of one who already knows [per scientiam scientis]."[9] The intellectual principle that is the form of man (in the Aristotelian sense), "is the beginning and end of the preparations." With the saffron color it appears precisely that "man is the principal and greatest force in the spagyric Work."[10] "Our Work is interior and exterior," confirms another text.[11] It is not a question then of processes that are exhausted in a mass of external determinisms. In alchemical processes the psychic energy and the "dignity" of the operator play an essential role. They exercise an efficacious influence on the mineral forces, thanks to an inner relation with them that is absolutely beyond the reach of normal consciousness.[12]

As for technology, it is necessary only to recall and apply certain principles already known to us in connection with human palingenesis. The first teaching is: "Change the nature of the body on which you want to act." Equivalent sayings include: "Extract the nature hidden within"; "Make the hidden manifest and the manifest hidden"; "Remove the darkness"; "Unclothe it"; "Make the visible invisible and the invisible visible"; and one of the most ancient renditions of this idea: "If you embody the incorporeal substances without making the corporeal substances incorporeal, none of the expected results will take place."[13]

It is evident that this mutation in the substances on which you must act does not refer to making them pass from one physical state to another, but to make them pass from a physical state to a nonphysical state. And this is equivalent to saying that the true preliminary operation concerns the operator more than the substances themselves. An alchemical mantram goes: *transmutamini in vivos*

---

[9] *Theatrum chemicum*, 5:647.

[10] *Liber Platonis quatorum* in *Theatrum chemicum*, 5:114ff.; Dorn, *Speculativae philosophiae*, ibid., 1:485.

[11] *Livre de la clémence*, *CMA*, 3:135. In this same text (p. 136) it is said that the "removal of its corporeal and material form from a thing" is the foundation of "all operations, *internal and external*," whether it be exercised on the principles of man, or on substances. Cf. later, page 218.

[12] The Greek alchemists declared that what words like ξήριον—an ancient name for the "powder of projection" that changes common metals into silver and gold—meant is the *spirit* (*CAG*, 2:258). And they added that only the Stone (that is, only the human organism) in which resides the φαρμακὸν τὸ τὴν δύναμιν ἔχον—the Remedy of the *just* power—can produce the "Mithraic Mystery," that is, the Sun and the Gold, here and now in a real sense. (ibid., 2:114)

[13] Olympiodorus, text in *CAG*, 3:110. Cf. the same theme in Zosimos (*CAG*, 2:114); Flamel (*Désir désiré*, §§1, 6); Arnold of Villanova (*BCC*, 1:665); Rosinus (*Artis auriferae*, 1:300); B. Valentine (*Dodici chiavi*, 20); etc.

lapides philosophicos—Be ye transmuted into living philosopher's stones—and consists in reaching that condition of the consciousness by virtue of which is precisely realized the psychic aspect of physical things, the "subtle soul" hidden by their exterior. This is the hidden that is made manifest, while the manifest—that is, the sensory and corporeal aspect—is made hidden; this is the appearance of the "hidden nature within," the "underneath" that is brought "up," etc. Only after this condition is realized does it become possible to act hermetically on substances. "Life,"says Basil Valentine "is nothing more than a Spirit; for, all that which the ignorant considers to be dead must live (for thee) with an incomprehensible life, visible all the same, and spiritual, and in that must he be saved."[14]

In the same sense other authors speak of "the vision in the Light of Nature," and the *Novum lumen chemicum* relates the operation "of removing the shadow from hidden things" to an act that must be at once intellectual and imaginative.[15] We find in the texts frequent and quite explicit allusions to the "magical imagination," which is opposed to simple fantasy. Sendivogius, in *De sulphure*, says that it is the key that the ancients have not revealed, and we must remember that Albertus Magnus teaches that all the magical techniques, which alchemy comprises, act only when man is in a sort of ecstasy or active trance.[16]

So we can understand the relation of "Transform the natures and thou wilt obtain what thou seekest," to the injunction to "mix" the substances with *our* Mercury, or Divine Water: it is a question of referring the perception of the substances to the consciousness transported to the state that corresponds to the symbols of Water and Mercury (the White Work), which we have seen in the initiatic work.

Comarius teaches that in the vapors of the Divine Water the spirits (of the substances) are revealed as divine mysteries—θεῖα μυστήρια—and celestial bodies—οὐράνια σώματα. It is this, *the appearance of the "roots,"* about whose equivalence to the resolution in Mercury we are told in the *Seven Chapters of Hermes* (chap. 1). "The water changes the Bodies into Spirits, stripping them of their gross corporeality" says Artephius,[17] "you have need only of the released and subtle nature of the dissolved bodies, which you will obtain by means of our Water."

---

[14] B. Valentine, *Dodici chiavi*, 37 (second key, §5). Cf. Agrippa, *De occulta philosophia*, 3.10: "It is necesary to know how to *intellectualize* exactly the perceivable properties by means of a secret analogy."

[15] *Musaeum hermeticum*, 574.

[16] Here, one could also cite the three conditions that Thomas Aquinas himself, in following Avicenna, considered necessary for the exterior materia to obey the prophet: to know the clarity of intelligence, a perfect creative imagination, and a mightiness of the soul. Cf. M.-L. von Franz, *Aurora consurgens*, 154-57.

[17] *Livre d'Artephius*, BPC, 2:128, 135.

Clearly, Zosimos tells us that the "tincture" of Gold (the metallic transmutation) cannot be obtained in the *solid state* (that is, the material state) of the bodies: "they must first be subtilized and spiritualized," until "the spiritual forces, which cannot be perceived by the (physical) senses,[18] have been made effective." It is necessary to "dissolve the substances and what then must be transmuted to obtain the physical transmutation are the *celestial natures.*"[19]

Moreover, for what makes the conversion of the incorporeal into the corporeal (apart from the corporeal into the incorporeal prescribed in the formula), it is necessary to understand, by analogy with everything that pertains to the purely initiatory experience, that the consciousness must not be the pure "spirit" aspect of the substances but, after being elevated to that aspect, it must be put back in rapport with the same substance as the body in such a way that "the two are made one." Otherwise, the results would be but a step to other forms of consciousness without direct relationship to the physical plane, which is necessary for the alchemical operation. It is necessary then to form "intermediate substances" or "androgynous" substances both "spiritual and corporeal" (perception of the substance and perception of its "psychic" dimension, the one in function of the other):[20] and thus has been established the first condition for the operations of physical alchemy.[21]

Also important, in this regard, is the reference to a "true and not fantastic imagination" and to an "intellectual vision," the first being accomplished in the "Light of Nature."[22]

---

[18] *CAG*, 2:285. Cf. Braccesco, *Espositione*, fol. 80a: "Neither metals nor stones receive celestial virtues when they are in the form of metals and stone, but only when they are in the form of vapors."

[19] *Livre de la miséricorde, CMA*, 3:180. Cf. *Livre de El Habir, CMA*, 3:107.

[20] Syrian texts, in *CMA*, 2:1.

[21] Interpretable in relation to this, in one of its aspects, is the symbolism of the "circular distillation," which results in "the external becoming internal and the internal, external," and everything "is in a circle, so that inner can no longer be distinguished from outer, or higher from lower." from *Tractatus aureus* (Leipzig, 1610), 43.

[22] *Rosarium philosophorum* in *Artis auriferae*, 2:214; *Novum lumen* in *Musaeum hermeticum*, 534.

Forty-Nine

CORRESPONDENCES, TIMES, AND RITES

The premise for transmutation is the ἔν τὸ πᾶν ("One, the All").

This premise is that at the root of all things having form, quality or individuality there lies an undifferentiated principle. This principle is without form or individuality, above and at the same time prior even to the opposition between I and not-I, between materiality and spirituality, between inner and outer. For the alchemists, to go back, or as they also say, to dissolve their substances in this "prima materia" is the fundamental aim of all their art.[1] So in order to "transmute" it does not suffice to pass beyond the perceivable types of substances to the state of "spiritualized bodies" or "androgynes," it is also necessary to know how to go beyond their detailed specifications to reach the undifferentiated principle, and then to execute, by an act of the spirit, a "projection" that unties the knot of those invisible powers manifesting themselves as a given minerality.

---

[1] Cf. Arnold of Villanova (*Semita semitae*, §10): "They are correct who assert that transmutation is not possible if the metals cannot be returned to their prima materia"; Raymond Lully, (*Clavicula*, 21): "The metals cannot be transformed, unless they are reduced to the first matter"; Zacharias, (*Philosophie naturelles des métaux*, BPC, 2:501): "If you know not the true dismantling of *our body*, do not begin the work: because if this remains a stranger to you, the rest will be useless."

The consequence will be a "precipitation" on the material and sensory plane that precisely determines the passage of this materiality from one species to another: for example, from copper or lead, to gold.

It is thus evident that for physical alchemy to succeed, one must know how to pass correctly through the successive stages that mark the transmutation in a spiritual sense. The power to remove the individuality of a particular metal is quite strictly measured by the suspending of the same human individuality, so far as to realize, in an active ecstasy, the *pure* Mercury that contains the "seeds" [or *signatures*] of all things, beyond the opposition between the physical body of a man and that of natural things separated in space.[2] Specifically, there are three points of correspondence. First, there is the power to "extract the natures," making manifest that which is hidden with regard to the physical metallic substances and which corresponds to the power of carrying out in itself the "mortification" and of producing the "Black Materia" and then, little by little, the white from the black. Second, there is the power of returning the metallic soul to the prima materia, which is the power to be maintained in the "Great Sea" and to dominate the Mother, that is to say, to fix the "matter" in the whiteness. And finally, there is the power of projecting from the undifferentiated prima materia a new qualification, obtaining thereby the transmutation of the metal, which we find in the Red Work and the regime of Fire, in which there is enough primordial energy for every individualization.

So much for the general sense and scheme of metallic transmutation. There is no cause to go into the technical details here because it is very difficult to pry them loose from the labyrinth of texts and requires a very specific competence. Apart from what we have said about the required inner qualifications for palingenesis—about ascetic preparation, about the two lives, about the difficulties, dangers and uncertainties—we would also now have to deal with astrology and magic in the same way, but these themes fall outside the scope of the present work.

Actually, although in a higher realization all operative virtue proceeds—according to the teaching of Agrippa—out of the "stable and not declining soul" of the regenerated without any external help, in other cases we are presented nevertheless with the opportunity of a meeting of elements. And if they do not immediately create the act, they serve to favor and guide it effectively in the desired direction. So then, in some alchemical texts, in addition to physical and mental purity and integrity, and in addition to spiritual dignity, there are also *rites* mentioned, and prayers, conjurings, magical herbs, special substances—in this case not symbolic

---

[2] From this arises the error of those who think that the foundation of the alchemical will-o'-the-wisp is the forerunner of the scientific truth of the unity of matter and energy. This "truth" is limited to external reality, that is to say, to a mere sector of reality that modern science has methodically isolated from everything else.

but real—and finally the "proper time and felicitous moment" determined by particular positions and conjunctions of the stars. Here a true science comes into play that seeks to create favorable conditions for moments of *sympathy* and *syntony* between the various orders of conciliating forces, exterior and interior, individual and cosmic, to the point of "oneness" in which the action of the spirit can be vibrated efficiently and without hindrance.

We can now come back to what we were saying about the correspondences of the "Seven": certain groups of subtle dynamics of the human organism (that can be energized by the appropriate magical rituals) are found to correlate with powers that are also manifested in the mineral kingdom in the form of typical metallities and, in heaven, by the various planets and the invisible influences proceeding from their movement.

With the astrological aspect in particular, the principle is the actualization linked to a specific meaning occurring at the exact moment in the which the exterior (stellar) reality is presented as a symbol that objectively parallels it, then by syntony a hidden circuit is closed, as it were, multiplying the effectiveness of that same expression in the physical world.

The planets, on fixed dates, with their conjunctions—especially in aspect to the Sun and Moon—are presented precisely as great symbols of particular hermetic or alchemical operations; and when these are conducted on such dates they have a major probability of succeeding.[3] Naturally, cold calculation is not enough for this. A lively sense of nature is needed, the living Fire of "communications." As for the moment of the "coincidence" or "oneness"—and transmutation—this will always be a culmination, an apex of the whole being.

For beginning the Work, Razi and Rudienus recommend the period when the Sun is in Aries, following the tradition of the Greek alchemists. The Cosmopolite and the *Hermetic Triumph* extend the time to cover the whole period of the spring signs: Aries, Taurus, and Gemini. In his *Theatrum chemicum britannicum* Ashmole provides a table of the favorable celestial aspects with respect to division, separation, rectification, and conjunction of the Elements. The first purifications take place when the Sun is in Sagittarius and the Moon is in Aries, while the work is completed at the conjunction of Sun and Moon in the sign of Leo.[4]

All this may—or rather, must—have both a hermetically symbolic value and a strictly astrological value at the same time—for the reason already given: that the astrological factor is effective only at the moment when a rigorous and mutually

---

[3] Cf. *Introduzione alla magia*, 2:89ff.

[4] Among the various reasons for the notable differences between astrological prescriptions are those deriving from the fact that a propitious date for one particular individual may not be propitious for another: the different ascendent of each individual constitutes, strictly speaking, a factor of primary importance.

reciprocal correspondence has been established between reality and symbol, thought and thing.[5] In addition, the counsel of Agrippa must be observed, that to invoke the stars one agrees to become like them, to the point of participating inwardly in their light, the soul fleeing the darkness that seeks to take advantage of the body.[6]

As for the magical rituals, their aim, in the idea of the Greek alchemists, is on the one hand to obtain the cooperation of the natures, and on the other to resist the influence of the "demons."[7] In the first case it is a question of indirect methods to activate those correspondences between the macrocosmic and microcosmic manifestations of an identical force, correspondences that otherwise can also be actualized directly by the "drawing out" of the consciousness hidden in a given "center" of the invisible man. And as for the *demons*, these are considered visionary dramatizations of the obstacles and resistances in the deeper strata of the human entity.[8] So the conjuring ritual, in the final analysis, has only a symbolic value and the effectiveness of an indirect method.

Regarding *prayer*, of which mention is sometimes made in the texts, we may recall what has already been said: in this tradition prayer has a value essentially as a compelling mental act (similar to a spell) and not as a sentimental effusion of devotion. It is an element of technique, executed at the correct moment, with the right attitude and a clear "direction towards effectiveness." Finally, with respect to the aforesaid use of magical herbs, this is a matter of potions which, according to the function we have explained for the "corrosive waters," facilitate the state of spiritual exaltation summoned by the alchemist for his operation. Different substances, such as perfumes, etc., may also be used, in an ambience consecrated to the work (the "laboratory"); these are substances that, in particular circumstances, also serve as "condensers" for certain occult influences.

Elsewhere, we have touched on the power that solutions of metals, introduced into the organism in particular physical and psychic conditions can manifest: for every metal exercises an action on its corresponding "center" in the body. The metal natures of Gold, Tin and Iron affect, for example, vital energies that act respectively in the region of the heart, the brow, and the larynx. If when this happens the consciousness remains concentrated in the subtle state, it can be

---

[5] Another common element for the determination of the "right time" can be furnished by the symbolism of the seasons: to winter, spring, summer, and fall, as we have said (p. 85), correspond respectively the Works in black, white, red, and gold (as fixation of the red). In antiquity the Lesser Mysteries (White Work) were celebrated in spring, and the Greater Mysteries (Red Work), in autumn.

[6] Agrippa, *De occulta philosophia*, 2:60.

[7] Cf. *CAG*, 2:72, 74, 79, 86, 87, 95.

[8] Thus they correspond to those "clouds," "poisonous vapors," winds, or eclipses that in the hermetic work occur when the Water goes again to quench the thirst of an earth not entirely purified (see page 127ff.).

introduced and transformed in the "mystery" of the center corresponding to the metallic substance that has been introduced into the body[9] by means of the specific reactions that are manifested. So we arrive at some equivalent to that which in antiquity was the initiation according to the various planetary gods; an initiation that among other things conferred the virtual possibility of the relation with the "inner nature" of given metals, and therefore of the action on them.[10]

On the other hand, we can also consider special *physical* or *chemical* conditions to which it is convenient to subject the metallic substances, in order that even their physical condition offers less resistance to the operation of transmutation than, for example, when they are submitted to a vibratory state of molecular instability. The alchemical teaching, according to which the "projection" would be effected on *heated* metals, can also be interpreted from this angle.

There is more to be said about the time necessary for the completion of the Work, but on this particular the opinions of the Philosophers are much divided. And that is only natural given the difference between the action of spirits and machines. Frequently, the indications are reduced to symbols, as when in place of days, months or years, the numbers three, seven, twelve, etc. are used. Roger Bacon[11] says that transmutation "is a thing of a day, an hour, a moment." Others, on the contrary, speak of long, long years of work that cost them health and property. Besides, it is neccessary to bear in mind that because one may have succeeded once, that is not to say, in the majority of cases, he can succeed many times at will, precisely because of the necessity of reuniting in one *fateful* moment a rather complex conjunction of physical and psychic factors, and because of the character of the *culmination* of the realization itself. It is true that all the philosophers agree to discourage rashness, and advise patience, perseverance, and tenacity, without neglecting a "subtle intelligence." Pseudo-Democritus, Zosimos, Pelagius, and the *Turba* declare: "If you don't succeed, don't put the blame on the Copper, but on yourself; because that means you have not labored well." In any case, it is useless to hope for any result before having acquired illumination.

And on this illumination must focus every effort of the true alchemist, since— according to the texts—only this enlightenment affords that penetration into the "mystery of the Egyptian priests," which is incommunicable, and has always been passed over in silence, but once understood, makes the Opus child's play or woman's work—παιθίου παιγινιον καὶ γυναιὸς ἔργον.

---

[9] Cf. R. Steiner, *Initiatenbewußtsein*, 56–82, 116–26.

[10] We might again recall in this regard the words of Agrippa (3.36) who, with Geber, teaches "that one cannot excel in the alchemic art *without knowing its principles in himself*"; cf. this Taoist text: "The five elements that operate in nature, creating and destroying, also operate in the mind, objectifying the same nature. So the whole world lies [potentially] in our hands." (*Yin fu Ching*, 1.2).

[11] R. Bacon, *Speculum alchimiae*, §7.

. . . .
Fifty
. . . .

silence and
the tradition

T he law of silence has always been maintained by the
Philosophers. In the writings of the ancient Egyptian
masters we find descriptions and expositions of
the teaching, but its practice—ἔργα—was always silent.[1] In their own writings,
the hermetists have addressed none but the initiates: "They have written only
for those who have been initiated into their mysteries and because of that they
have intentionally filled their books with enigmas and contradictions."[2] "Wherever it seems that I have spoken most clearly and openly about our science,"
says Geber, "that is where I have spoken most obscurely and where I have
hidden it. . . . I declare that neither the Philosophers who have preceded
me, nor I myself, have written for others, but only for ourselves and our successors."[3]

Although it is true that the sages "have mixed in with the process of inves-
tigation the means of arriving at the perfect understanding of the science" and
although "they have indicated a certain path and have prescribed rules by which
a Sage can understand what they have enigmatically written and reach the

---

[1] *CAG*, 2:79.

[2] Salmon, Introduction to *BPC*, iv, v.

[3] Geber, *Summa*, 4, §10 (*BCC*, 1:383). Cf. d'Espagnet, *Arcanum hermeticae*, §§9, 15; Flamel, *Figures
hiéroglyphiques*, §2; *Livre de Artephius*, *BPC*, 2:144ff.

proposed objective even after making many mistakes"[4] nevertheless, the reader is always assumed to be an initiate or person of prepared mind.[5]

The *transmission*—originally restricted to persons of rank: kings, princes, and priests[6]—is only given directly; the key, says Agrippa, "is not transmitted by writings, but is infused in the spirit by means of the spirit [*sed spiritui per spiritum infunditur*]."[7] Who receives it swears never to reveal it to anyone who is not one of them.[8] Quite drastic is the *Turba philosophorum:* "Who has ears let him open them and listen, who has a mouth, let him keep it shut." And Bernard of Treviso adds, "I could not speak more clearly of that which I've said to you if I were to show you. But understanding does not permit it. And you yourself, when you know it (I tell you in truth), will hide it even more than I."[9]

Concerning all this, we have to realize that the "secret" had nothing to do with any exclusivity of sect or unwillingness to speak, but rather that it was a question of not *being able* to say, in addition to having to prevent the inevitable incomprehension of those who would profane or distort the teaching. Since the alchemical technique, in its truth, consists of an Art made possible by higher powers set in motion by superior and nonhuman states of consciousness, it is natural to declare that the secret of the Great Work cannot be transmitted, but is the privilege of the initiates, who by virtue of their own experiences, can alone understand what is hidden behind the jargon and symbolism of the technical texts. For the profane the only counsel was to be prepared and to pray, in the hope that through some spontaneous enlightenment[10] their eyes might be opened at last. As for the possibility, admitted by the

---

[4] Zacharias, *Philosophie naturelle des métaux*, BPC 2:495; *Livre de Synesius*, BPC, 2:177; cf. *CAG*, 2:315: "Having written in enigmas, they have left it to you, who hold this book in your hand, to labor constantly to create the subject of the mystery."

[5] *CAG*, 3:62, 63.

[6] *CAG*, 3:97.

[7] Agrippa, *Epistolae*, 3:56.

[8] *Livre de Cratès*, *CMA*, 3:57.

[9] B. Treviso, *Philosophie des métaux*, BPC, 2:385. See Agrippa (*De occulta philosophia*, 3.2) concerning the hiding of the doctrine and the secret that "must be kept in the heart": "It is a sin to divulge to the public in writing the doctrine of those secrets that must only be transmitted orally, down through the ranks of the Sages. . . . The gods themselves detest things exposed to the public and profane, and love things kept secret: so each experience of magic flees from the public, wants to remain unknown, *is fortified by silence and destroyed by declaring it* and does not produce the complete effect. . . . It is agreed that the operator be discreet and reveal to no one either his work, or the place, time or the goal being pursued, except to his master or his coadjutor, who must also be faithful, believing, taciturn and worthy of such knowledge through nature or cultivation."

[10] When some texts speak of "election," "grace," "divine inspiration," and the like, almost always they must be understood as a religious version of the brusque and unintentional character that some experiences can present.

hermetic Philosophers themselves, of the direct transmission of the secret on the part of a master, there is the matter of one of the powers proceeding from the hermetic reintegration that we have hinted at above: the *projection* into the spirit of another a given psychic state, which in this case is a state of illumination. This corresponds, however, to one of the meanings of the "multiplication" symbolism: the transmutation that multiplies the quantity of the precious substance because it induces in other bodies the quality of this one, can be interpreted equally from the point of view of the "initiation by transmission" on the part of a master. To transform the base metals into Silver and Gold is the equivalent, from this point of view, of transmitting to others the interior state relative to the White Work or the Red: that is to say, to initiate into the Minor Mysteries (those of the Mother or the Moon) or the Greater Mysteries (those of Amun or the Sun).

What has been said about the "transmission of the secret" being conferred only on the "worthy" need not be interpreted moralistically. It has to do with the fact that the consciousness of the one who is to be transformed has to be at the level of readiness to enter the new state and to be transformed within it; or else, either the operation will fail, or it could well provoke violent and dangerous dissociations in the natural unity of the different components of the person. Regardless of the so-called natural dignity that must be attributed to privileged qualities preserved in the higher castes of antiquity, there remains the aforementioned fact that certain moral qualities, apart from their ethical value, produce in the person who cultivates them certain subtle, objective conditions that are propitious for the "transformation." So much for the "acquired dignities."

In this same order of things it is also necessary to remember another interpretation of the hermetic prescription, according to which the projection only happens with "heated metals." Here the metals are the candidates for initiation and allude to an intense emotional vibration, which itself constitutes an inclination to transcendence through, so to speak, an ambience propitious to the reception of the initiating teacher being transmitted to an action of the student and fully completed in the transformation that this produces.[11]

---

[11] In this case the hermetic multiplication is equivalent to the "univocal generation" about which Agrippa says (*De occulta philosophia*, 3.36): "In this univocal procreation the son is like the father in every respect and, engendered according to his kind, in the same way as the parent. And this offspring is the power of the Word formed by the *mens*, a Word well received in a subject ritually prepared, as a seed by a matrix, for the generation and birth. I say well disposed and *ritually prepared*, because all things do not participate in the word in the same way. . . . And these are secrets too recondite by nature to be bruited further in public." The designation "sons of Hermes" takes us back to the same idea, with the warning that, here "Hermes" should not be considered an actual historical personage, but the special spiritual influence that defined the initiatic chain and the organization. In the important work of A. David-Neel, *Initiations lamaïques* (Paris, 1930), there is ample information about these procedures that are states practiced in Tibetan esotericism.

Finally, we must mention something that will leave many perplexed: the elixir of longevity and the powder of projection, not as symbols of spiritual powers, but as real substances. Here there comes into play the supernatural possibility already alluded to (see page 194) of attracting to or liberating from one's own being certain subtle forces and of connecting them to specific physical materials that are charged with them objectively in the form of spiritual condensers. This possibility is confirmed by all magical traditions (in primitive people we find the idea of the supersaturations of *mana* that things or persons can bear), and betrayed by the positive religions themselves as necessary prerequisites of the powers that they attach to rites of consecration and the like.

This means that these substances converted into an "elixir of life" or "powder of projection" are no longer mere physical substances; despite the fact that a chemical analysis would not reveal any supplementary quality in them, these substances have received an occult "vitalization" in relation to a "direction of effectiveness" determined by means of a certain rite (recall the Rite of Epiclesis[12] in the ancient Church), which in turn presupposes the existence of a person capable of being raised to transcendent states. The supernatural action of such substances is not considered completely automatic, *ex opere operato*. A certain degree of exaltation and disposition is always necessary in the person for or in whom they must act, in order to awaken and transfer to his being the force that, it is hoped, above all will then be that which will act objectively.[13]

From this can be deduced some interesting consequences about the fact that the "powder of projection," understood to be a real substance and when utilized in a certain manner, produces the chemical transformation of the metals into gold, whereas when it is used on man can equally serve as one of the means—a dangerous one if the subject is not "prepared according to the rite," as Agrippa says, or there is no one to help him—of producing in him the "separation."[14] Generalizing this idea we arrive at the hermetic concept of the Universal Medicine fully capable of acting in an analogous way on the three kingdoms of nature, to overcome imperfection, infirmity, and "privation."

The renovation and prolongation of physical life ("physical immortality" is, naturally, an absurdity) assumes thereby the character of one of the possible

---

[12] [The calling down of the Holy Ghost in the Mass, who thereupon changes the bread and wine into the body and blood of Christ.—Trans.]

[13] In alchemy reference is also made to the opposite possibility, that is to say, to desaturate the substances by releasing their vital principles: as when we think of a supernatural nourishment based not so much on physical nutriments as—above all—on the nutritive virtues supposed to be dissociable from the physically and psychically aspirable parts. (Cf. Della Riviera, *Mondo magico*, 150).

[14] Cf. this idea expressed in connection with the life of the alchemist John Dee in G. Meyrink's novel, *Der Engel vom westlichen Fenster.*

symbols of a spiritual reintegration. Thus various traditions teach that the terrestrial life becomes shorter the farther man is removed from the primordial state. And even among certain primitive peoples there persists the idea that death in general is always a violent event, an act against nature.

Fifty-One

ᴄhe iɴvisibᴌe ᴍasᴄers

After associating the hermetic Philosophers with the Rosicrucians, Salmon says of the latter: "We have been told that they can spiritualize their bodies, transport themselves in an instant to distant places, make themselves invisible whenever they wish and do other things that seem impossible."[1]

The abbot Langlet du Fresnoy, in the *History of Hermetic Philosophy*, relates that according to the Rosicrucians "the meditations of their primeval founders surpass by far all that has ever been known since the creation of the world: that they are destined to accomplish the general reestablishment of the universe. They are subject neither to hunger, nor to thirst, nor to age nor to any other infliction of nature. They know by revelation those who are worthy of being admitted into their society. They live in all times as if they had existed from the beginning of the world, or as if they must remain in it until the end of time. They are able to press into their service and control the most powerful spirits and demons."[2]

And Cagliostro says: "I belong neither to any century nor to any particular place; my spiritual being lives its eternal existence outside time and space. When I immerse myself in thought I go back through the Ages. When I extend my spirit to a world existing far from anything you perceive, I can change myself into

---

[1] Salmon, introduction to *BPC*, xix.

[2] Langlet du Fresnoy, *Histoire de la philosophie hermétique* (The Hague, 1742), 1:371-72.

whatever I wish. Participating consciously in absolute being, I regulate my action according to my surroundings. My country is wherever I happen to set foot at the moment . . . I am that which is . . . free and master of life. There are beings who no longer possess guardian angels: I am one of those."[3]

Association with the Rosicrucians, those enigmatic personages whose custom was to appear in the world as ordinary beings, hiding their true being and their real mission, must serve again here as a warning to those who, on the basis of the extraordinary possibilities attributed to the hermetic Art, seek in past epochs or even the present, some tangible and convincing manifestation of it to remove their suspicion that the whole thing is nothing more than the mere fantasy of exalted imagination.

Those who adopt this attitude will find few confirmations and little proof. They are proceeding from a dramatic, theatrical concept of the magus or initiate: as if the adept is preoccupied, above all else, with "exhibiting," or manifesting—in forms that will astonish, amaze, or terrify—everything within the power of heaven and earth so that all eyes will converge on him.

On the contrary, if there is anything radically opposed to the style of a true initiate, it is precisely such behavior. By definition, the initiate is an occult being and his path is neither visible nor penetrable. He is elusive, not to be pigeonholed. He arrives from the direction contrary to that towards which all gazes are fixed and takes the most natural seeming vehicle for his supernatural action. He may be an intimate friend, companion, or lover; he may be sure of possessing all your heart and confidence. But he will always be something different, other than what he lets be known. We will perceive this "other" only when we have penetrated his domain. And then perhaps we will have the feeling of having been walking on the edge of an abyss.

Men desire that what they are be known, that what they do be acknowledged, and that we be pleased by the quality of their performance. In the words of Agrippa, we have learned how different the law is that governs the magus and the hermetist. They judge all exhibitionism and personality to be puerile. There is no adept. He does not exist. He does not speak. They but seek to net the wind, who are diverted by such things. The hermetist has reached a state that categorically avoids all reaction to human judgment. He has stopped taking an interest in what others may think of him, or say about him, just or unjust, good or bad. He knows only that certain things must *happen*: he provides the precise means and conditions for them and that is all. He does not pretend the action is his *own*. He is pure instrumentality. "Self-affirmation" is a mania he does not recognize. And the

---

[3] M. Haven text (*Cagliostro: Le maître inconnu*, 282–84), reproduced in *Ignis*, no. 8–9 (1925). Of course it remains to be seen, without prejudging, whether it is the right of Cagliostro or not, to attribute to himself his own eligibility for initiation.

farther he advances, the more deeply his center sinks into a superindividual and superpersonal range, like one of the great forces of Nature, while those on whom he acts will have the impresson of being free.

Of the hermetic quality itself, since their texts are as if they have been written only for themselves, we have to rely for the most part on what the alchemists say of themselves and their works. And once a certain attitude is assumed one can always find a way to convince oneself that the hermetic texts lack all inner meaning and have been reduced to an incomprehensible jargon in the service of superstition, chimeras, and muddles; just as, with a similar attitude, we can always convince ourselves that nothing in history shows us "positively" that we can completely prove that persons of such extraordinary possibilities have ever existed. Actually, in the very fact of the miserable human existence led by so many alchemists we can see an ironic argument for the opposite contention. A hermetist would guard himself from dissuading anyone who thought him to be an ordinary person; this is precisely what helps to make the mask behind which the tradition is hidden still more impenetrable.

As for what might astonish some people—instead of furnishing sufficiently documented cases of actual metallic transmutations as proof, true accounts from a not so distant past[4] that indicate some "phenomenon" regardless of the hermetic commandment to disdain the vulgar magic associated with such and such a particular result, to let things happen outwardly according to "nature and author-ity" and to be directed, instead, to "know oneself and to dominate the nameless triad"[5]—instead of focusing on all this, it might be useful to consider how many "random" and unpredictable elements are the germs of sometimes great revolution-ary changes in life and history. It might also be useful to consider how much there is in the natural order of phenomena, beyond the laws that explain the *how*, but never the *why* of their happening. All that constitutes an empty space, *which might not be so empty after all*.[6] Behind the scenes of the consciousness of men

---

[4] Metallic transmutations have been attributed to Raymond Lully, to Nicholas Flamel, to Philalethes (which seems to have been the pseudonym of Thomas Vaughn [sic]), to John Dee, who would have also worked with the Hapsburg Emperor Rudolph II in Prague, to the Cosmopolite (Alexander Seton), to those unknowns who executed the work on their visits to Van Helmont, to Helvetius, and to Poisson, to the enigmatic Lascaris and Delisle, to Richthausen who had connections with the emperor Ferdinand III, himself very versed in the Art, to the Swede Paykull (of whom the chemist Hierse gave notice), to the enigmatic Aymar, also known as the Marquis of Bethunar, to Borri (who seems to have been the personage whose transmutations gave origin to the Porta Ermetica of the Piazza Vittorio in Rome), to Count Manuel Gaetano. It can be seen in regard (although the references contained in it are in need of revision) to the work of N. Poce, *Alchimia e alchimisti* (Rome, 1928).

[5] Text of Zosimos in *CAG*, 2:230.

[6] Cf. *Introduzione alla magia*, 2:315ff., (concerning positions and solutions to the contrast between positive science and magic).

and their history, where the physical eye and doubt alike dare not stretch, *there may be someone*. Homer said that the gods often travel through the world in the guise of strangers and pilgrims and turn the cities of men around. This is not just mythology. There is reason to believe that no historical or social event of any importance, no phenomenon that has followed a determined course of terrestrial events comprising certain "discoveries" or the birth of new ideas, has not had a casual or spontaneous origin, but on the contrary has obeyed an *intention,* if not an actual plan conceived behind the scenes and realized via paths we can scarcely imagine today, under the sign of the Light, as well as—according to circumstances— under the sign of Darkness.

Now then, whoever, peradventure, comes to accept ideas so meagerly "positive," it could be said to him that "the Transcendent Man," created by the hermetic Royal Art, instead of playing with little phenomena to astound the profane—like the sleights-of-hand of the music hall—or making "metaphysical investigations" his objective, he might very well prefer to focus his possibilities on the invisible world. He should not pay any great attention if some shock or rebound from above comes to alter the more or less happy course of his terrestrial existence even if it result in the spectacle of a life that perhaps few would envy. "Ye are not here to struggle with things, but with gods," said Boehme.[7]

Given the nature of this work, we have said enough. For some we need only quote from a master of the Far East: "Just as the fish cannot live outside the gloomy depths, so the common man knows not the weapon of this 'Noble Wisdom.'"[8] For others, for those who despite everything wish to learn more, there is only one way to direct them: to create in themselves the capacity for a vision in which what is *beyond* their consciousness and thought be made as clear and distinct as objective things are for the eye and for the mind tied to the body.

But it is time now to enter into the adventure and to become one of the links in the royal, golden, occult chain of the tradition of the sons of Hermes: for which, there only remains for us—and thus we come to the end—to repeat these words of the second Rosicrucian manifesto: "Anyone who comes looking for us simply out of curiosity, will never find us. But if his will truly and in fact is to inscribe himself in the registry of our fraternity, we, who judge by thought, will fulfill our promises to him. We do not divulge the place of our residence, because thoughts, united to the real will of the reader, are capable of letting us know him, and him us."[9]

---

[7] Boehme, *Aurora,* 21, §121.

[8] Lao-tzu, *Tao te Ching.*

[9] In Langlet du Fresnoy, op. cit., 1:377.

index

. . . .